To my father,
Norman P. Auburn
and
to the memory of my mother,
Kathleen Montgomery Auburn (1908–1974)

Contents

Acknowledgments

I WISH TO THANK the College of the Humanities and the Graduate School of The Ohio State University for a grant-in-aid and a Faculty Development Summer Fellowship which enabled me to carry out part of the research for this book. For arranging time off, I am indebted to my then-chairman, John B. Gabel, to Dean Arthur E. Adams, and to Provost Albert J. Kuhn. My colleagues Richard D. Altick, James L. Battersby, Ernest Lockridge, Bernice J. R. Lubin, Edwin Robbins, and John Harold Wilson generously read and criticized the manuscript at various stages. James R. Kincaid and Richard M. Weatherford read portions at crucial junctures and offered valuable advice. Robert D. Hume and Arthur H. Scouten read the final draft carefully and made many useful suggestions which I have incorporated. Barbara M. Austin typed the final manuscript with intelligence and precision.

My interest in Sheridan and the eighteenth-century stage was nurtured by Arthur Friedman, Gwin J. Kolb, and Edward W. Rosenheim, Jr.—men "whom I ought not to mention but with the reverence due to instructors and benefactors." To Professor Friedman especially this study owes many of its insights; it will meet, I hope, that standard of precision his example inspires.

Throughout the process of learning and writing, the "weariness of copying" and the "vexation of expunging," Sandra K. Auburn has given the perspective of an intelligent social scientist and the love and support of a loyal helpmate.

SHERIDAN'S COMEDIES

CHAPTER I:

Sheridan and the Georgian Comedy

> MRS. DANGLE. The PUBLIC is their CRITIC—without whose fair approbation they know no play can rest on the stage.
>
> *The Critic*, 1.2.80–82[1]

AFTER TWO CENTURIES *The Rivals*, *The Critic*, and *The School for Scandal* continue to play on the stage and to satisfy in the study. Together these comedies represent a vital dramatic creation which surpasses in popular endurance in the repertory the output of any other English comic playwright between Shakespeare and Shaw. Intrinsically the plays are as fascinating as the man who wrote them, Richard Brinsley Sheridan, playwright and politician, romantic lover and scapegrace wit, literary friend of Johnson and Byron.

Thanks to the work of Thomas Moore, Walter Sichel, and R. Crompton Rhodes, we know the man quite well.[2] Thanks to scholars such as George Henry Nettleton, Iolo Williams, Sichel, Rhodes, and especially Cecil Price, we have an acceptable canon and definitive texts of the plays.[3] And thanks to Jean Dulck, Jack D. Durant, and John Loftis, we have a renewed interest in the plays themselves as literary objects.[4] The work of these later scholar-critics is particularly important, for the appreciation of Sheridan's achievement as comic playwright was long marred by a general ignorance of many of the retrievable and verifiable contexts, those myriad factors that bear on the construction of a work of art before, during, and after its completion.

Most older critics approached Sheridan from one particular and limited context: the perspective provided by some apparently similar "costume comedies," the wit plays of the late Restoration. Because Sheridan was called the "modern Congreve" in his own time, because people still read today the

3

works of William Congreve, Sir George Etherege, William
Wycherley, Sir John Vanbrugh, and George Farquhar but not
the works of Sheridan's own contemporaries, many com-
mentators, in assessing Sheridan's works, have tended to gen-
eralize far too quickly from their experience with Restoration
comedies. In Sichel's and Price's studies, references to Congreve, Wycherley, Vanbrugh, and Farquhar abound, but there
are few references to such major Georgian playwrights as
Samuel Foote, George Colman, David Garrick, or Arthur
Murphy, and fewer to lesser contemporaries whose plays
Sheridan must have seen and whose audiences supported
Sheridan's plays. Moreover, since Oliver Goldsmith, puffing
the appearance of his then-unfashionable comedy *She Stoops to
Conquer*, articulated a critical position aimed at an ill-defined
group of plays which had some popularity in the early 1770s,
many have assumed that Goldsmith's great fellow playwright
shared his reaction to "sentimental comedy" and wished to
return instead to a style of drama three-quarters of a century
old.

Sheridan, of course, helped to form this impression. In the
prologue to the tenth-night performance of *The Rivals*—a
prologue which was performed only after his comedy had
proved successful—Sheridan deplored "The Goddess of the
woeful countenance—/ The sentimental Muse" (ll. 21–22).
Then, when burlesquing the theater of his time and of all
time in *The Critic*, he commented indirectly on various sentimental and didactic forms recently exhibited on stage. These
two oblique criticisms—and there are hardly any others, almost no comments in his letters or memoirs, no critical
essays—provide the basis for widely accepted and sadly mistaken critical opinions: that both Sheridan and Goldsmith
were reactionaries against the dramatic comedy of their day;
that their works are chiefly interesting as last gasps of the
comic spirit of the Restoration, as gallant but ineffective
attempts to reform English comedy, to rescue it from the
clutches of sentimentality, melodrama, didacticism, and de-
based farcical entertainment. Goldsmith and Sheridan were
unable to kill the tradition of sentimental comedy, one critic

tells us, but they set up an "effective protest"; another brands
Sheridan and Goldsmith as "exponents of the old comedy";
"like Goldsmith, Sheridan defied . . . 'the sentimental Muse' "
writes another; Sheridan's and Goldsmith's comedies were
"reactions" against the comedy of their time, a fourth tells us;
writes a fifth, both dramatists were fellow reactionaries, but
whereas "Goldsmith endeavours to revive the spirit of *As You
Like It*, . . . Sheridan strives to create another *Way of the
World*."[5]

Of course, by no means all students of Sheridan have
ignored the "high Georgian comedy," the best comedies of the
two decades between 1760 and 1780. Studies like those of
Harold Routh, Ernest Bernbaum, James Lynch, Harry Pedicord, and Ricardo Quintana demonstrate a knowledge of the
drama produced by Sheridan's contemporaries.[6] Unfortunately, none of them devote much space to Sheridan.

That so little attention has been paid to the Georgian drama
when assessing Sheridan's work is puzzling. Sheridan was a
practical playwright whose talents were exercised largely if not
exclusively toward the end of making money in the theater.
He first turned to the stage, in spite of prejudices against
associating himself with an ungentlemanly occupation, as the
easiest way to support himself; he only turned from the stage
when he had the money to fulfill his lifelong ambition to enter
Parliament; and he always returned to the stage, or at least to
the box office, when his purse was empty. A monetarily
motivated playwright, far more than a playwright whose
economic livelihood does not depend upon the immediate
financial success of his work, must attend carefully to the
tastes, expectations, and desires of his audience. A rich di-
versity of kinds may entertain, and novelty may frequently
please, but continued success is more likely if his works do not
radically shock or challenge his audience. Hence the works of
such a playwright are likely to resemble most closely in their
content, their moral assumptions, and their aesthetic devices
and forms those works which have demonstrated the ability to
please his audience. For Sheridan such works are to be found
in a wide and varied comic repertory of plays by Shakespeare

and by Cibber, by Congreve as well as by Susanna Centlivre, by Jonson, Farquhar, Sir Richard Steele, Isaac Bickerstaff, Garrick, Colman, Richard Cumberland, and Hugh
Kelly.

Of course, the literary and theatrical contexts in which we
might judge the works of a practical, monetarily motivated
playwright like Sheridan always stand in jeopardy of becoming
reductive. We may recognize that the state of a play is
protean, that it manifests itself as a script which details the
order of words to be spoken, actions to be represented, and
effects to be portrayed; that individual productions result
from timebound collaborations among many different theatrical personages; and that a play has an imaginable performance, predicted by the script, which might have been
achieved under the author's direction and which each subsequent production can but approximate. But even if we bear
this appreciation of the special nature of drama as theater in
mind, when we judge the works of a practical playwright who
involved himself in his productions we must beware the trap
of considering external influences exclusively. Like Sheridan,
both Shakespeare and Cibber were practical men of the
theater who needed to make money by their dramatic talents,
but this common motive in no way explains the considerable
aesthetic and moral differences between their respective bod-
ies of work. An understanding of the need to eat will not
particularly illuminate the artistic discrepancy between Molière's adequate works and his great plays any more than will
the knowledge that he was an actor who wrote his plays with
specific companies in mind. Hence a careful critical consideration of each individual work taken as a whole must be
judiciously balanced against all the theatrical and literary
contexts. In the case of Sheridan such an attitude does not
mean ignoring his need to make money, or failing to speculate about his knowledge of contemporary and older comedies, or avoiding the search for difficult problems of interpretation in the experience and capabilities of the actors
and actresses he chose to create his characters; but it also does
mean not simplifying complicated artistic choices merely by
reference to the concrete particulars of production or the

precedents of the forms. Most important, such an approach should draw together all the information of source studies, biography, bibliography, literary historical criticism, and theatrical history to provide the contexts within which to assess Sheridan's achievement as comic dramatist.

Of these many contexts, only one will not arise naturally from a detailed discussion of the inception, creation, casting, production, construction, and reception of each of Sheridan's comedies. That context is the repertory of Sheridan's day, both the older plays which were so frequently before the public and the newer plays which strove to gain attention. The characteristics of the older and the newer comedies surely interested Sheridan, and by their success or failure influenced the directions he would choose to take.

Consider the repertory of older plays. In the 1770s, each major patent house offered about fifty different mainpieces in a season of about 180 nights. On an average, thirty of these were older comedies long established in the repertory. In the 1779–80 season, for instance, a spectator could have seen twenty-two five-act comedies which had been playing in the 1747–48 season (Garrick's first as manager of Drury Lane). Thus the repertory was fairly static. New comedies had great difficulty breaking into the repertory: of the fifty-two new five-act comedies produced from the Licensing Act in 1737 to Sheridan's assumption of the management of Drury Lane in 1777, twenty-seven did not survive beyond the season and only seven lasted ten seasons or more.[7]

The bulk of the repertory consisted of early eighteenth-century plays, Shakespearean comedies, a few Jacobean comedies in adapted, chastened forms, and a handful of contemporary productions. Two of Congreve's plays were offered with some frequency, but many people were no longer entertained by what they considered the smuttiness of Etherege or Wycherley, let alone the frankness of Shadwell or Dryden.

Let us examine the popularity of five-act comedies (despite the growing influence of farce and comic opera, still the heart of the repertory) in the thirty-three seasons from Garrick's assumption of the management of Drury Lane (1747–48) through Sheridan's last active year as playwright and manager before he entered Parliament (1779–80).[8] For this representative period, in sheer numerical terms *The Beaux' Stratagem* was the most popular five-act comedy, with Cibber's adaptation and completion of Vanbrugh's *The Provok'd Husband* close behind; each play received slightly over 200 performances in London from 1747 to 1780. Next on the list are Benjamin Hoadly's *The Suspicious Husband* with more than 190 performances, Susanna Centlivre's *The Busy Body* with more than 180, Steele's *The Conscious Lovers* with more than 170. Of Shakespeare's comedies, *The Merchant of Venice* was most popular (170 performances), then *Much Ado About Nothing* (123), *The Tempest* (109), *As You Like It* (101), and *The Merry Wives of Windsor* (94).[9] Jonson's *Every Man in His Humour* (165) and Vanbrugh's *The Provok'd Wife* (147) were each nearly as popular as *The Merchant of Venice*, while two other of Mrs. Centlivre's plays, *The Wonder* (130) and *A Bold Stroke for a Wife* (84) had considerable success among the older plays. Farquhar's *The Recruiting Officer* (121), *L'Avare* in Henry Fielding's adaptation as *The Miser* (111), Beaumont and Fletcher's *Rule a Wife and Have a Wife* (111) were about as successful as Congreve's *The Way of the World* (114) and *Love for Love* (105). Other popular Cibber plays included *She Wou'd and She Wou'd Not* (78), *Love Makes a Man* (73), *The Careless Husband* (73), *Love's Last Shift* (44), and *The Refusal* (37). Farquhar was also represented by *The Constant Couple* (64) and *The Twin Rivals* (34), while Steele's *The Funeral* (58), Jonson's *The Alchemist* (76), Vanbrugh's *The Relapse* (49) and *The Confederacy* (52) all swell the totals of the respective authors. Dryden's *Amphitryon* (39) and *The Spanish Friar* (49; both in purified versions) earned him only a minor place among the comic writers popular in the period. Two sets of figures may suggest a perspective: *The Beggar's Opera* received 464 performances in the thirty-three seasons, a notable indication of the audience's fondness for ballad operas and a surprising contrast to the most popular of tragedies, *Romeo and Juliet*, which was performed 340 times; of the new comedies which entered the repertory during the period, *The School for Scandal* (114 performances in four seasons), Cumberland's *The West Indian* (96 in twelve), Colman and Garrick's *The Clandestine Marriage* (120 in fourteen), Colman's *The Jealous Wife* (117 in eighteen), *She Stoops to Conquer* (57 in eight), and Murphy's *The Way to Keep Him* (73 in eighteen) and *All in the Wrong* (58 in eighteen) achieved success.

The total number of performances each of these comedies received over the thirty-three season period of the Garrick-Sheridan era reflects a steady, year-in and year-out popularity rather than bursts of long runs or frequent repetition. For instance, Sheridan could have seen a major production of any of the comedies mentioned except three: during the period he spent with his father in London after he left Harrow (the seasons 1768–69 and 1769–70); during the time he spent in Bath (ca. September 1770 to August 1772); or during the two London seasons 1772–73 and 1773–74, just before his marriage to Elizabeth Linley and just after their return to London following their honeymoon (e.g., August 1772 to April 1773 and about February 1774 through the end of the season).[10] Many of Sheridan's early dramatic efforts were composed in this six-year span, and though we can definitely place him at the theater on only one night,[11] he must have gone frequently. Two of the three comedies he probably could not have seen, Farquhar's *The Constant Couple* and Vanbrugh's *The Mistake*, were produced in London while he was in Bath; of the forty most popular mainpiece comedies only Cibber's *The Refusal* was not produced in either London or Bath when Sheridan might have seen it before his first play appeared.

The repertory of comic mainpieces is remarkably varied; moreover, many of the comedies were popular only for local reasons such as topicality, spectacular production, or commendable acting. Nevertheless, we can extract from the group three common characteristics. All three of these characteristics appear singly or in combination in every mainpiece comedy popular between 1747 and 1780. First, we find within most of the comedies a plot with at least one line of action designed to evoke strong comic anxiety. Next, we discover an abundance of characters whose "humour" or idiosyncrasy is strongly drawn but who are not objects of harsh satiric attack. And finally, all the comedies lack explicit sexual reference or implicit sexual innuendo, or use them very sparingly, particularly the sort typical of "high Restoration comedy."

To illustrate these common characteristics negatively, consider some enduring comedies which were not popular in the Georgian repertory: *Volpone, The Man of Mode, The Country Wife,* and *The Plain Dealer.* Each of these plays lacks a comic plot productive of the sort of anxiety typical of, say, the Claudio-Hero line of *Much Ado About Nothing* or the Shylock-Antonio line of *The Merchant of Venice.* Each presents humours characters who are satirically attacked. And each deals with matters of sexuality with frankness or even license. The Georgian period did recognize the great comic potential of each of these plays; either adaptations or near analogues such as Cibber's innocuous fop plays held the boards throughout the era. But the originals could not be played.

All of the characteristics shared by the older comedies popular in the repertory are present in two of the greatest new Georgian comedies, *She Stoops to Conquer* and *The Rivals.* Both of these plays offer subplots evocative of fairly intense comic anxiety; to those willing to be moved by the real or imagined sufferings of the virtuous, the dilemmas of Miss Neville and Hastings or Faulkland and Julia produce much concern. Both of the comedies portray strongly drawn humours characters who are revealed as "amiable humorists" by the conclusion.[12] And both treat sex in a decidedly careful, almost prudish manner, never mentioning or suggesting adultery, basing marriages on love rather than finances, and avoiding sexual jokes.

But some of the older comedies and some of the less successful new comedies emphasized various aspects of the characteristics of the popular comedies to such a degree that they fell under critical disapproval. The plays of their contemporaries which Goldsmith and Sheridan supposedly attacked were excessive in one aspect or another. In "An Essay on the Theatre; or, a Comparison between Laughing and Sentimental Comedy" (1772), Goldsmith complained about "a new species of Dramatic Composition . . . in which the virtues of Private Life are exhibited, rather than the Vices exposed;

and the Distresses, rather than the Faults of Mankind, make our interest in the piece."[13] Sheridan, in *The Critic*, ridiculed such plays:

DANGLE. [*reading*] "Bursts into tears, and exit." What, is this a tragedy!

SNEER. No, that's a genteel comedy, not a translation—only *taken from the French*; it is written in a stile which they have lately tried to run down; the true sentimental, and nothing ridiculous in it from the beginning to the end.

[1.1.114–18]

Neither Sheridan in *The Critic* nor Goldsmith in his "Essay" was creating an imaginary category of plays; a few of these plays did exist and occasionally held the boards. But both writers objected to calling such works comedies, and in fact the forms of the plots of such plays were often melodramatic rather than comic. One such play is William O'Brien's adaptation of Sedaine's *Le Philosophe sans le Sçavoir* entitled *The Duel* (DL, 8 Dec. 1772) which appeared within a month of the publication of Goldsmith's "Essay."[14]

O'Brien's play tells how George Melville's desire to defend his family's honor against a slight passed on merchant bankers upsets the marriage plans of his sister, causes his beloved great distress, brings his family to tears of despair, and at last is settled only by the chance that George's opponent is the son of a man his father had generously helped. In the "Advertisement" to the printed play, O'Brien wrote that "It did not escape observation that it was a new species of *drama*, turning altogether upon a single incident, in some passages warm and interesting, but free from the theatrical bustle so much relished in this country, and in the less important scenes, exhibiting a draught of life and manners, easy, natural, but unadorned." Nor did it escape observation that the play was, to tastes prepared for something else, dull and maudlin. The audience hissed it off the stage in one hearing, and the *London Magazine* wrote as its epitaph that "In a word, the author was bewildered in a French mist, and it led him astray."[15]

O'Brien's play does not fully deserve such treatment: its successors held the nineteenth-century stage and influenced

even the early works of Oscar Wilde. O'Brien's attempt to
create in George a character of some depth, troubled by the
dilemma of familial duty and honor in which he finds himself,
was partially successful; and the scenes of domestic life with
such fine actors as Spranger Barry in the role of the generous
and noble elder Melville, Mrs. Ann Barry as the tender Maria,
George's beloved, Mrs. Elizabeth Hopkins as George's mother,
and Thomas King as the kindly old family retainer and best
friend to his old master, Melville, could have been touching
and at the same time very anxiety-provoking.

But O'Brien had been too much of a revolutionary. Other
recent plays had presented similar lines of action designed to
maximize the audience's apprehensions and to bring them to
tears—stories in which they never know until the dénouement
whether to expect a fortunate or an unfortunate outcome.
These plots were melodramatic, that is, neither distinctly
comic nor definitely tragic in construction.[16] They were, as
Horace Walpole put it, examples of *"tragédie mitigée,"* a "melancholy story in private life . . . with a cheerful conclusion."[17]
Such "sentimental comedies" as Mrs. Frances Sheridan's *The
Discovery* (DL, 3 Feb. 1763), Mrs. Griffith's *The Platonic Wife*
(DL, 24 Jan. 1765), *The Double Mistake* (CG, 9 Jan. 1766), *The
School for Rakes* (DL, 4 Feb. 1769), and *A Wife in the Right* (CG,
5 March 1773) all have lines of serious action concerned with
the distresses of private life which reach an unassured cheerful conclusion. But each of these plays has other lines of
action with more distinctly comic expectations. For instance,
Mrs. Sheridan's play portrays an amusing, long-winded *senex
amans* of the chivalric school whose antics help assure that
Louisa will escape a forced marriage, while the spoiled young
married couple, Sir Harry and Lady Flutter, present an
amusing contrast and rather easily avoid embarrassing complications. The serious line of action depicts the self-inflicted
financial woes of Lord Medway, causing constant apprehension until the dénouement that those woes will force young
Colonel Medway to abjure his beloved and embattled Miss
Richly in order to marry her wealthy sister, Mrs. Knightly,
and thereby repair the family's fortunes. Mrs. Griffith's plays
contain similar juxtapositions of lines of action. But O'Brien's

play banishes *all* comic expectations by banishing subsidiary lines of action and subsidiary comic characters. His audience, accustomed to plays like Mrs. Sheridan's or Mrs. Griffith's, was denied the important assurances that made their anxiety more nearly comic. In creating what we might call "crypto-melodrama," O'Brien sought to exercise the same kind of emotional apprehension works like *Jane Shore* and *Pamela* had evoked. Both those works were created around lines of action designed to abate either tragic or comic expectations, to prevent the audience from knowing if the outcome will be fortunate or unfortunate, and to force some auditors to cry. The first, because its outcome was unfortunate, was commonly viewed in the eighteenth century as tragic; and the tears of distress auditors undoubtedly shed at its conclusion were confused with an effectively defined catharsis of pity and fear. The second, with its fortunate outcome, was seen by many such as James Dance, the adapter of an early stage version, as a comedy; the tears of distress many shed at Pamela's trials gave way to tears of joy whose pleasure could be heard in the sound of tolling village church bells when the volume containing Pamela's marriage arrived.

Few if any "sentimental comedies" written in the Georgian period are *tragédies mitigées*, and those that remotely resemble examples of the category are constructed not like *The Duel* ("*taken from the French*") but like Dryden's *Marriage a la Mode*, with serious and comic lines of action juxtaposed. By far the greater number of late eighteenth-century "sentimental comedies" are constructed along the lines of *Much Ado About Nothing* with two or more lines of distinctly comic action, one of which maintains comic expectations but portrays the sufferings of the virtuous in such a way as both to bring its auditors to tears and to assure them of an eventual fortunate outcome. In this category belong such Georgian comedies as Whitehead's *The School for Lovers* (DL, 10 Feb. 1762), Mrs. Sheridan's *The Dupe* (DL, 10 Dec. 1763), William Kenrick's *The Widow'd Wife* (DL, 5 Dec. 1767) and *The Duellist* (CG, 20 Nov. 1773), Mrs. Charlotte Lennox's *The Sister* (CG, 18 Feb. 1769), Cumberland's *The Fashionable Lover* (DL, 20 Jan. 1772)[18] and *The Choleric Man* (DL, 19 Dec. 1774), Kelly's *A Word to the Wise*

(DL, 3 March 1770) and *The Man of Reason* (CG, 9 Feb. 1776), Colman's *The Man of Business* (CG, 29 Jan. 1774) and *The Suicide* (HM, 11 July 1778), Francis Waldron's *The Maid of Kent* (DL, 17 May 1773), the anonymous *The South Briton* (CG, 12 April 1774), Mrs. Hannah Cowley's *The Runaway* (DL, 15 Feb. 1776) and even Samuel Foote's *The Bankrupt* (HM, 21 July 1773). Indeed, many Georgian auditors would have found tears of distress at scenes of the sufferings of the virtuous, and tears of joy at the eventual and always expected fortunate outcome, the appropriate response to such more artistically successful comedies as Colman's *The Jealous Wife* (DL, 12 Feb. 1761), Colman and Garrick's *The Clandestine Marriage* (DL, 20 Feb. 1766), Colman's *The English Merchant* (DL, 21 Feb. 1767), Kelly's *False Delicacy* (DL, 23 Jan. 1768) and *The School for Wives* (DL, 11 Dec. 1773), Cumberland's *The West Indian* (DL, 19 Jan. 1771), and even Sheridan's *The Rivals*.

These "sentimental comedies" can be compared in structural and psychological terms to *Much Ado About Nothing*, itself the tenth most popular older comedy in the Georgian repertory. Shakespeare's play loosely links two distinct kinds of comic lines of action, the one a typical witty-lovers-outwitted story, the other a more thrilling intrigue involving a virtuous heroine in scenes of distress brought about by the machinations of a villain and the excessive credulity of a proud lover. Both of these lines are distinctly comic in that we are constantly aware that the probability of a fortunate outcome is far greater than the probability of an unfortunate outcome. Neither line is serious in the sense of "melodramatic". Despite the anxieties we have for Hero, for instance, we always expect that eventually her sufferings will prove no more than temporary, a discomfort to be endured (and for which to punish mildly the erring Claudio and more severely the villainous Don John) before the happy outcome is achieved. All the techniques of dramatic representation are designed to produce such emotional effect and yet maintain fully comic expectations. O'Brien could have altered the last act of *The Duel* in such a way as to bring about George's death and increase the suffering of the Melville family, and conceivably

Mrs. Sheridan could have allowed Lord Medway's financial insolvency to force young Colonel Medway to marry Mrs. Knightly; these changes could have been made without alterations in the preceding material because the probabilities of a fortunate outcome to the respective lines of action were always in doubt: their plots were designed as melodrama. But Shakespeare could not have allowed the accusations of lechery to stand, or permitted Hero to die, or failed to marry Hero and Claudio happily at last without making so many changes in the foregoing representation as to alter the play completely from beginning to end. Both his plots were designed as comic.[19]

No doubt part of Goldsmith's and Sheridan's objections to some of the comedies of their day were levelled against artistic incompetence rather than formal design; what they appeared to resent were the attempts of the dull scribblers of their age to evoke tears or sighs in their plots by artificially inept means. So many of those third-rate productions used distinct improbabilities to resolve complicated sentimental lines of action that Steele's long-lost daughter device in *The Conscious Lovers* seems masterful in comparison. Mrs. Sheridan, for instance, can resolve Lord Medway's trouble only by discovering in the rich Mrs. Knightly his bastard daughter; Kelly in *A Word to the Wise* must show that Villars is Willoughby's long-lost son to resolve one love match; Cumberland must make Aubrey return late in the action in time to expose the villainous Bridgemores, who bilked him of his fortune, and rediscover his suffering daughter, victim of the Fashionable Lover; Kenrick must produce a long-lost father in order to plant suspicions that a match is incestuous, then relieve those suspicions and reunite the father with the Widow'd Wife; a brother in *The Sister*, a wife in *The Brothers*, all lost and all miraculously found. Such improbabilities, when not a part of the fabric of the play and postulated early as grounds upon which the whole action depends (as with Marlowe's mistaking Hardcastle's house for an inn or Stockwell's concealing his relationship in order to test Belcour), are poor indeed when revealed merely to unravel complications. *Coups de théâtre*, not tears, cause the objections. Indeed, in support of his attack on "bastard tragedy," even Goldsmith cites for an alternative the "laughing comedy" of Cibber—a playwright whose practical knowledge of the theater led him to create the tearful scenes between Lord and Lady Townly in *The Provok'd Husband*, the second most popular stock comedy in the Georgian repertory.

Like plots designed to evoke intense comic anxiety, the portrayal of strongly drawn humours characters who are not the objects of harsh satiric attack is another index of both the older comedies popular in the repertory and the new comedies of the Georgian era. Again, an intensification of one aspect of this characteristic marks the Georgian dramas against which many critics reacted: the expansion of the principle of avoiding satiric attack on an amiable humorist to the forgiving of a character's faults simply because he happens to be good-natured. Of those plays where this abuse was most evident, Goldsmith wrote:

> . . . almost all the Characters are good, and exceedingly generous; they are lavish enough of their *Tin* Money on the Stage, and though they want Humour, have abundance of Sentiment and Feeling. If they happen to have Faults or Foibles, the Spectator is taught not only to pardon, but to applaud them, in consideration of the goodness of their hearts; so that Folly, instead of being ridiculed, is commended . . . .[20]

Certainly late eighteenth-century comedy suffers from no dearth of generous and good-natured characters whose faults are forgiven in consideration of the goodness of their hearts. Sheridan's Charles Surface is one of the best examples. Some, like Cumberland's Belcour, are portrayed with a modicum of psychological depth; but many, like Kelly's young Captain Dudley (*A Word to the Wise*), Colman's Beverly (*The Man of Business*), or Mowbray in *The South Briton*, are one-dimensional figures whose sexual rapacity or lack of concern for their social and business obligations are their most believable traits, while their generosity and good nature seem no more than assumptions. Goldsmith takes worthy exception to the poverty of moral vision which constructs such characters and involves them in culpable actions, the consequences of which they are ultimately forgiven.

In the presentation of such characters, we can see the influence of the doctrine of universal benevolence that underlay so much of the thinking of the time. This curious product of anti-Puritan, anti-Stoic, and anti-Hobbesian divines of the Latitudinarian school in the late seventeenth and early eighteenth centuries held that universal benevolence or good nature was supreme. Benevolence toward all humanity was made to encompass all other virtues. Benevolent feelings themselves became as important as benevolent actions. And those benevolent feelings which we have for the sufferings of others were thought to give the good-natured man the highest pleasures, what David Fordyce called in 1754 "a sort of pleasing Anguish, that sweetly melts the Mind, and terminates in a Self-approving Joy."[21] This philosophy surely influenced the selection of plots designed to evoke tears and the creation of characters forgiven their faults because of their good nature; but even more pervasively it spread the faith that most people are basically good-natured and naturally benevolent, that through such good nature they will, if not prevented by insurmountable external difficulties beyond their control, solve their problems. Tony Lumpkin aids Miss Neville and Hastings in *She Stoops to Conquer* not just to prevent his marriage to Miss Hastings, but also to prove to them that "if you don't find Tony Lumpkin a more good-natured fellow than you thought for, I'll give you leave to take my best horse and Bet Bouncer into the bargain" (4.1). No motive but good nature can lead Sheridan's fiery Sir Lucius O'Trigger, after he has been tricked in love and forced to second a coward, to declare that "as I have been disappointed myself, it will be very hard if I have not the satisfaction of seeing other people succeed better" (5.3.235–36). Nor can we attach to Charles Surface any characteristics more typical than his good-natured sentimentality about the "ill looking little Fellow over the Settee" and his spontaneous generosity to his relative Stanley. Indeed, when even Goldsmith set out to satirize benevolence, he bore with him a respect for the sentimental virtues and attacked not those virtues but the vices which resembled them; of Honeywood's folly his uncle Sir William can say: "There are some faults so nearly allied to excellence, that we can scarce weed out the vice without eradicating the virtue."[22] I do not know of any late eighteenth-century comedy which does not in some form accept this aspect of the doctrine of universal benevolence; even many of the satirical farces of Samuel Foote and the dark productions of Charles Macklin show evidences of it.

Again, Goldsmith, Sheridan, and their contemporaries seem to be criticizing artistic ineptitude rather than expressing deep philosophical disagreement. It is acceptable to create characters whose good nature and generosity are abundant, and indeed, these qualities can serve as partial mitigation for acts of folly or for idiosyncratic behavior. But those characters must not be portrayed in such a way that the action of the comedy shows generosity and good nature to be their only redeeming traits or forgives vicious behavior merely on the basis of the goodness of their hearts. Most of the comedies that repelled Goldsmith attempt to mitigate foolish or vicious behavior by showing a thoroughly repentant character at last, but they fail because the repentance is almost always unbelievable. The comic discomfiture which the character undergoes either consists in so mawkish a scene as to be unbelievable, given what we know of the character, or is so subordinated to other demands of the action as to be unrecognizable as sufficient punishment. The moral effect is what Goldsmith identified—the approval of faults or foibles—largely because of a failure to motivate characters in a probable and believable manner.

Such failure of characterization is not just the result of artistic ineptitude or commonly held assumptions related to the doctrine of universal benevolence; the failure results in part from the shift in conception of the purpose of comedy. And this shift in conception is related surely if subtly to the third mark by which the comedies popular in the repertory may be characterized: the eschewal of bawdry. For in creating comedies designed to meet new standards of propriety or in criticizing older comedies with whose root assumptions or superficial freedoms critics could no longer agree, playwrights and critics tipped the Horatian balance between pleasure and instruction far too often in favor of the didactic. Many

Georgian dramatists of the 1760s and 1770s portrayed *raisonneur* figures from whose lips flowed the "sentiments" which give a literal etymology to "clap-trap." These authors were often attempting to use the imitative form for a rhetorical, didactic end. An erring Lord Eustace in *The School for Rakes*, constantly doubting himself, is matched by a repentant and reformed rake in Frampton—a noble lesson for us all. In *A Word to the Wise*, Captain Dudley's pale rakishness—from which he is ultimately converted—must be opposed constantly by the honorable goodness of the noble Villars, the sententious suffering of old Willoughby, the pious moral truths of Sir John, and the spontaneous generosity of Sir George. In such works the informing principle of dramatic comedy is seen as positive moral instruction: avoid vicious figures, for they present to the young or unwary dangerous models, even if they are comically chastened for their faults; present instead *exempla* for emulation. Sheridan's laugh at "The Reformed Housebreaker," an imaginary didactic comedy which Sneer champions in *The Critic*, is directed at precisely this failure to intuit the proper ends of comedy:

DANGLE. . . . But what have we here?—This seems a very odd—
SNEER. O, that's a comedy, on a very new plan; replete with wit and mirth, yet of a most serious moral! You see it is call'd "THE REFORMED HOUSEBREAKER;" where, by the mere force of humour, HOUSEBREAKING is put into so ridiculous a light, that if the piece has its proper run, I have no doubt but that bolts and bars will be entirely useless by the end of the season.
DANGLE. Egad, this is new indeed!
SNEER. Yes; it is written by a particular friend of mine, who has discovered that the follies and foibles of society, are subjects unworthy the notice of the Comic Muse, who should be taught to stoop only at the greater vices and blacker crimes of humanity—gibbeting capital offences in five acts, and pillorying petty larcenies in two.—In short, his idea is to dramatize the penal laws, and make the Stage a court of ease to the Old Bailey.
DANGLE. It is truly moral.

[1.1.138–54]

Sheridan's joke follows his assertion in the tenth-night

prologue to *The Rivals* that Comedy is not "form'd to teach" (l. 13). He apparently agreed with Goldsmith's statement in the "Essay on the Theatre" that "Amusement is a great object of the theatre," and that such sententious characters and didactic plots do not amuse. Goldsmith certainly bows to the Horatian assumption of delight and usefulness, but his instructive end in comedy is negative; comedy "should excite our laughter by ridiculously exhibiting the follies of the lower part of mankind." Comedy is not just to delight, not just to instruct, but to blend both through the ridicule of follies; in such a view, the failure to amuse is the failure to fulfill the informing principle in both its aspects. Clearly the "mulish productions" to which Goldsmith was reacting in his "Essay on the Theatre" failed to fulfill the final cause of comedy.

So Goldsmith called for the return of the "laughing, and even low Comedy, which seems to have been last exhibited by Vanbrugh and Cibber," and thereby evoked the "reigning word," as Colman called it, in the current battle over comedy. Colman writes in 1775 that

> I am old enough to remember when the word LOW was this Scare-crow. *Genteel* Comedy, and the *politest* Literature, were in universal request; and every writer who attempted to be *comick*, dreaded the imputation of buffoonery. If a piece had strong humour—Oh, Sir, it's damned *low!*—was its sentence of condemnation.[23]

In the days of Congreve and Vanbrugh, "the term, *genteel comedy*, was then unknown amongst us, and little more was desired by an audience, than nature and humour, in whatever walks of life they were most conspicuous," Goldsmith writes in 1768.[24] But in the present age, "by the power of one single monosyllable, our critics have almost got the victory over humour amongst us. Does the poet paint the absurdities of the vulgar; then he is *low*: does he exaggerate the features of folly, to render it more thoroughly ridiculous, he is then very *low*."[25] The dichotomy of "low" versus "genteel" comedy colors Goldsmith's objection to "weeping" comedies and neatly divides the adherents on two sides of the complicated debate about the nature of comedy. To lovers of "genteel" comedy, "low" meant coarse, bawdy, and indelicate—but as the objections to the bailiffs' scene in *The Good-Natur'd Man* (CG, 29 Jan. 1768) showed, it also meant dealing with persons of vulgar classes; and as the attack on *She Stoops to Conquer* for its "low mischief and mirth" demonstrates,[26] it also meant farcical. To its supporters "low" meant "humourous" in all senses, including its eighteenth-century sense of dealing with idiosyncratic characters whose "humour" constituted the foible to be ridiculed. It certainly did not mean "bawdy," for even supporters of the "low" in Georgian drama eschewed sexual innuendo. To adherents of the "low," "genteel" comedy was weeping comedy strewn with pious but meaningless sentiments, lacking in vigorous ridicule of comic faults or foibles, and not designed to make audiences laugh. To adherents of the "genteel," the word referred to all that was sensitive, refined, dignified, morally uplifting; both laughter and tears were admissible if these qualities were upheld. The vast majority of late eighteenth-century comedies with plots designed to evoke tears were "genteel," particularly in the tearful line of action; but not all comedies including such plots were totally "genteel," for the subordinate lines of action frequently included characters and situations that were "low." The best example I know of a nearly completely "genteel" comedy is Hugh Kelly's *False Delicacy*, a comedy which certainly had some influence on Sheridan.[27]

The motivations of the major characters in *False Delicacy* present an elaborate tangle. Because Lady Betty Lambton feels she would be indelicate as a widow to receive the addresses of Lord Winworth, she denies herself the pleasure of marrying him; because Lord Winworth feels he would be indelicate to press his attentions where he still loves but has been once denied, he turns to Miss Marchmont, Lady Betty's grateful friend and ward. Miss Marchmont cannot refuse the advice of her protector Lady Betty, who has been asked by her erstwhile suitor Lord Winworth to intercede on his behalf, so Miss Marchmont admits Lord Winworth's addresses and denies herself the pleasure of marrying her beloved Charles Sidney; in turn Charles Sidney thinks he would be indelicate to tell his friend Lord Winworth of his love for Miss Marchmont. We would expect from this summary of the situation and from the title of the play a slightly satiric and rather absurd comedy of mistakes and misapprehensions, ridiculing that delicacy which is one characteristic of the "sensibility" so often attributed to sentimentalism. Indeed, we seem to have confirmation of our expectations when the spirited Mrs. Harley accuses Lady Betty and Miss Marchmont of being "unaccountably fond of these half-soul'd fellows, who are as mechanically regular as so many pieces of clock-work, and never strike above once an hour upon a new observation—who are so sentimental, and so dull—so wise and so drowsy" (act 1); when Mrs. Harley tells Lady Betty that if she were asked to marry Lord Winworth, "I would make sure work of it at once, and leave it to your elevated minds to deal in delicate absurdities" (act 4); and when she comments on the lovers by asking, "Did ever two fools plague one another with their delicacy and sentiment?" (act 4). Lady Betty is termed "Lady Sentimental," Charles Sidney "Master Sobersides," and Miss Marchmont "Madam Gravity": who would not expect a satire of the sentimental? Faulkland's delicacy about dancing or being cheerful in a lover's absence hardly seems more absurd. Yet in fact, the action of *False Delicacy*, like that of the Julia-Faulkland line of *The Rivals*, serves in part to vindicate the delicacy closely allied to generosity and suggests that Kelly had a positive didactic intent, much like that of the author of "The Reformed Housebreaker."

Lady Betty's motive for urging Lord Winworth on Miss Marchmont is her belief that Miss Marchmont wishes to receive his addresses; Lord Winworth's motive for addressing Miss Marchmont is his belief that Lady Betty has retired in her favor; Miss Marchmont's motive for receiving Lord Winworth's addresses is her belief that Lady Betty wishes her to. As Colonel Rivers says at the conclusion: "The principal moral to be drawn from the transactions of to-day is, that those who generously labour for the happiness of others, will, sooner or later, arrive at happiness themselves" (act 5). No real satire of delicacy is here; and in the final lines, at least, we find evidence of a positive didactic intent.

Moreover, much of the play's action upholds precisely the circumspect delicacy of personal conduct the benevolent practitioners of sentimentalism approved. Miss Rivers's lack of delicacy in contemplating elopement with Sir Harry Newburg leads to difficulties for herself, for her father, and for Sir Harry; the delicacy of old white-haired Cecil (himself with Mrs. Harley a ridiculer of the excessive delicacy of the lovers) prevents him from making a fool of himself by declaring to Miss Marchmont that his fatherly affection has changed to something warmer. Delicacy is not attacked, for generous delicacy of personal and social conduct eventually produces a satisfactory dénouement.

The subject matter and its treatment account for the play's "genteel" quality. That both lines of action (Lord Winworth–Miss Marchmont–Lady Betty–Sidney, and Sir Harry–Miss Rivers–Sidney–Colonel Rivers) are designed to produce tears for the sufferings of the virtuous (Miss Marchmont's denying herself the marriage with Sidney; Miss Rivers's *crise de conscience* over the elopement) might be taken by themselves as an indication of the play's "genteel" qualities. But more important is the tone of the piece, its *vis comica*, that truly makes it "genteel." Cecil is mildly twitted for refusing to wear a wig, but simultaneously granted such generosity, common sense, and good nature as to relieve him of any satiric attack on account of his dress; Sir Harry momentarily stoops to the notion of stealing Miss Rivers away, but, when Cecil reproves him, repents instantly: "But I was distracted:—nay, I am distracted now, and must entirely rely upon your assistance to recover her. . . . What a contemptible figure do I make!" (act 5). The dull sentimental folk offer sentiments, some of them accepted in seriousness, such as Lady Betty's "The woman that wants candour where she is address'd by a man of merit, wants a very essential virtue; and she who can delight in the anxiety of a worthy mind, is little to be pitied when she feels the sharpest stings of anxiety in her own" (act 2).[28] Indeed, the only sort of "low" humor like that which Goldsmith wished to revive in comedy is in the character of the irascible Colonel Rivers, an absolutist father similar to Sheridan's Sir

Anthony; even he is inexplicably turned into a maudlin mor-
alist on hearing of his daughter's plan of elopement and
piously confronts her, giving her the £20,000 which is her
dowry while tearfully turning away from her forever.

All in all *False Delicacy* is not an absolutely wretched play,
and Kelly proved himself a competent playwright of the
"genteel" school in such entertaining pieces as *The School for
Wives*. What hampered him was not the ethical view which
posited a genial world in which most people were basically
good natured, or the aesthetic theory which suggested that the
good found the highest pleasure in tearfully and benevolently
sympathizing for the sufferings of the virtuous, or even the
strictures against bawdry, farce, or vulgarity preached by the
followers of the "genteel": what hurt Kelly in *False Delicacy*
(and many writers of this kind of social problem comedy
popular in Sheridan's time) was a design which demanded
psychological depth, depth Kelly was incapable of creating.
Characters such as Lady Betty, Lord Winworth, and Miss
Marchmont might have been made real, but they certainly did
not appear real when a didactic motive in creation flattened
them and failed to answer the demands of an imitative form.
Goldsmith took much the same problem, motivated his character by a slightly improbable yet psychologically explicable
lack of self-respect, called it bashfulness, and found far more
success—not just because in *She Stoops to Conquer* he admitted
comic devices his time thought "low," but because he chose
first and foremost to amuse, not to instruct through positive
exemplary figures. Sheridan in *The Rivals* tried to make
his Faulkland a comic yet pitiable character and failed.

Three qualities, then, seem to be typical of the plays which
Goldsmith attacked in his "Essay on the Theatre" and Sheridan pilloried in *The Critic*. Each is related closely to the
qualities by which we may characterize the older popular
comedies in the repertory. The first quality—plots or lines of
action designed to evoke tears of distress or joy—is most
representative of comedies universally labelled "sentimental."
While it is easy to identify the philosophical justification which
the Georgian period offered for revelling in the "pleasing

Anguish" and the "Joy too exquisite for Laughter" (as Steele called them in the preface to *The Conscious Lovers*[29]), the eighteenth century did not have a special right to call this sort of sentimentalism its own. The pleasant sigh of pleasure at the relief of comic or melodramatic anxiety belongs to all times, and its more intense expression—the tears of joy—are common to almost everyone, even Rochester, Sedley, and their Royal Patron. But the eighteenth century, and particularly the Georgian period, is justifiably seen as a time in which such tears frequently were emphasized in comedy. It was the misfortune of the two decades from 1760 to 1780, which saw more than fifty new mainpiece comedies first produced, to lack a Shakespeare to handle both tears of distress and tears of joy. In the hands of a Mrs. Griffith, lacking the artistic skill necessary to make the evocation of tears seem more than insincere, poorly conducted plots of this nature deserve all the opprobrium Goldsmith and Sheridan can heap upon them.

The second quality—the portrayal of comic characters whose faults and foibles are forgiven on the basis of their good hearts—does not by itself identify "sentimental" comedy. Such appeals are so common and so prevalent that we hardly notice them in comic works whose other qualities far outweigh this blind spot in moral vision. When a period defines generosity as a cardinal virtue, we can expect to find generosity influencing all facets of dramatic literature. But surely we are justified to close the playbook on works whose artistic ineptitude allows this quality to be the only redeeming feature of a major character or the only probable basis on which to accept a significant change in personality.

The third quality—the eschewal of bawdry, indelicacy, the improbabilities of farce, and characters from common life in favor of an emphasis on the refined, sensitive, dignified, and morally uplifting—does not by itself identify "sentimental" comedy or characterize the mass of late eighteenth-century comedy. Nor does it suggest that an aesthetically pleasing dramatic comedy written along these lines is not possible: certainly many successful narrative comedies have been so written. But when used by the practitioners of the "genteel" to make imitative works serve the rhetorical end of presenting figures for emulation, it vitiates greatly the potentialities of comedy.

The concurrence of these three qualities in a single play was very rare in late eighteenth-century comedy, despite the attacks of Goldsmith and Sheridan, and indeed, in the comedy of any time. While there are a number of plays with plots designed to evoke tears and a number of plays whose actions and characters could only be called "genteel," there are few which include both qualities exclusive of other comic techniques. In fact, though every play of the period portrays characters who are generous and good-natured, and many forgive their faults on that basis, at least fifteen of the thirty new comedies produced in the immediate seasons before Goldsmith's essay (1760–72) are based on plots which are neither "genteel" nor designed to evoke tears. And while every play shows positive didactic impulses, most subordinate these impulses to occasional speeches which can be deleted without seriously altering the imitative end for which the comedy was created. The most obvious of such didactic excrescences are the "moral tags" that end almost every one of these comedies; Sheridan's obscure rose-thorn-wreath metaphor for the problems of love that ends *The Rivals* is a good example of such a tag.

In fact, the general character of Georgian comedy is not much unlike that of third-rate comedy of any period. A stereotypical plot might be concerned with the distresses of a pair or two of lovers. Their plight is the fault of insensitive or venal parents, or of villains motivated by obscure crotchets or pure evil. Through the agency either of chance or a benevolent person—an uncle, a family friend—the obstacles are rather suddenly removed. The agent generally seriously believes in something like the "holiness" of young love, but is usually aware that financial comfort is superior to love in a cottage; through arguments outwardly based on "sense" and "reason" he convinces the parents of their fault or by trickery helps to neutralize the power of the villain, thereby freeing the young people to marry. The resolution is applauded by the young lovers' servants who, though possessed of the right attitude concerning love and marriage for the hero and heroine, are generally unable themselves (like the young people) to effect the changes the benevolent agent had brought about.[30]

A line of action of this nature is not necessarily a recipe for aesthetic disaster. True, most of the obstacles are external and therefore not likely to lend themselves to the development of characterization: we will have few Beatrices and Benedicks wittily battling one another, few Rosalinds and Orlandos playing pastoral romantic love games to plumb the depths of mutual commitment, fewer Harriets and Dorimants or Millamants and Mirabels duelling for ascendency in relationships each knows to be inevitable. True, since the obstacles are merely external and since the hero and heroine are mostly incapable of altering them, many plays will have plots in which sympathy for the distresses of the protagonists overshadows interest in the contrivances advanced to overcome them or dampens delight in the ridiculousness of follies which prevent their mutual acceptance of one another. True, the presence of benevolent agents may lead to excessive moralizing, sententiousness, and artificiality of atmosphere. But small variations in any of these features can lead to effective stage pieces if not artistically first-rate comedies.

For instance, make the benevolent agent a foppish and foolish old rake, ridiculously described by a witty servant and ludicrous in his own appearance and manners, but possessed of a good heart. Make the characters who play the insensitive and venal parent-roles in part realistically motivated (so that the situation does not seem merely artificial) and in part themselves ridiculous—he could be a cit with pretentions to the aristocratic life which include a misdirected taste and an unjustified pride of his accomplishments in architecture and landscaping, motivated otherwise by a comical miserliness which makes him act unwittingly in accord with the hero and heroine's desires and puts him into other people's power; she could be his sister, a widow with aristocratic yearnings herself, blinded in part by her own amatory stirrings at fifty, and characterized by pretentious pronunciation. Make the hero and heroine capable of acting in their own interests to a small degree, avoid dwelling on their distress by presenting them

together only when action and not passivity is demanded, and
marry them before the commencement of the representation
so that their worst possible fate is to be banished in a state of
poverty, a fate distinctly improbable because their good nature
and appealing qualities immediately win the favor of generous, good-natured men. Add a mildly witty servant of
common sense, another lover of honor and good nature, a
ridiculous and generally impotent sister for a subordinate
villain; shake well with a series of misunderstandings and a
carefully prepared discovery scene involving all the characters
around a chamber door at midnight, dressed in their bed-
clothes, each expecting a different discovery while the audience all the time is aware of what will be disclosed. These
slight variations on a stereotypical Georgian comic plot form
the basis of George Colman and David Garrick's *The Clandestine Marriage*, one of the best of the new high Georgian
comedies.

While many late eighteenth-century comedies are designed
along these lines, many others vary the pattern in other
directions. A favorite device is to introduce a small but
corrigible fault into the character of the protagonist, thus
adding an internal obstacle to an external one. Charles Oakly
(*The Jealous Wife*), for example, drinks a bit too much and
hence is somewhat indiscreet; Belville (*The School for Wives*),
like Lord Belville (*The Married Libertine*, Charles Macklin, CG,
28 Jan. 1761), Lovemore (*The Way to Keep Him*, Murphy; as
five acts DL, 10 Jan. 1761), and Belcour (*The West Indian*), is a
man of sexual appetite whose attempted affairs complicate the
action; Millamour (*Know Your Own Mind*, Murphy, CG, 22
Feb. 1777) is delightfully irresolute both on marriage and on
the proper choice. Occasionally the fault is placed in the
female protagonist. Lady Restless (*All in the Wrong*, Murphy,
DL, 15 June 1761), like Colman's Mrs. Oakly (*The Jealous Wife*),
is comically jealous; Lady Frankland (*The Platonic Wife*), like
Sheridan's Lydia Languish, dwells on romantic absurdities to
express love. Faults of this nature provide the stuff for psychological depth in characterization, even though such depth
is rarely achieved in these Georgian comedies; and the use of
such faults can diminish reliance on external obstacles to the

happiness of the people we value, and hence diminish potential sentimentality.

Another variation on the stereotypical plot is to make the external obstacles people who are themselves ridiculous. Thus Lady Freelove, while vicious, is matched with the absurd if vicious Lord Trinket in *The Jealous Wife*; General Savage, principal obstacle to the marriage of his son and Miss Walsingham in *The School for Wives*, is not only a *senex amans* but the timid mouse of his mistress, Mrs. Tempest; the villainous Fulmers of *The West Indian* not only prove impotent because overreaching, but like the hypocritical puritan, Lady Rusport, are objects of our laughter.

Always available to the competent Georgian playwright is the leavening of ludicrous or ridiculous idiosyncratic and national characters. The generous, or occasionally as in Macklin and Foote, more harshly satiric treatment of such characters was common practice in many of these comedies. Whether included within the principal line of action or developed outside, such characters gave enough comic interest to sustain many a play whose plot or subplot was designed to evoke tears and to embellish many designed simply to amuse. Anyone can name his own favorite country booby, blustering Irishman, irascible father, rich nabob, virtuoso, or antiquated lover—amiable humorist or affected hypocrite.

Not surprisingly, many of the features of Georgian comedy are those which make the contrast with "high Restoration comedy" so plain. (It is well to remember that the plays of Etherege, Wycherley, and Congreve by which most of us have formed our opinion of high Restoration comedy are but a few of the many comedies written in the Restoration, and that the cynical or libertine attitudes they portray and the high level of witty dialogue they maintain is not characteristic of the mass.) In contrast to the relatively few Restoration comedies which we still read and see, Georgian comedy is noticeably devoid of wit: few and far between, even in Sheridan's comedies, are scenes in which the dialogue does not depend upon concealed information or the idiosyncratic characteristics of the participants, and hence is not purely witty. Similarly, few of these late eighteenth-century comedies contain characters who have succeeded in seduction or adultery and none, to my knowledge, who actually accomplish either in the course of the representation. I do not know of a Georgian comedy where cuckoldry is the final comic punishment, or of one which does not view marriage as a generally desirable institution to be entered with emotional as well as financial stability; indeed, there are a surprising number of relatively happy marriages which occurred before the representation and are discussed or portrayed in these plays. And I can name only three "keepers" in the whole literature: Lord Belville of *The Married Libertine*, Sir John Woodall of Mrs. Sheridan's *The Dupe*, and General Savage of *The School for Wives*. All are shown the error of their ways.

But "caparisons," as Mrs. Malaprop says (*The Rivals*, 4.2.6), are odious, and in assessing late eighteenth-century comedy we should not assume simply because the bulk of such comedies are "costume" plays dealing with fashionable or upper-middle-class life that they are comparable only to high Restoration comedy. Indeed, to one who has read widely in it, Georgian comedy is a logical development of an English comic stream that arises in the Elizabethan and Jacobean period, flows quietly beneath the impressive torrent of high Restoration comedy, and trickles into the twentieth century through the early plays of Wilde, the social comedies of Maugham, and the wit comedies of Coward. It is in the comedies of Richard Brinsley Sheridan that we see at once the limitations and the highest achievement of Georgian comedy.

CHAPTER II:

The Rivals

SNEER. . . .—But pray, Mr. Puff, what first put you
on exercising your talents in this way?
PUFF. Egad sir,—sheer necessity—the proper parent
of an art so nearly allied to invention. . . .
The Critic, 1.2.97–100

For my own part, I see no reason why the Author
of a Play should not regard a First Night's Audience, as a candid and judicious friend attending, in
behalf of the Public, at his last Rehearsal.
Preface to *The Rivals*

The Rivals is the production of a young man in possession
of a good wife who was in want of a fortune. On 13 April
1773, Sheridan had secretly married his beloved Elizabeth
Linley, the "siren of Bath" and the most admired popular
singer of the day. Their marriage upset Elizabeth's father,
Thomas Linley, who had hoped to continue exploiting her
rare talents (she was offered as much as £1,500 for a series of
concerts), and enraged Richard's father, Thomas Sheridan,
whose inflated notions of social propriety did not admit his
younger son's marrying a musician's daughter. He broke off
relations with his son; her father countenanced the marriage
with a small dowry. Sheridan abandoned his legal studies, and
since he refused to allow his wife to sing publicly for hire, the
fashionable young couple whose house in Orchard Street had
become by mid-1774 the center of an impressive London
social circle soon knew the pressures of poverty.

Raised with many of the advantages of a gentleman, money
excepted, Sheridan was suited to no career which required
more than wit, charm, and intelligence. Though his decision
to write for the stage may seem abrupt, he had tried his hand
at journalism and playwriting in his late adolescence. His
epistolary announcement to Thomas Linley on 17 November

1774 that "There will be a *Comedy* of mine in rehearsal at
Covent-Garden within a few days" constitutes a perfectly predictable clarion from the son of a playwright mother and a
player/playwright father. He claims that he had been "very
seriously at work" on several projects and is hopeful for the
comedy "that the least shilling I shall get (if it succeeds) will be
six hundred pounds."[1]

In the same paragraph, Sheridan says *The Rivals* was specifically written at the request of Thomas Harris, the shrewd
principal manager of Covent Garden. Whether or not Harris
commissioned it, certainly he treated the comedy with care,
for he helped cast the play with five performers who had
created starring roles in the theater's best recent comic success, *She Stoops to Conquer*: Mrs. Jane Green was both Mrs.
Hardcastle and Mrs. Malaprop; Mrs. Mary Bulkley created
Kate Hardcastle and Julia Melville; Ned Shuter added Sir
Anthony Absolute to his Mr. Hardcastle; John Quick made
Bob Acres rival Tony Lumpkin in fame; and Lee Lewes took
certain features from his Young Marlowe to create the pompous Fag. Other characters were cast with similar care.

But the first night, 17 January 1775, was unsuccessful. Ned
Shuter was not "perfect" as Sir Anthony (that is, he did not
know his lines, either because he had not rehearsed properly
or possibly because he was drunk) and John Lee was not
effective as Sir Lucius O'Trigger. Indeed, newspaper criticism
makes clear that the audience was dissatisfied not only with
the actors but with the inordinate length of the play, the
crude portrayals of Sir Lucius and Sir Anthony, the occasional
reliance on bad puns, bawdry, and grossness. In short, many
found it both too careless and too "low." Sheridan, needing
money and wishing fame, was perfectly willing to let his muse
serve the drama's patrons. Within eleven days he had carefully answered each criticism, shortening the comedy, remoti-
vating and recasting Sir Lucius (Lawrence Clinch, an old
family friend of the Sheridans, took the part), toning down
Sir Anthony's licentiousness, cleansing the dialogue of flabby
near-wit, and strengthening the characters to whom the response had been particularly good—Fag, and especially the

"genteel" Julia and Faulkland.[2] The result was a comedy whose success was not spectacular but solid: *The Rivals* failed to remunerate its backers at the rate of *The Duenna* or *The School for Scandal*, but it did not, like *The Duenna*, fade from the stage in the nineteenth century, and it has been performed at least as frequently as *The School for Scandal* in the last two hundred years.

That Sheridan utilized his own experiences in creating his first produced comedy is obvious. He had been involved in a long courtship filled with jealousy and self-doubts; he and Elizabeth had eloped (though they did not marry until a year later) as romantically as Lydia Languish could wish; he had fought two duels over his beloved; and during the period in which he wrote his comedy his relations with his father were far worse than those of Jack and Sir Anthony. For those reasons, and because of his Irish background and tenuous social position, throughout his adolescence and young manhood Sheridan had a variety of reasons for thinking himself a country bumpkin, an Irish adventurer, an intrepid intriguer, or a fretting, captious skeptic in love. Though his own experience provides plenty of material for a comedy, Sheridan perhaps drew as well on a variety of plays produced on stage in the late eighteenth century. Scholars have named three near contemporary farces—Garrick's *Miss in Her Teens* (1747), Colman's *The Deuce Is in Him* (1763) and *Polly Honeycombe* (1760)—as the sources of the mainplot and subplot of *The Rivals*, and the portrait of Lydia. Jonson's *Every Man in his Humour*—popular on stage in Garrick's version (1751)—has been suggested to explain the origin of Bob Acres. Farquhar's plays and Congreve's, especially *The Old Batchelor*, also have been mined for correspondences. One of the first newspaper reviews points out the similarities of Jack Absolute to characters in plays by Cibber and by Steele. Frances Sheridan's unfinished play, *A Journey to Bath*—which was in Sheridan's hands when he lived in Bath with his father, brother, and sisters—has been cited as yet another source. And Faulkland has been found in Murphy's *All in the Wrong*.[3]

Perhaps Sheridan's denial of plagiarism is responsible for so

diligent a search for sources. In the Preface to the first
printed edition of *The Rivals* he wrote that

> as my first wish in attempting a Play, was to avoid every
> appearance of plagiary, I thought I should stand a better
> chance of effecting this from being in a walk which I had not
> frequented, and where consequently the progress of invention
> was less likely to be interrupted by starts of recollection: for on
> subjects on which the mind has been much informed, invention
> is slow of exerting itself. —Faded ideas float in the fancy like
> half-forgotten dreams; and the imagination in its fullest enjoy-
> ments becomes suspicious of its offspring, and doubts whether
> it has created or adopted.
>
> [*Plays*, p. 6]

In whatever fashion Sheridan mined the rich vein of eighteenth-century comedy, he certainly refined the ore far better
than his contemporaries.

One reading of *The Rivals* suggests that its appeal lies in a
distinctly amiable plot peopled by charming, artificial, idiosyncratic characters. Though the plot is complex, it is not
overwhelmingly intricate or powerful in construction. To
identify plot as the primary source of pleasure would be as
foolish as to conceive of the action as one structured so as to
compare implicitly two equally wrong-headed views of love—
Lydia's romanticism with Faulkland's false delicacy and tor-
tured self-doubts. Some might point to a certain unified
aesthetic design or thematic coherence by noting the parallel
quality of the scenes between Jack and Lydia and Julia and
Faulkland or by pointing out the fortuitous resolution of both
lines of action in a single event (the duel), after which a
difficult and somewhat obscure metaphor tries to make clear
the similarities of the four lovers' plights. But these readings
cannot account for the excrescences to the design.

Again, a reading might show how the plot of *The Rivals*
resembles those of other Georgian comedies. Like the others,
The Rivals derives from Roman New Comedy, concerning
itself with the distresses of two pairs of lovers who wish to
marry. Like many comedies of the Georgian pattern, here the

obstacles to their happiness are internal rather than external: though Mrs. Malaprop and Sir Anthony serve brief roles as blocking agents, the real obstacles are within the lovers themselves. And Sheridan, like Goldsmith in *The Good-Natur'd Man* or Colman in *The Jealous Wife*, seems willing to postulate rather than make believable changes in character in order to remove the internal obstacles. Moreover, most of those necessary changes occur because the characters are good-natured. As in some other Georgian comedies, this principal line of action with its good-natured characters is joined to a "genteel" and nearly melodramatic secondary line, that of Julia and Faulkland. Both plots are resolved in an amiable way so as to include rather than exclude all characters in the new society created by the resolution. Irascible Sir Anthony, pedantic Mrs. Malaprop, pugnacious Sir Lucius, and cowardly Bob join hands with clever Jack, lively Lydia, self-doubting Faulkland, and sensible Julia to celebrate two marriages which misunderstandings and misguided notions rather than real evil or lasting intractibility have heretofore prevented.

But a reading of *The Rivals* that compares its plot to those other Georgian comedies is no more satisfying than one which locates the source of satisfaction in a structural or thematic view of plot, for plot in any sense is not sufficient to explain the power of *The Rivals*. Who would ask these questions of its plot? "Why does Lydia change her mind and accept Jack even after she has been tricked?" or "What is the affront which motivates Sir Lucius to duel with Jack?" or "Why does Julia agree to marry Faulkland when he has given no clear evidence that his jealousies will cease?" or "What is the function of Mrs. Malaprop's vocabulary in the plot?" Such questions about the probable connections between events in the plot of *The Rivals* seem irrelevant, while in most plays they reveal the sources of aesthetic satisfaction. They seem irrelevant because the confusing welter of circumstances is much less interesting than the exposures of characters' foibles and idiosyncrasies. *The Rivals* is, simply, a comedy of character, not a comedy of plot.

Of course, except in the loosest sense, character cannot be separated from plot. The judgments made about characters

are founded upon what they do as well as what they say. In
any comedy constructed as a coherent story, what characters
do affects the course of the action. Much pleasure in a
coherent story is provided by the successful resolution of relationships among characters and by the satisfying if mild comic
punishment dealt to characters who deserve to be tricked or
exposed, not only for their eccentricities, but also because they
have stood in the way of sympathetic characters. But in *The
Rivals*, local exposures of characters' peculiarities and follies in
themselves, and not just through their influence on the course
of the action, constitute the major sources of pleasure.

In short, *The Rivals* is one of those particular stage comedies like, for example, *Every Man in his Humour*, *The Old
Batchelor*, *The Recruiting Officer*, or *L'Etourdi* in which pleasure
derives from individual effects and not from a sophisticated
overall informing aesthetic design. Only the fun of seeing
comic crotchets exposed can explain audiences' delight in Mrs.
Malaprop's language, their willingness to forgive improbabilities of plot, and their obliviousness to the complete irrelevance
in the plot of such scenes as Jack's meeting with Sir Anthony
on the South Parade (5.2).[4] To understand *The Rivals* it is
necessary, then, to examine individually the characters and
the ways in which Sheridan provides opportunities for them
to expose their singularities.

Sheridan's first serious critic was his biographer, Thomas
Moore. In 1825 Moore pointed out the artificiality of the
characters:

> The characters of *The Rivals* . . . are *not* such as occur very
> commonly in the world; and, instead of producing striking
> effects with natural and obvious materials, which is the great art
> and difficulty of a painter of human life, he has here over-
> charged most of his persons with whims and absurdities, for
> which the circumstances they are engaged in afford but a very
> disproportionate vent.[5]

But Moore (and other contemporary critics) missed the point:
Sheridan was not aiming at psychological realism. *The Rivals*

does not seek to explore the human heart as do *As You Like It* or *Candida*, but instead seeks to please our sense of comic absurdity as do *The Comedy of Errors* or *The Importance of Being Earnest*. In Julia and Faulkland, perhaps, there are hints of the first kind of comedy, though handled little better than by Kelly in *False Delicacy*; but in the best known characters of *The Rivals* the second sort of comedy is brought to its highest pitch. Sheridan's achievement was to create new stage archetypes, the two best being Bob Acres and Mrs. Malaprop.

Though Mrs. Malaprop is strikingly original, her character is an amalgam of traits seen many times before on the Georgian stage. One tradition from which she springs is that of the foolishly amorous older woman, such as Lady Cockwood or Lady Wishfort; in contemporary plays harsh portraits had given way to the sexually less suggestive autumn loves of Mrs. Heidleburg in *The Clandestine Marriage*, Lady Autumn of Charlotte Lennox's *The Sister* (CG, 18 Feb. 1769), or Lady Dove of Cumberland's *The Brothers* (CG, 2 Dec. 1769). Sheridan could have seen Jane Green, the actress cast to play Mrs. Malaprop, create the role of Lady Dove and recreate the role of Mrs. Heidleburg for the Covent Garden performances of Garrick and Colman's play. He could also have seen Mrs. Elizabeth Hopkins, who became the first Mrs. Malaprop at Drury Lane under Sheridan's direction, portray Lady Wishfort; one performance in that role occurred 15 March 1774, during the period Sheridan was probably working on *The Rivals*.

However, Mrs. Malaprop's passion for Sir Lucius is central neither to the plot nor to her character, though it contributes to both. For example, at the end of the first act, when Mrs. Malaprop gives a letter for Sir Lucius to Lucy, the encounter is dramatically placed not so much to call attention to Mrs. Malaprop's absurd amorousness as to provide an opportunity for "Miss Simplicity" to display her talents. The old woman's protestations of affection, both verbal and written, serve more to display her tongue than her heart; and Sir Lucius's reading of her letter is amusing not so much for Mrs. Malaprop's misdirected passion as for her language, and for the imposture being practiced on the Irishman. Sheridan, as a practical playwright, knew that to stress her love for Sir Lucius beyond the bounds of mere comic suggestion was to run the risk of giving physical characteristics to their relationship in an age when a chaste embrace was a dangerous piece of stage business and sex outside marriage could hardly escape critical censure, no matter what its treatment.

The other tradition on which Mrs. Malaprop's characterization draws to a minor extent is that of the falsely learned lady. This type of character had been strong in English comedy long before even Congreve's Lady Plyant and still found expression in contemporary comedy. Sheridan's first Mrs. Malaprop, Mrs. Green, had recently created in William Kenrick's *The Duellist* (CG, 20 Nov. 1773) Lady Bauble, a crypto-feminist who is proud of her writing and her knowledge. Mrs. Malaprop's pretensions, however, are not very far-reaching. Her attitudes on the education of young ladies are dictated in part by Lydia's novel-bred romantic foibles, and are also stridently antifeminist. She does not—like Congreve's Lady Plyant or Hugh Kelly's recently displayed Lady Rachel Mildew (*The School for Wives*)—write; her conversation uses only the most common of Shakespearean quotations, and no other literary learning serves further to ridicule her affectations; nor is she any kind of virtuoso or antiquarian. Not false learning but a trait closely allied to it produces the effectiveness of the character—and that trait made her name a part of the English language.

The comic tradition of characters who misuse words extends across the history of English comedy. In its simplest aspect, it is exemplified by a host of chambermaids in the comedies of the 1760s and 1770s. Sheridan might have seen either of two servant-maid characters in plays by Samuel Foote: Betty in *The Lame Lover* (HM, 22 July 1770) who calls apothecary "potter-carrier," remarks on "satirical" (i.e., hysterical) fits, and is apparently familiar with the title of Ambrose Phillips's tragedy, *The "Distrustful" [i.e., Distressed] Mother*; or Kitty in *The Bankrupt* (HM, 21 July 1773) whose "purry-funalia" and "rippartees" are little better than mispronunciations. Such characters were so common in late eighteenth-

century comedy that David Garrick in 1766 was able to tell
Elizabeth Griffith that her "*Civil* is too like many Chambermaids of lat[e] who mistake Words, and I think that humour
very nearly Exhausted."[6]

    Mrs. Malaprop's words, however, are "ingeniously *misap-
plied*, without being *mispronounced*" (1.2.130–31). Her antecedents here are Dogberry in *Much Ado About Nothing*, Mrs. Slipslop in *Joseph Andrews*, and Winifred Jenkins in *Humphrey
Clinker*. (Of course, Sheridan also reworked Mrs. Tryfort, his
mother's character in *A Journey to Bath*; she shares the same
ancestors.)

    What differentiates Mrs. Malaprop from her predecessors
who misapplied words? Dogberry generally uses or interprets
words as their antonyms—thus Borachio and Conrade should
be damned to "everlasting redemption" for their actions—
though his near misses frequently create amusing puns: the
rag-tag constables certainly are a complete "dissembly." Winifred Jenkins, sounding like Mrs. Slipslop, attempts to spell
hard words she has heard Tabitha Bramble use and achieves a
similarly appropriate punning effect—surely Smollett effectively laid the groundwork for a Freudian analysis of Matt
Bramble when he had Win write that the "whole family have
been in such a constipation." Mrs. Malaprop, like Dogberry,
has antonyms—"malevolence" for benevolence, "controverti-
ble" for incontrovertible, "persisted" for desisted—but these
are few; almost all of her malapropisms are of the second
sort—words whose misapplication conveys with them other
meanings which are amusing. Thus "allegory" and "antistro-
phe" are literary puns; Sir Anthony's fear that romance
readers will become romantic is "laconic" as well as ironic; the
servant who will escort Mrs. Malaprop and the girls to the
scene of the duel has offered to "exhort" them there already.
One can easily believe that the stalactites found in damp and
dank Derbyshire pits were "putrefactions." There is something
"intricate" as well as ingrate about Lydia and something
"oracular" as well as vernacular about Mrs. Malaprop's
tongue, for hers is indeed a "nice derangement" of language.

    But such "derangement" alone is unlikely to create a character
as memorable as Mrs. Malaprop. We enjoy *Much Ado About*

Nothing for much more than just Dogberry's appearances; Mrs. Slipslop is minor; Winifred is a correspondent and character, but hardly the center of *Humphrey Clinker*. Yet Mrs. Malaprop has served as the chief character of many a farcical abridgement of *The Rivals* and apparently with good effect, even though her appearances in the play are hardly more frequent than Faulkland's and contribute but little to the plot. Indeed, the only scene in which she materially contributes to the action is the third scene of the third act, when her presence is necessary to interrupt Jack and Lydia. The basis for Mrs. Malaprop's continuing comic appeal is made clear by Jack's comments on her character in the letter to Lydia which she intercepts: "the same ridiculous vanity, which makes her dress up her coarse features, and deck her dull chat with hard words which she don't understand . . . does also lay her open to the grossest deceptions from flattery and pretended admiration" (3.3.59–70). Dogberry is merely ignorant: he does not know his mistakes are mistakes and he would not be particularly abashed to learn so. Win Jenkins attempts to mimic her ridiculous mistress and fails without making herself sound ridiculous too; she is merely ludicrous, while we recognize Tabitha as the truly ridiculous figure, for *she* should know better. But Mrs. Malaprop speaks as she does from her "ridiculous vanity," her desire to appear "queen of the dictionary," a "mistress of orthodoxy," and indeed, a "progeny of learning." The actress playing Malaprop is well-advised to emphasize each malapropism with self-satisfaction, vain pluming and preening, and conscious stress: in this way the incredible vanity will provide absurd contrast to the learned ignorance which complements the character's amorous stirrings. Only then will she be open to the "grossest deceptions" which Jack, Lucy, and even Sir Anthony (when he gently compliments her) practice upon her.

Sheridan provided another imaginative combination of characteristics—country naturalness, naiveté, foppishness, and false bravado—in the other great idiosyncratic character of *The Rivals*, Bob Acres. Country naifs were common on the Georgian stage; before Tony Lumpkin, Sir Harry Beagle of

The Jealous Wife and Squire Richard of *The Provok'd Husband* were probably the best known. All three of these roles had been performed at Covent Garden by John Quick, the creator of Bob Acres. Of the most recent country bumpkins after Tony Lumpkin, Jack Nightshade, one of two sons in Cumberland's *The Choleric Man* (DL, 19 Dec. 1774), and Toby Aircastle (an obvious take-off on Tony) in Foote's *The Cozeners* (HM, 15 July 1774) were both created by diminutive Tom Weston, famous as Scrub in *The Beaux' Stratagem*; though he might have seemed the logical actor to recreate Bob Acres when Sheridan produced *The Rivals* for his new company at Drury Lane, he died in 1776, one year before that production. Portraying Bob on that occasion was James Dodd, whom Sheridan would use as Lord Foppington in his revison of *The Relapse* and who had done naifs like Cloten in *Cymbeline* and Dupely in Burgoyne's comic opera, *The Maid of the Oaks* (DL, 5 Nov. 1774), as well as fops like Tinsel in Addison's *The Drummer* and Sparkish in Garrick's adaptation of *The Country Wife*.

The choice of Dodd for the recreation of Bob Acres explains even more than the choice of Quick for the creation of Acres: Sheridan's first intention seems to have been to combine the characteristics of a fop with those of a country bumpkin. The thought was original, but it was also typical of his time. The late eighteenth-century audience was no longer stimulated by a character who was merely a fop. Sir Fopling Flutter's polishing is too subtle for an era when dressing to the fashion without overaffecting was no longer a sign of wit and intelligence; the careful differentiation between wit and would-be wit practiced by the dramatists of high Restoration comedy would not work on a stage where such intellectual distinctions went unappreciated. Hence the fops of the Georgian stage had to be something else—a superannuated roué like Lord Ogelby in *The Clandestine Marriage*, a returning nabob who wishes to "polish" like Zachary Fungus in Foote's *The Commissary* (HM, 10 June 1765; reminiscent of *Le Bourgeois Gentilhomme*), or a bumpkin like Bob Acres who wants a place in what he thinks is fashionable society. The combina-

tion of country naiveté, foppishness, and cowardice is especially clear in Acres' relations with his servant David, in the
ornamental introductions to 3.4 and 4.1.

The humor of Bob's character springs from his failure to
realize the discrepancy between what he is and what he wishes
to be. Much of his characterization is purely visual, the stuff
of farce. His "hair in training" (2.1; done with his hair in curl
papers, as later acting texts indicate) presages his "cooked
head" in a subsequent scene (3.4); he is a perfect "Devon
monkeyrony" (i.e., "monkey" or fop plus "macaroni," the
London expression for fop) as David calls him.[7] He must
physically handle the letter he pens for "Beverley" in as
gingerly a fashion as David would, as if it did indeed smell of
gunpowder and might go off. The potential for visual stage
business in the last scene of the play is obvious: if the actor
does not use the practice duel with Sir Lucius for a great deal
of farcical effect, he has failed to capitalize on what Sheridan
clearly intended.

Since most of Bob's scenes are only tangentially related to
the plot, he is a perfect example of Sheridan's exploitation of
an idiosyncratic character for its own sake. Bob is technically,
but only technically, one of the four rivals for Lydia's hand
(the others of course are Sir Lucius, Jack, and "Beverley"); his
unconscious tormenting of Faulkland in the first scene of the
second act provides a probable but not necessary link between
the two lines of action; and while his undramatized dismissal
in form by Mrs. Malaprop motivates the challenge and the
duel, the duel is only a probable and not a necessary facet of
the resolution. We are unlikely to think about Bob in terms of
his relationship with Lydia, even though that imagined relationship is in part the reason for his whims and oddities.
Instead, the focus is on his amusing peculiarities and affectations. The sprightly, unconscious fop with his eccentric
"oaths referential" (another of the subtly comic uses of language in the play) gives way to the polisher whose partially
acquired social skills so befuddle honest David; in turn the
country bumpkin whose courage fires apace while his valor
rises gives way to the young man whose valor quickly vanishes
and who then tries vainly to retain some shreds of dignity
while asserting his good nature.

The conglomeration of all these comic traits produces a likeable, if highly farcical, character. He does not inspire the scornful superiority aroused by cowardly braggarts like Jonson's Captain Bobadil or Congreve's Captain Bluffe, nor does his country naturalness inspire the derision with which one may react to the drinking and fox-hunting excesses of Colman's Sir Harry Beagle or Macklin's satiric portrait of Squire Groom (*Love a la Mode*, CG, 12 Dec. 1759, still popular at Covent Garden in the 1770s). Neither does his foppishness have the selfish overtones of a Sparkish or a Fopling Flutter. His attempt to learn to dress and dance seems genuine but unfortunately misplaced; his participation in challenges and duels seems justified by his naive understanding of the situation. He is a passive and helpless character whom others spur to action. In short, he is drawn to evoke the same emotional responses as those evoked by such typical eighteenth-century amiable humorists as Parson Adams, my uncle Toby, and Dr. Primrose, and by the warm and sympathetic portraits of Falstaff with which Ned Shuter pleased Covent Garden audiences.

That Bob Acres is treated sympathetically, and that little is made of those qualities of Mrs. Malaprop which could be treated in harsh or bawdy terms, is indicative of the informing principle of this comedy. Sheridan is not yet attacking discernible external particulars, as he would with the satire of *The School for Scandal* and *The Critic*; in *The Rivals*, mild ridicule of stage types suffices. Both characters are amusing for linguistic reasons, but neither for linguistic reasons exclusive of character. And neither is likely to offend anyone—prude, countryman, or London wit.

With two other crotchety characters Sheridan was both less original and less careful not to offend, especially in the initial performance. Sir Anthony's bawdry struck the first night's audience as grossly "low" and indelicate; Sir Lucius's calculated fortune-hunting seemed an unfair attack on the Irish. In the revision, Sir Anthony's luscious description of Lydia's charms remains, but his inference from Lydia's anger in act 4 scene 2 that Jack has been too sexually aggressive with her mellows to the merest of suggestions. Sir Lucius now has the feelings of a gentleman, and hence Lucy has to make him believe he is courting Lydia while his letters really come from Mrs. Malaprop so that he will not feel he is sacrificing pride and delicacy to the necessities of his fortune. In addition, Sir Lucius has been given an inconsistently drawn motive to explain his participation in the duel: before, he fought Jack because he interpreted the same letter of challenge he dictated for Acres to be a challenge to him from Beverley when it was accidentally delivered to him; now he fights either to revenge a slight passed on the Irish by Jack or to "ask the gentleman, whether he will resign the lady" (5.3.143). Neither this father nor this Irish adventurer is particularly original in conception, but each is given manifold opportunity to expose his crotchets and oddities.

Perhaps no character in Western comic tradition is more common than the irascible father. The pattern of young people circumventing parents and guardians to marry appears so frequently that among the eighteenth-century comedies popular in the Georgian era one can quickly name seven irascible fathers characterized by a single additional trait. Sir Francis Gripe (Centlivre's *The Busy Body*), Obadiah Prim (Centlivre's *A Bold Stroke for a Wife*), Lovegold (Fielding's *The Miser*), and Peachum (*The Beggar's Opera*) are all miserly. Justice Woodcock (Bickerstaff's *Love in a Village*) is gouty; Sir Francis Wronghead (Vanbrugh and Cibber's *The Provok'd Husband*) is political; Croaker (Goldsmith's *The Good-Natur'd Man*) is pessimistic. All seven of these roles were popular as played by Ned Shuter at Covent Garden. Sheridan, when he was a young man and in London (1768–70), could have seen Shuter perform in any one of the roles; and perhaps he saw Shuter as the miserly city father, Grub, playing opposite Mrs. Green as the social-climbing Mrs. Grub in William O'Brien's harmless and popular farce, *Cross Purposes*.[8] Though Shuter was also skillful in roles as diverse as those of Polonius, Dogberry, and Cimberton (the fop of *The Conscious Lovers*), he gave highly sympathetic characterizations not only in his famous Falstaff role but in such gruff-but-good roles as O'Flaherty in *The West Indian* and Major Oakly in *The Jealous Wife*. Of course, his most recent old father was the good but old-fashioned Hardcastle of *She Stoops to Conquer*. It may well be significant that

Thomas King, who would create Sir Anthony for Drury Lane, had portrayed absolute fathers in Kelly's *The School for Wives* (General Savage) and Cumberland's *The Choleric Man* (the irascible Andrew Nightshade), and was capable of playing sympathetic roles like Belcour in *The West Indian* (DL, 19 Jan. 1771) or Captain Lloyd in *The School for Rakes* (DL, 4 Feb. 1769). Irascibility, with good nature at base, is Sir Anthony's distinguishing characteristic.

The pleasure audiences derive from Sir Anthony is clearly produced by the way in which his crotchety absolute disposition at first thwarts and then is circumvented by his clever son. He is important as a blocking agent in the plot, or rather, as an imagined blocking agent; he is not, like Congreve's Sir Sampson Legend, a serious threat, nor is he characterized by any particular quality other than his quick temper. Thus he is miserly, but he does not act upon his avarice; he proposes "kicking up his heels" like a *senex amans* to Mrs. Malaprop (4.2), but never appears particularly ridiculous for his autumnal rebirth; naturally he is gouty—as his leaning on David's shoulder for the walk to King's Mead Fields (5.2) makes clear—but his gout is no more than a visual accoutrement, for his irascibility springs from more than a sore foot. Surprisingly, Sir Anthony's quick temper has little to do with the plot; it merely provides an opportunity for the red herring of Jack's "forced marriage" (2.1 and 3.1). His other acerbic speeches—when he recommends starvation and confinement for Lydia and calls a circulating library a tree of diabolical knowledge (1.2), when he berates Jack (2.1) and is tricked by Jack's pretended phlegm (3.1), when he wonders at Jack's identity (4.2), when he is again tricked by Jack as Jack is going to duel (5.2), or when he tries to find the origins of the duel (5.3)—are simply good theatrical entertainment.

His basic good nature makes it even better entertainment. Sir Anthony can threaten to cut Jack off with a quarter guinea, but he can also gently flatter Mrs. Malaprop when she realizes Jack is the writer who called her "an old weather-beaten she-dragon" and can also tell her she is still in her prime when she declares that "men are all barbarians." He can demand that Jack marry sight unseen, but he can also admit that when he ran away with Jack's mother, he "would not have touched any thing old or ugly to gain an empire" (3.1.65–66). He can forgive the duel, and can reconcile Julia and Faulkland by reminding Julia that Faulkland, beneath his jealousy, needs the security their marriage will afford him. All of this is in perfect keeping with the amiable comedy of Sheridan's time, and except for its brilliant handling, none of it is particularly original in theatrical type or penetrating in psychological perception.

Nor is Sir Lucius particularly original. The first choice of John Lee to portray the character is puzzling.[9] But the choice of John Moody to recreate Sir Lucius in the Drury Lane revival of *The Rivals* sheds some light on Sheridan's Irishman as he conceived him subsequent to the first abortive performance. One of Moody's most famous roles was as Cumberland's Major O'Flaherty in *The West Indian*. O'Flaherty is a good-natured fortune-hunter who thinks he might marry the rich Lady Rusport; his essential honor—not his pique at being refused—leads him to expose her villainy in the end.[10] Moody also created Hugh Kelly's amusing, good-natured, and honorable Connolly in *The School for Wives*. Both these characters are conventionalized depictions free from the hate and satire with which the Irish were assaulted earlier in the century; Sir Lucius, as he was redrawn for the second opening, is not much different.[11] His function is almost completely ornamental: he exists to characterize Mrs. Malaprop and Bob Acres, to provide an occasion for the duel, and to show off his hot head, glib tongue, swaggering courage, and the good-natured honor which leads to his good-hearted declaration of reconciliation at the conclusion of the play.

All four of the principal idiosyncratic characters have fairly tangential roles in the plot, and the same is true of the three servants, Fag, Lucy, and David. Lucy disappears after her demonstration of her "Miss Simplicity" character at the conclusions of 1.2 and 2.2; Fag has little to say after 2.2, except for his part in bringing the news of the duel to Mrs. Malaprop and the women (5.1)—and his role there was soon excised from acting texts.[12] David does not appear until 3.4, then is present again in 4.1, 5.1, and 5.2, but has only a single line in the concluding scene. Each of these memorable place-holders is important for bringing crucial information to central characters at important junctures, and for providing contrast and elucidation where necessary.

Lucy is a hypocrite and the only character in the play who is motivated solely by selfishness—in her case, avarice. Though the clever deliverer of books is so ignorant as to think sal volatile the title of a novel rather than fashionable smelling salts, she recites a string of novel titles and cleverly intrigues for her mistress. Later she reveals herself as a practiced dissembler who has bilked Jack, Bob, Mrs. Malaprop, Sir Lucius, and Lydia of tips and favors. That the part was cast to Jane Lessingham, an actress who in 1774 had played successfully important roles like Constance Neville in *She Stoops to Conquer*, Hero in *Much Ado About Nothing*, and Lady Grace in *The Provok'd Husband*, is indicative of Harris's or Sheridan's care.[13]

David is little more than a "natural," a servant of country extraction who remembers far better than his master the pleasant life built around eating, drinking, and hunting to which any country squire is likely to become accustomed. His commonsense reactions to Acres's polishing provide an excellent contrast to Bob's misguided efforts to win Lydia. John Dunstall's performances as Lockit in *The Beggar's Opera*, Sir Jealous Traffic in *The Busy Body*, Tradelove, one of the four jealous guardians of *A Bold Stroke for a Wife*, or especially John Moody, the honest country servant of *The Provok'd Husband*, certainly qualified him for this rich if hackneyed role when he created it in the original production of *The Rivals*.

Fag is perhaps the most interesting of the servants. He lords it over Thomas the Coachman, who he assumes is illiterate;[14] he prides himself on his own forays among the lower classes of fashionable Bath society; he thinks it amazing that Mrs. Malaprop would look at Sir Lucius rather than himself who has "walked by her window an hundred times" (2.2.73). His delightfully circumstantial explanation of Jack's presence in Bath, leading to expansions of their success at recruiting, and his pedantic circumlocutions in the first scene of the fifth act, come close to Mrs. Malaprop's foibles but do not detract from

them. Lee Lewes, who created Fag, also created Charles
Marlow, and played both Tibalt in *Romeo and Juliet* and Osric
in *Hamlet*. Fag's was an important role to director and playwright.

Even in his first play, Sheridan knew that every part
counted, and like Garrick and Colman in *The Clandestine
Marriage*, or their predecessors Congreve and Farquhar, he
seldom allowed a servant's role to be empty. Colman and
Garrick created the amusing Brush, Lord Ogleby's vain and
conceited servant; Congreve's Waitwell is the epitome of the
dramatically useful servant; Farquhar's Scrub in the hands of
Weston at Drury Lane or Shuter at Covent Garden was
delightful to behold. Sheridan used almost all of his servants
effectively, enhancing the character-centered qualities of *The
Rivals* by giving each theatrically viable foibles and rarities.
Even Thomas the Coachman is granted amusing and characteristic comments on Bath society. The only placeholder in the
piece is the anonymous maid who announces Julia to Lydia in
act 5 scene 1—and one wonders why this is not Lucy.

Despite its character-centered qualities, *The Rivals* also conveys a story, a story concerned largely with the plight of the
four lovers. In examining their importance to the informing
design we can dismiss passive Julia, although Sheridan's audiences were delighted with her common sense and delicate,
feminine distress. Today we are only surprised that she
endures Faulkland's absurdities so long; then she was interpreted as a sentimental heroine of depth and perception.
Certainly she understands Faulkland, and despite her tears at
the conclusion of both their dramatized meetings, perhaps she
understands herself. A dignified passive character of this
nature was an accustomed role for Mrs. Mary Bulkley, who
had recreated the similarly oppressed Louisa Dudley for
Covent Garden's production of *The West Indian*, but who was
also capable of creating Kate Hardcastle, or for Mrs. Sophia
Baddeley, who had created Louisa Dudley, and who became
the second Julia for Sheridan's revival of *The Rivals* at Drury
Lane. Julia may not, like Louisa Dudley, have her virtue
assaulted, but she certainly undergoes all the mental turmoil

that besets Cumberland's character, and more. "Chaste," "elegant," "tender," and "affecting" are the adjectives of praise with which Mrs. Bulkley's and Mrs. Baddeley's performances in the role were met.[15]

A subtle eye, a dashing handsome exterior, and a sense of self-possession are necessary for the portrayal of Jack Absolute, and for its Covent Garden introduction, the role was entrusted to an aging but competent comic performer, Henry Woodward. Woodward was the successor to John Rich in the many Harlequin roles of the Covent Garden stage, though gradually Lee Lewes was winning the characters which the sixty-five-year-old Woodward could no longer play night after night. The elderly performer was, however, still popular as the clever and witty Tom of *The Conscious Lovers*, as the rash Mercutio, and as Iago's dupe, Roderigo; he was still capable of roles as diverse as fiery Captain Bobadil, Mrs. Centlivre's blundering Marplot, or Macklin's selfish fox-hunting Squire Groom in the popular farce *Love a la Mode*. In recent seasons he had created Lofty, the social climber of Goldsmith's *The Good-Natur'd Man*, the brusque but good-hearted Captain Ironsides in Cumberland's *The Brothers*, and the honest Tropick of Colman's *The Man of Business*. When Captain Absolute was given new life at Drury Lane, he was portrayed by John Palmer, who later would create the hypocritical Joseph Surface and who lately had created such roles as Sir Harry Newburg, the slightly foppish, rash, good-hearted suitor of Hugh Kelly's *False Delicacy*, the noble Colonel Evans of Mrs. Griffith's *The School for Rakes*, and the essentially honorable young Leeson of Kelly's *The School for Wives*. Indeed, Palmer created yet a third Kelly hero—Captain Dormer, the pale rake of *A Word to the Wise* (DL, 3 March 1770). Like Jack, this character hypocritically employs a self-parodying romantic vocabulary in his love-making and is at last exposed when he is "in the meridian of all his nonsense" while making high-flown love to the clever Miss Montagu.[16]

Jack is clearly the center of the play. He appears in eight of the thirteen scenes, and in cutting his role for performance only one of those may be removed (5.2, the ornamental scene

on the South Parade). This, the most active character, ma-
nipulates all the others before being exposed himself and is
responsible for exposing the foibles and whim of every idiosyncratic character but Sir Lucius. Jack is a clever intriguer
whose assumption of a disguise is but slightly more culpable
than Archer's masquerade as Aimwell's servant; the discomfiture he receives—temporary loss of Lydia, exposure before
his father and Mrs. Malaprop—is minor. He loves Lydia; his
instinctive reply to Sir Anthony is not to give her up, and his
understanding of the sprightliness and beauty that underlie
her absurdity is humanly warm. He clearly intends honorable
marriage, not seduction. His commonsense attitude toward
the idiosyncratic characters and his witty, bemused tolerance
of them are transmitted to the audience. When Faulkland
insists that a truly modest woman would join only her near
relatives in a country dance, Jack drily replies, "Aye, to be
sure!—grand-fathers and grand-mothers!" (2.1.227). When Sir
Anthony insists that he would not touch anything old and
ugly for a fortune, Jack asks, "Not to please your father, Sir?"
(3.1.67). In the height of his romantic frippery with Lydia, he
tells the audience, "If she holds out now the devil is in it!"
(3.3.151). And when Sir Lucius finds himself disappointed
that there may not be a duel after all, Jack coolly advises
Faulkland, "O pray, Faulkland, fight to oblige Sir Lucius"
(5.3.100).

Typical of the comic heroes of high Georgian comedy, Jack
is not only mildly clever, motivated by honest, not entirely
selfish desires, but also humanly warm. The anger he displays
toward Fag after Sir Anthony leaves (2.1), the embarrassment
of meeting Lydia in his own person at last (4.2), the fretful
disappointment he displays while answering Sir Lucius's prov-
ocations and rebuking Faulkland (4.3) remind us that the
cool-headed intriguer is only a man, subject like most men to
his emotions; and his honorable replies to Sir Lucius's challenges (4.3 and 5.3) are those of a man who respects his
reputation but would not consciously set out to insult a man to
prove it. His treatment of Faulkland's jealousy and Acres's
newly acquired social graces is actually rather gentle; Jack's
reactions to neither are malicious so that, for instance, Faulk-

land's pique (2.1) seems entirely of his own making yet
understandable, and the irony of Acres's application to Jack
for advice in his suit with Lydia hardly apparent. In short,
there is almost nothing unlikeable about Jack Absolute.

While Julia and Jack are attractive in their various ways,
Lydia and Faulkland present some difficulties. Each is characterized by a single set of traits which seems a bit fantastic. In
Lydia's case the result is the creation of a distinct stage type,
in Faulkland's the attempt at a delineation of a character of
psychological depth. The original performer of each role was
a relative newcomer to the Covent Garden stage. Jane Barsanti had arrived for the 1772–73 season and was popular as
Estifania, the clever serving woman who dupes Michael Perez
in *Rule a Wife and Have a Wife*; she also attempted Mrs. Oakly
in *The Jealous Wife* but was not well received. Nevertheless, by
the end of the season she had earned for herself a fair
following, as the nearly £150 she brought in at her first
London benefit suggests. W. T. Lewis apprenticed on the
Dublin stage and arrived at Covent Garden for the 1773–74
season. His specialty appears to have been romantic roles. In
1773–74 he was seen as Mercutio, Lothario (Rowe's *Fair
Penitent*), Florizel in an adaptation of Garrick's adaptation of
The Winter's Tale, and Posthumus in *Cymbeline*; by the next
season he had earned a chance to perform Romeo, Orlando,
Cassio, and Claudio (*Measure for Measure*). Also in that 1773–
74 season, Miss Barsanti and Lewis appeared with each other
in contrasting parts in six different plays. Once they were
lovers when Miss Barsanti appeared as Dorinda (a notorious
"try-out" part for actresses) and Lewis took Aimwell in *The
Beaux' Stratagem*; but the rest of the time they merely shared
the boards, as they do in *The Rivals* (Faulkland and Lydia are
on stage together only in 5.3). A benefit performance of *Love
for Love* failed to establish either of them in the parts of Mrs.
Frail or Valentine, but the Covent Garden introduction of *The
West Indian* brought better luck for both: Miss Barsanti gained
popularity as a rather spirited Charlotte Rusport, while Lewis
made Belcour one of his famed roles. Kenrick's unsuccessful
The Duellist gave both their first opportunity to create a
character, Miss Barsanti as the spiteful and mildly hypocritical

Lady Lovemore, Lewis as the noble, cautious Counsellor Witmore. When Mrs. Bulkley chose *The South Briton* to make its sole London performance at her benefit, she called upon Barsanti and Lewis to create two roles for her.

That Miss Barsanti had begun to specialize is suggested by her choice of Steele's *The Funeral* for her 1774 benefit; the £175 she earned came from her performance of the witty, scheming Lady Brumpton. Lewis did her the favor of performing for his first time the noble, generous Campley—the kind of role in which he had begun to specialize. Therefore it would seem that entrusting Lydia to Miss Barsanti was chancey; the role was not really within her specialty, but she was young enough, spirited enough, and perhaps seasoned enough for success. Casting Faulkland to Lewis was taking no chance at all: his experience in romantic heroes and his range of noble Shakespearean characters suggests that he was perfectly equipped to do the part. Sheridan's choice of actors to portray these roles two years later at Drury Lane suggests that he still wanted youth, liveliness, and adolescent freshness for Lydia, and comic, romantic, but psychologically sensitive power for Faulkland. Frances Abington, successful as hoydens like Miss Prue and Laetitia Fondlewife, performed Lydia; handsome Samuel Reddish, who had created the nobly reformed rake Frampton in Griffith's *The School for Rakes*, the pious Sir John Dormer in *A Word to the Wise*, the conscientious young George Melville in William O'Brien's ill-fated *The Duel*, and Belville in *The School for Wives*, was given Faulkland.

Lydia Languish is a distinct stage type, though her novel-reading habits are not merely Sheridan's invention: a correspondent to the *Morning Chronicle* of 27 January 1775 declared that "almost every genteel family now presents us a Lydia Languish."[17] Several characters of this nature had been portrayed on stage before *The Rivals*. One is George Colman's Polly Honeycombe (in the farce of the same name), a bumptious, fractious intriguer who lacks the charm of Sheridan's Lydia. Jane Pope, who would many years later become Mrs. Candour, created Polly and was still playing her in the late 1770s. Sheridan might have seen her in the 10 February 1773 revival; and certainly before then he had written the following lines for an aborted adaptation of Goldsmith's *The Vicar of Wakefield*. The speaker is the budding dramatist's version of Moses Primrose:

> Why no Mother you are always gibing me because I was six months at the university, it would be better if you would take a little care of my sister and not let her be filling her head [with] novels. I never knew any good come of such stuf[f], they get their hands so plaguy full of pu[r]ling streams and dying swain that w[h]ere they can't find an Oroondates they'll pack of[f] with Thomas.—[18]

Lydia's novel-reading habits serve almost solely to define her character broadly, not to provide direct objects for parody: after the initial scene with Lucy and Sir Anthony's few comments on circulating libraries, the novels themselves are forgotten, and what becomes a matter of concern are the expectations, derived from the novels, that Lydia has of a lover. In this regard her character appears very like two others, both the "genteel" creations of a woman who followed in Frances Sheridan's dramatic footsteps, Elizabeth Griffith. One is Lady Frankland in *The Platonic Wife* (DL, 24 Jan. 1765), the other Lady Louisa of *The Double Mistake* (CG, 9 Jan. 1766).

Like Lydia, Lady Frankland has been strongly influenced by her reading habits; she is described as sitting up all night tearfully reading a new romance, and she "dies for sentimental passion." On her first appearance in the play she misquotes Pope's "Eloise to Abelard" and expresses her desire for an "ardent love which lifts us to the skies upon its seraph's wings." She has left Lord Frankland because she doubts his love; in fact he loves her still, but realizes that she must overcome her "fond wishes to inspire a vain, romantic passion." Not so comic as Lydia, Lady Frankland is evidently the result of an attempt on Mrs. Griffith's part to portray a character motivated in a complex manner by conflicting understandings of romantic, sentimental, and self-love. The unachieved complexity has little to suggest Lydia, but two other similarities are striking. First, Lady Frankland prefaces many of her sentences with "heigh-ho," a tag which Sheridan uses in Lydia's early lines. Second, her sensible friend Emilia tells her this story:

Indeed, my dear lady Frankland, you talk strangely, and put
me in mind of a young lady of my acquaintance, deeply versed
in romance, who, with a large fortune, ran away with an ensign;
but when they had got clear off, she would not be content
unless he returned and suffered her to leap out of a window to
him: The experiment was made, and the poor lady discovered,
and confined, till a more suitable match could be found out for
her.

[Act 1]

Luckily, Lydia planned for an "amiable ladder of ropes" to
descend rather than leaping to her Ensign Beverley.[19]

In *The Double Mistake*, Mrs. Griffith creates another romantic, Lady Louisa Belmont. Again the correspondences
with Sheridan's character are entirely on the ground of a
romantic conception of love; Lady Louisa is attracted to fashionable London life (just as Lady Teazle would be) and believes that "Secrecy is the very essence of love, and like all
other essences, it will evaporate, the moment it gets the air"
(act 1). This belief provides the motivation for her romantic
affair with the younger Freeman, who unfortunately is not
very attractive since he lacks entirely the sober industriousness
that characterizes his older brother or the grave good nature
of Louisa's brother Lord Belmont and sister Lady Mary. The
sympathetically drawn Lady Louisa believes "there is something
so indelicate in public courtships and weddings, that I cannot
bear the thought," and so refuses Lady Mary's request to
introduce him to the family because "the approbation of her
friends [will] prevent her liking" him (act 3). A convenient
conversion saves Louisa from young Freeman, and while they
will apparently never be married, young Freeman agrees to
pursue the mercantile business that is his station and responsibility.[20]

Lydia Languish is no more directly indebted to Lady Frankland and Lady Louisa than to the two other characters so
frequently cited—Biddy Tipkin and Polly Honeycombe. She
does share their romantic foolishness: she fomented a quarrel
with Jack because they had never had one; she dreams of him
"stuck like a dripping statue" in the garden, "shivering with
cold, and I with apprehension"; and she hopes for a romantic

elopement "with such surprise to Mrs. Malaprop—and such paragraphs in the News-papers!" (5.1.146–48, 133). But she has other characteristics that distinguish her from them. Underlying her fripperies is a quick-witted intelligence without which she would be no proper match for Jack; she remarks that Julia should not be grateful for Faulkland's having saved her from drowning: "Why a water-spaniel would have done as much" (1.2.119). Neither her disobedience of Mrs. Malaprop nor her scorn for Acres are likely to arouse the audience's disapproval—and just at that point where the audience may begin to tire of her caprices, Sheridan provides grounds for sympathy: in the first scene of the fifth act, she wonders how, as an heiress, she is to know that she will not be a "mere Smithfield bargain" at last.

Her final line in the play acknowledges the difficulties her attitudes have created in her relationship with Jack, but in a playful fashion. Faulkland has compared his situation with Jack's, saying they have both been lucky at love in overcoming their obstacles; Jack replies that "we have both tasted the Bitters, as well as the Sweets of Love—with this difference only, that *you* always prepared the bitter cup for yourself, while *I*— [LYDIA:] Was always obliged to *me* for it, hey! Mr. Modesty?" (5.3.249–52). Lydia's is an "easy and elegant," and "agreeable" character;[21] she inspires gentle, not harsh laughter, in a manner appropriate to the best of amiable Georgian comedy.

In its way, Faulkland's character is a male reflection of Lydia's—not on the ground of its appearance but on the ground of its motivation. But while he did not try to expose the human heart in Lydia, in Faulkland Sheridan attempted to plumb the emotional depths of jealousy, particularly that sort of jealousy arising from insecurity. And he evidently wanted to achieve both psychological depth and comic amusement. The audience is supposed both to sympathize with Faulkland and to laugh at him when he allows his awareness that Julia was promised to him by her now-dead father to lead him into exaggerated fears that she may now feel no real love but an obligation to that promise and to his having saved her from drowning. Similarly, his behavior when Acres unconsciously disturbs him (2.1) is supposed to appear ridiculous, as is his quixotic soliloquy following Julia's tearful exit (3.2). Earlier in that scene he catches upon Julia's words ("ingratitude," "quality," "contract," "liberty") and misinterprets them as his false delicacy and self-doubt would wish. Faulkland's self-torture resembles the excessive sentimental delicacy of feeling which beset Hugh Kelly's characters in *False Delicacy*; the language is remarkably similar and the quality of amusement in the scene is very like that which Kelly evokes in his interview between Lady Betty and Lord Winworth (4.1).

Jack characterizes Faulkland as a "captious sceptic in love,—a slave to fretfulness and whim—who has no difficulties but of *his own* creating" (4.3.112–14). Lydia accuses him of jealousy,[22] but Julia's view is different:

> . . . he is too proud, too noble to be jealous; if he is captious, 'tis without dissembling; if fretful, without rudeness. —Unus'd to the fopperies of love, he is negligent of the little duties expected from a lover—but being unhackney'd in the passion, his affection is ardent and sincere; and as it engrosses his whole soul, he expects every thought and emotion of his mistress to move in unison with his. —Yet, though his pride calls for this full return—his humility makes him undervalue those qualities in him, which would entitle him to it; and not feeling why he should be lov'd to the degree he wishes, he still suspects that he is not lov'd enough:—This temper, I must own, has cost me many unhappy hours; but I have learn'd to think myself his debtor, for those imperfections which arise from the ardour of his attachment.
>
> [1.2.100–111]

Jack's view leads to a good comic character; Julia's view of Faulkland as basically insecure, because of its depth of perception, produces a Faulkland requiring the most subtle of interpretations, and consequently clashes with the broader and more farcical portraits of the rest of this comedy of character. When Sheridan saw an acting script of the play around 1787, he noticed that Julia's explanation of Faulkland's character had been cut by the actresses and was infuriated: "The only speech in the play that cannot be omitted. The pruning-knife, Damme, the Axe! the Hatchet!" he wrote in the prompt-script.[23] But the actresses were right, from their viewpoint.

Without Julia's explanation, Faulkland can be played as almost low comic; with it, and with his motivation understood, he becomes too complicated for a play whose essence is fast-moving, broad, almost farcical characterization only barely dependent upon plot.

In the prologue to the tenth night's performance of *The Rivals*, Sheridan claimed that he sought to prevent "the Goddess of the woeful countenance—the sentimental Muse" from displacing "gay Invention," "amorous hint," "wit," and "Satire's strokes." Comedy was not designed to teach: "Bid her be grave, those lips should rebel prove,/ To every theme that slanders mirth and love." To tragedy belongs moral truth:

> Can our light scenes add strength to holy laws!
> Such puny patronage but hurts the cause:
> Fair Virtue scorns our feeble aid to ask;
> And moral Truth disdains the trickster's mask.
> [Lines 37–40]

The informing principle of this comedy, as he viewed it *after* success had been gained, was gay comic laughter, and perhaps just a *soupçon* of satire.

But the comic criticism of *The Rivals* rarely becomes true satire, if by satire is meant an attack upon discernible historic particulars—the ridicule of objects in the external world. Mrs. Malaprop, Sir Anthony, Bob Acres, and Jack are merely theatrical types, representative of human nature only in the most general sense. The comic criticism which is directed at them as stage characters is mitigated greatly by their own good nature and by the sympathetic views we are asked to take of them. The Sir Lucius who might stand for Ireland has been softened to an amiable humorist whose Irishness is merely conventional; and Julia, of course, is never criticized.

Nor is there much recognizable satire of social institutions or practices. Bath society gets some licks in the first scenes, but few elsewhere (and the Bath satire disappeared quickly from the script on topically oriented stages); of arranged marriages there is no disapproval, for two of them work out successfully. And duelling, a practice vigorously, if didactically, attacked in three recent plays (*The Duel*, *The Duellist*, and

The School for Wives) is not attacked here; a duel to preserve
one's reputation when one is the object of an unprovoked
attack (as is Jack) seems perfectly acceptable. Indeed, in avoiding satire of any definable external object, Sheridan the monetarily motivated playwright avoided offending anyone.

If there is satire in *The Rivals*, it attacks sentiment; but even
that is considerably muted. Though there is ridicule of Lydia's
misdirected notions of romantic love bred by her reading of
popular "sentimental" novels, and of Faulkland's absurd delicacy of feeling, the faults are handled gently, with sympathy
for the characters and with little attempt to motivate self-
realizations. In fact, in view of the sensible but sentimental
feeling of Julia, the amiable good nature which all characters
reveal, and the didactic metaphor that ends the play ("When
Hearts deserving Happiness would unite their fortunes, Virtue would crown them with an unfading garland of modest,
hurtless flowers; but ill-judging Passion will force the gaudier
Rose into the wreath, whose thorn offends them, when its
Leaves are dropt!" [5.3.256–60]), we are inclined to agree with
Richard Little Purdy: if Sheridan was satirizing sentiment or
even writing in reaction to sentimental, weeping comedies,
then "he left important hostages in the camp of the enemy."[24]
More likely, the camp of sentimentalism was his own and, if
all the forces there were not his native countrymen, at least
they were friendly mercenaries.

Whatever his attitude toward sentimentalism, in *The Rivals*
Sheridan proved himself a master of comic technique, particularly of comedy of situation. While some of the scenes, like the
exchange between Mrs. Malaprop and Sir Anthony (1.2), are
built upon good comic theatrical dialogue unshaped by irony
of situation, the most effective scenes are those in which the
essence of the created comic situation lies in dramatic irony—
scenes in which truths are concealed from some of the characters but are known to others, and to the audience. Consider
how such a technique works in the third scene of the third
act. Jack passes himself off to Mrs. Malaprop as Absolute, but
continues in his disguise as Beverley to Lydia. The humor of
the scene arises mostly from Mrs. Malaprop's mistaken assumption of Jack's identity. She makes herself appear ridicu-

lous by triumphantly proclaiming her invincibility as a guard-
ian to Lydia. "Elude my vigilance, will he" (3.3.73–74), she
chortles as "Beverley" stands in her very drawing room,
preparing with her assistance to meet privately with Lydia. A
mild comic anxiety that Jack will overextend himself and be
caught, with discomfiting if not disastrous consequences, is
increased by Mrs. Malaprop's secret arrival on the scene while
Jack as Beverley woos Lydia. Jack escapes this time, and by
the end of the scene each character is in possession of only
part of the essential knowledge we as audience have. Mrs.
Malaprop knows Jack is Absolute, but not that he is Beverley;
Lydia knows Jack is Beverley, but not that he is Absolute; and
only Jack knows that he is both, but he is unaware of the
depth of Lydia's commitment to the romantic imposture. The
two women both see themselves as clever—Mrs. Malaprop in
preventing Beverley from seeing Lydia, Lydia in duping her
aunt—while both are really dupes of Jack. And we, in our
mild comic anxiety, see the probability that Jack's cleverness
will be overborn at last when the truth is equally distributed.

The technique of letting the audience in on the joke—
rather than surprising them as Congreve does with Mirabel's
deed at the conclusion of *The Way of the World* or as Colman
and Garrick do with Lord Ogleby's unexpected support of
Fanny at the conclusion of *The Clandestine Marriage*, for instance—allows the audience the pleasures of both anticipation
and expectation. Sheridan would work diligently with this
technique in his farce *St. Patrick's Day*, his comic opera *The
Duenna*, and his adaptation of *A Trip to Scarborough* until he
achieved its greatest realization in *The School for Scandal*.

The Rivals, then, is a supremely practical play, lacking for
the most part any moral seriousness or effectively realized
psychological depth, but admirably suited to please on the
stage. It is wholly typical of high Georgian comedy: in it two
lines of action—the one a brisk intrigue, the other a genteel,
problematic, and only partially successful comic sentimental
line of action which appears designed to evoke strong comic
anxiety if not tears for the sufferings of a virtuous heroine—
are subordinated to the portrayal of comic characters whose

purely local exposure constitutes our chief pleasure in the piece. The characters in turn are all amiable humorists, good-natured at base, but not particularly representative of any external reality which would serve either to identify them as objects of satiric attack or as portraits of typical human behavior. The situations into which these characters are put allow for a good deal of light, farcical fun which is neither licentious nor particularly witty, but for the most part humorous (in its eighteenth-century sense) and occasionally built upon complex dramatic ironies. The informing principle of the whole is harmless theatrical fun, not as aesthetically pleasing as, say, *She Stoops to Conquer*, but certainly not burdened by the didactic impulses inherent in plays like *False Delicacy*. It is easily understood as the production of a young man serving an apprenticeship and desirous not of securing posterity's approval or of reversing contemporary trends in dramatic comedy, but of making money. And as the innumerable echoes in *The Rivals* to other late eighteenth-century comedies suggest, Sheridan, like Congreve and Farquhar, was very familiar with the comedy popular in his day. Moreover, "*il ne se pose pas en révolutionnaire. . . . Il se soumet au goût du jour.*"[25]

CHAPTER III:

St. Patrick's Day and The Duenna

> PUFF. In short, we are at a loss which to admire most,—the unrivalled genius of the author, the great attention and liberality of the managers— the wonderful abilities of the painter, or the incredible exertions of all the performers!—
>
> *The Critic*, 1.2.175–78

The *Rivals* announced Sheridan's professional career and proved him a brilliant apprentice. In the ten months following its production, Sheridan became a competent journeyman, involving himself in all aspects of production and writing comic pieces for every part of the varied program. It was a time to grow and learn, to avoid the mistakes that led to the initial failure of his first comedy, to strengthen friendships with actors and producers, to become further acquainted with his audiences, and to prove himself competent enough to warrant the enormous financial backing another full-length piece would need.[1]

Part of that proof came in his two-act farce, *St. Patrick's Day; or, the Scheming Lieutenant*, which was introduced for a benefit performance at Covent Garden 2 May 1775. The merits of this distinctly occasional work earned it a minor place in the afterpiece repertory. Sheridan is said to have written it in forty-eight hours, and to have given it in gratitude to Lawrence Clinch, the family friend who had recreated the softened Sir Lucius O'Trigger.[2] Clinch portrayed Lieutenant O'Connor, the scheming officer from whom the farce gets its subtitle, while Lee Lewes, Quick, and Dunstall—all actors from *The Rivals*—took the roles of Justice Credulous, Dr. Rosy, and Serjeant Trounce. Ann Pitt, who specialized in lower-class women with biting tongues like the nurses of *Romeo and Juliet* and *Love for Love* or Dame Quickly of *I Henry*

IV, or in upperclass women of vanity, affectation, and spite like Lady Wronghead of *The Provok'd Husband*, Mrs. Sealand of *The Conscious Lovers*, and Lady Freelove of *The Jealous Wife*, portrayed Bridget, wife to Justice Credulous with whose daughter, Lauretta, Lieutenant O'Connor is in love. Lauretta was taken by Ann Brown, a relative newcomer to Covent Garden and to the stage in general, who had begun in the 1769–70 season as a child singer portraying nymphs, cupids, and fairies, had appeared in comic dramatic roles like Louisa Dudley in *The West Indian* and Cherry in *The Beaux' Stratagem*, and had had some success playing ingénues in farces and English burlettas. This was the first season in which she was allotted a benefit, and luckily for Sheridan's farce Miss Brown was successful in the role—so competent, in fact, that Sheridan later featured her in *The Duenna*.

St. Patrick's Day revolves around a typical farcical action, the boy-gets-girl-in-spite-of-parents formula. Lieutenant O'Connor wants to wed Lauretta but Justice and Bridget Credulous object to the marriage. By disguising himself first as a bodyguard (the soldiers billeted in the area have been obstreperous of late) and then as a German physician, he tricks the mildly avaricious and cowardly Justice Credulous into giving him permission to marry. Talkative and pedantic Dr. Rosy is his confident and abettor in this design.

With a line of action so broadly typical, to distinguish Sheridan's exact debt to a farcical tradition is difficult. Many of Samuel Foote's and Charles Macklin's dark satiric farces use this sort of comic frame upon which to build their potent attacks on contemporary society. Garrick's *Miss in Her Teens* and Colman's *Polly Honeycombe*, both of which have been named as sources of *The Rivals*, are as similar to this piece as to Sheridan's first comedy. There is less originality here, in the use of the old device of a disguised lover attempting to circumvent parents, than in *The Rivals*, where Sheridan added the wrinkle of tricking the daughter as well. The disguise as a German quack brings to mind Sergeant Kite's masquerade as a soothsayer in *The Recruiting Officer*, and the old trick which O'Connor plays on Justice Credulous of making him believe he has been poisoned had been used recently in Foote's *The Englishman Return'd from Paris* (CG, 3 Feb. 1756) and would be used again by Colman in *The Suicide* (HM, 11 July 1778).[3]

Much of the structure and content of *The Rivals* appears to have been in Sheridan's mind when he wrote the farce. Lauretta, like Lydia, is a spirited girl who can argue amusingly with her equally temperamental mother and who thinks a military man the height of fashion; she is rather more like the harsh Polly Honeycombe than the sprightly Lydia, but she retains an attractiveness necessary to effect the amiable dénouement. Dr. Rosy, like Mrs. Malaprop, is characterized largely by a verbal tic—in this case, a propensity to spout three- and four-word moral phrases of the most prosaic kind (anticipatory, perhaps, of the pompously phrased sentiments of Joseph Surface)—and like Mrs. Malaprop's his "humour" his little to do with the conduct of the plot; it exists merely to embellish his playing character. Some of the comic situations arise as they do in *The Rivals* through the careful preparation of mistaken identity and misunderstanding. In both plays, for instance, the opening scenes establish the initial situation through exposition but also characterize peripheral agents in order to set up further local display of them later. In *The Rivals*, Fag's characteristic pomposity enlivens the opening scene, then appears on three other occasions, exclusively as embellishment; in *St. Patrick's Day*, Serjeant Trounce inflatedly assumes superior knowledge as he instructs the other soldiers in how to approach their lieutenant with their grievances, and later his cleverness both helps him to recruit and becomes the means by which he is exposed when O'Connor poses as a recruit. As with Fag's displays of pomposity, neither of the two dramatized incidents has much to do with the plot. The central scene of *The Rivals* occurs when Jack arrives at Mrs. Malaprop's and tricks her into admitting him to see Lydia; in *St. Patrick's Day*, there is a similar scene when O'Connor, disguised as Humphrey Hum, reveals himself to Lauretta. Sheridan again uses the technique of removing the parent (Justice Credulous) from the scene so that the lovers may come to understand one another, then returning him at the crucial moment in order to discomfit them just as success seems at hand. The compressed scope of *St. Patrick's Day* forces the discomfiture to be more immediate than that of *The Rivals*, where Jack does not receive his comeuppance until four scenes later.

As in *The Rivals*, and indeed in all of Sheridan's original dramatic work before *The School for Scandal*, the tone of *St. Patrick's Day* is distinctly amiable. Lieutenant O'Connor is immediately characterized as an essentially honorable fellow. He sympathizes with his soldiers, gives them money to buy liquor, and opines that "upon my Conscience, 'tis very hard, that these poor Fellows should scarcely have bread from the Soil they would die to defend" (1.1.69–71). Soon thereafter, we learn that his motive in trying to steal Lauretta from her parents is neither lust nor fortune-hunting but honorable love with marriage as its object: "I must marry the Girl . . . hang the Fortune, let that take its chance . . ."(1.1.80–83). Similarly, the dénouement is brought about not just by the trick O'Connor and Dr. Rosy play upon Justice Credulous, but by the Justice's willingness to accept his son-in-law on amiable terms; even though there is nothing so abhorrent to Credulous as an officer who is an Irishman, he agrees to their marriage, declaring, "Lauretta, you're a sly tricking little Baggage, and I believe no one so fit to manage you, as my honest friend here, who is the most impudent dog, I ever saw" (2.4.206–8). The sarcasm of "honest friend"—O'Connor was disguised as "Honest Humphrey"—gives way to Credulous's admission into the new society: he will continue to be plagued by his wrangling wife as he deserves, but we also know he will join Dr. Rosy and the rest at the fine dinner to celebrate the marriage. In keeping with the tone, satire is restrained. Rosy's practice as an apothecary comes in for little real attack, while Credulous's profession of justice of the peace receives but one heavy lash in the Justice's pocketing of a bribe intended for "Honest Humphrey."

Little here points to Sheridan's talent beyond the general compactness of the short piece and a few fine *bon mots*. Among these are Justice Credulous's replies to his wife's preference to follow him to the grave rather than have a quack attempt to cure him ("I'm sensible of your affection, Dearest—and believe me nothing consoles me in my present melancholy situation, so much as the thought of leaving you behind, my Angel" [2.4.124–26]) and to her assertion that dying is quick ("Ay, but it leaves a numbness behind, that lasts for a plaguy long time" [2.4.153–54]). But there is much in *St. Patrick's Day* that points to a deep and growing familiarity with what will immediately please upon the stage. First, the farce is designed for a hero whose specialty is not comedy. Though his is the title role, Lieutenant O'Connor carries little of the real humor of the piece: a handsome exterior, a slight ability to mimic theatrically obvious types like a country bumpkin or the quasi-Dutch, and the soberness of a straight man to the self-exposures of Dr. Rosy and Serjeant Trounce are all that is necessary for success in the role. Since Clinch specialized in tragedy, Sheridan designed for his benefit farce a character that required only enough comic talent to gain success through contrast with his accustomed roles. Second, theatrical coterie jokes abound. Rosy calls O'Connor "my Alexander," setting up a pleasant laugh for the audience which had just seen Clinch perform Alexander the Great in Nathaniel Lee's heroic *The Rival Queens*, his choice for the mainpiece of his benefit night. Dunstall, who portrayed Serjeant Trounce, might have mimicked Shuter's portrayal of Launcelot Gobbo in his lines "Dear Serjeant—or Dear Trounce—or Dear Serjeant Trounce (according to his hurry)...,"[4] while John Quick as Dr. Rosy may have imitated Shuter's performance as Croaker in Goldsmith's *The Good-Natur'd Man*, for Justice Credulous calls him "Dr. Croaker" on one occasion, and there is a strong resemblance between Rosy's frequent plaints about the vanity of life and those of Goldsmith's character.[5] Perhaps Lee Lewes purposely recalled David's gingerly handling of the "gunpowder" letter of challenge in *The Rivals* when, as Justice Credulous, he suggested that the letter from O'Connor was "Combustible Stuff," "Take it away—and bury it ...." (2.4.26–27). All in all, Rhodes's statement that *St. Patrick's Day* "was written for to-morrow night, not for posterity"[6] is accurate if we add that its author intended it specifically for the boards of Covent Garden theater, with which he was becoming so well acquainted.

That acquaintance shows in Sheridan's "Prelude on Opening Covent Garden next Season" (CG, 20 Sept. 1775). Here he was following a long tradition, and following it most likely at the request of the manager. Topical preludes frequently introduced the first performance of a season in the 1770s at the major patent houses. For the first night of the 1772–73 season, Colman provided a "New Occasional Prelude" for Covent Garden that proved popular enough to repeat several times that year and served to introduce Jane Barsanti to London audiences; for 1773–74, Woodward delivered a special "Address to the Town" as well as a "New Occasional Prologue," and in the 1774–75 season he gave another. For 1775–76, the prelude was a brief jumbled affair that traced the fortunes of the actors and actresses during the summer season. Sheridan claimed it was his but no printed or manuscript version has been discovered.[7] It probably appeared no more than twice, and its only significance here is as an indication of Sheridan's growing professional links with the practical stage. He had become, as it were, an in-house hack; but as his next dramatic offering would prove, he was a hack of great talents.

The Duenna opened on 21 November 1775 and played an unprecedented seventy-five nights in the 1775–76 season. It was an amazing success financially and critically, and though we cannot know exactly how much Sheridan (or Covent Garden manager Thomas Harris) made on the comic opera, we do know that he earned enough to be able to purchase part of the Drury Lane patent in concert with the composer of the music, his father-in-law Thomas Linley, and an "angel," Dr. James Ford.

Like *The Rivals* and *St. Patrick's Day*, *The Duenna* is both distinctively original and slavishly derivative. Set in the never-never land that Spain was for eighteenth-century comedy, the plot of *The Duenna* is even more involved than that of *The Rivals*. As in the earlier comedy, *données* of character are added to multiple disguises to develop amusing and amiable comedy of situation, complicated and recomplicated, dependent on chance. Where before there was one strict father, now there are two; where before there was one couple whose happiness depended upon circumventing their elders, now there are two; but where before it was character that interested us primarily, now farcical character is subordinated much more completely to plot, so that the tangled imbroglio is constantly before our eyes. As in *The Rivals*, the crusty old father—here, Don Jerome—is hoist with the petard he thought he had so successfully laid; but now all fortifications are blown up together, and the vain Jew Isaac is exploded by his own charge just as Don Jerome's bomb clears the way for Donna Louisa to marry the impecunious Antonio, her jealous brother Ferdinand to marry the slightly sober Donna Clara, and Margaret, the old and ugly duenna who has taken Louisa's place, to make her fortune from her marriage to Isaac.

The action of *The Duenna* has much in common with such mixtures of intrigue and farce popular in Sheridan's time as Susanna Centlivre's *The Wonder: A Woman Keeps a Secret*.[8] Centlivre's popular comedy tells of the escape of an imprisoned daughter from a father who intends to marry her to a rich fool, includes a less-than-attractive serving maid who is also witty, and introduces a pair of jealous lovers contrasted with a pair who find happiness without jealousy. Moreover, Don Felix, the jealous male lover, is the brother of imprisoned Donna Isabella, whom the dashing Colonel Briton eventually wins.

Despite these similarities of situation, *The Duenna* and *The Wonder* are like one another more in tone than in any specifics of action or character. Spanish intrigues of this sort were popular enough with Georgian audiences to allow the prolific Isaac Bickerstaff to leave his field of expertise, the comic opera, and attempt a full-blown farce-intrigue, *'Tis Well It's No Worse* (DL, 24 Nov. 1770), a comedy whose title the critics gleefully used to ridicule the play. In all three of these pseudo-Iberian comedies, the marks of the intrigue—external obstacles rather than internal flaws, heightened but more artificial concern, frequent reversal of situation, concealed truth producing multilayered comic dramatic irony—combine with an amiability bred of basically good-natured characters and a middle-class moral view to produce comedies typical of the Georgian era.

Analogues to *The Duenna* abound, though no single source leaps forth. A comic plot similar to one principal situation of *The Duenna*—a daughter turned out of doors while the maid passes as the mistress—is found in an Italian comic opera, Carlo Goldoni's *Il Filosopho di Campagna*. Goldoni's libretto with Galuppi's score had been popular in England at the opera house since its London introduction in early 1761 and had recently been adapted as *The Wedding Ring* (DL, 1 Feb. 1773) by Charles Dibdin.[9] Sheridan could have seen the Italian original while he lived in London during 1769 and early 1770, or he might have seen Dibdin's amusing piece (which maintained the Italian setting and characters) while he was near London at Waltham Abbey in the autumn and winter of 1772–73. Whatever the superficial resemblances— and there are few or none on a verbal level, as indeed, there are few verbal resemblances among any of Sheridan's comedies and earlier works—the peculiar admixture which reveals itself in the entanglements so amusingly sorted out in *The Duenna* is wholly Sheridan's.

As there are similarities to other plots, so there are to other characters. We can point from the two best playing characters of Sheridan's comic opera—Isaac the Jew and Margaret the ugly duenna—to similar roles already established and long popular on the Georgian stage, and to the actors who created them. One of the most successful comic operas written in the period before *The Duenna* is Isaac Bickerstaff's *The Padlock* (DL, 3 Oct. 1768).[10] Like *The Duenna*, *The Padlock* combines a farcical Spanish intrigue plot with original songs. This amusing piece of theatrical ephemera tells how Leander wins the love of the beautiful Leonora, the unwilling fiancée of wrinkled fifty-year-old Don Diego who locked her up to test her virtue. Ursula, an old and ugly duenna, is attracted to Leander and becomes their ally, while Mungo, a Negro man-servant, provides the first major comic blackface role in English theatrical literature—an amusing if demeaning caricature.

Though there is little connection between Sheridan's comic opera and Bickerstaff's beyond the similiarities of Spanish setting and characters, an old duenna, and a slightly exotic humours character, *The Padlock* deserves close attention for two reasons.

First, Sheridan had numerous opportunities to see it and, we are led to suspect by his actions, either liked it or—what is more important to this pragmatic playwright—respected its audience-drawing capacities, or both. It was twice performed in Bath during the period young Sheridan lived there,[11] and it was frequently performed while Sheridan was in or near London. On several nights when we can be almost certain Sheridan was at the theater, it was the featured afterpiece at Covent Garden: 18 March 1775, the night Sheridan's epilogue to *Edward and Eleonora* was spoken; 20 September 1775, the night Sheridan's season-opening prelude appeared; and most significantly, 13 February 1775, the ninth night of *The Rivals*, the third and final author's benefit in which all the profits accrued to Sheridan and in which, while he did not have the right to choose the afterpiece, his advice might have been asked.

These Covent Garden performances of *The Padlock* are important for another reason: in them Sheridan could have seen no less than five of the major performers he cast in *The Duenna*. John Quick, Isaac of Sheridan's comic opera, portrayed Mungo. Mrs. Jane Green, whose only other singing role was a walk-on as Mrs. Slammekin in *The Beggar's Opera*, created Sheridan's Duenna after appearing as Bickerstaff's aging Ursula. Charles Dubellamy was the romantic Leander of *The Padlock* as well as Sheridan's Antonio. Isabella Mattocks, the Leonora on most nights when Anne Catley chose not to play,[12] created Sheridan's Donna Louisa. Ann Brown, whose early career suggests she was being groomed as a replacement for Miss Catley in comic singing roles, portrayed Leonora in *The Padlock* for the first time on 20 September 1775, the opening night for which Sheridan created the lost prelude, and subsequently became Sheridan's Donna Clara. Of course, Sheridan could have known these actors' talents from other roles as well; four of them had previously created parts for

him, and the fifth (Dubellamy) appeared frequently in comic
opera. But that one old and ugly duenna preceded the same
actress's creation of another while one exotic humours character in the same comic opera preceded the actor's being cast as
an exotic humours character in Sheridan's play seems significant: the almost inescapable inference is that Sheridan must
have chosen to create Margaret and Isaac and to cast Mrs.
Green and Quick in the roles because he was influenced by
their success as Ursula and Mungo in *The Padlock*.

That John Quick took the role of Isaac Mendoza matters
not only for his previous performances as Mungo in *The
Padlock* or for his appearances as Bob Acres, Dr. Rosy, or a
host of comic opera idiosyncratics, but for another character
he portrayed. There were two famous Jewish characters seen
frequently on the late eighteenth-century stage. One was
Macklin's Shylock; the other was also Macklin's creation, Beau
Mordecai, the macaroni cit of *Love a la Mode*. Beau Mordecai
seeks the hand of Charlotte, but like her other false lovers,
veers off when it appears she is penniless. Macklin described
him as follows:

> The character is an egregious coxcomb, who is striving to be
> witty; at the top of dress, with an awkward fancy of his own, so
> as to be ridiculous and as badly matched or sorted as such a
> fellow ignorant of propriety can be. His manner is very lively—
> singing, conceited, dancing—throwing himself out, body, voice,
> and mind, as much as conceit and impudence and ignorance
> can effect.[13]

At Covent Garden, Beau Mordecai was portrayed by John
Quick. Sheridan could have seen his impersonation of the
macaroni cit as early as 1768 or as recently as 18 or 29 May
1775, just before the summer recess which he probably spent
composing *The Duenna*.[14] Conceit, affectation of fashion, and
vanity—the qualities Isaac and Mordecai share—were amalgamated in only these two Jewish characters among the many
Jewish caricatures popular on the late eighteenth-century
stage.[15] While Sheridan was original in his mixture of foppishness and country naiveté in Bob Acres, he followed Macklin's lead in mixing foppishness and Jewishness. And one
wonders if he would have done so had it not been for the
performances of Quick.

As I have indicated, *The Duenna* was a rousing success in its time. Boswell, characteristically using the anecdote to vindicate his hero against charges of selfishness and spite, relates the following:

> I have already mentioned, that Johnson was very desirous of reconciliation with old Mr. Sheridan. It will, therefore, not seem at all surprising that he was zealous in acknowledging the brilliant merit of his son. While it had as yet been displayed only in the drama, Johnson proposed him as a member of The Literary Club, observing, that "He who has written the two best comedies of his age, is surely a considerable man." And he had, accordingly, the honour of being elected; for an honour it undoubtedly must be allowed to be, when it is considered of whom that society consists, and that a single black ball excludes a candidate.[16]

Sheridan's election occurred in March of 1777; of his original full-length works, only *The Rivals* and *The Duenna* had appeared. Those of us who read *The Duenna* today might be surprised that the greatest critic of his age would consider this slim comic opera one of the "two best comedies" of the 1770s, as Boswell's syntax in relating the statement implies. Indeed (making allowances for the rhetoric of the occasion), Johnson appears to rank it above his dead friend's great comedy, *She Stoops to Conquer*. But consider also this assessment:

> The "Duenna" is a perfect work of art. It has the utmost sweetness and point. The plot, the characters, the dialogue, are all complete in themselves, and they are all his [Sheridan's] own; and the songs are the best that ever were written, except those in the "Beggar's Opera." They have a joyous spirit of intoxication in them, and a strain of the most melting tenderness.[17]

The writer is one of the most perceptive critics of the early nineteenth century, William Hazlitt. In an age more sensitive to anti-Semitism than Johnson's or Hazlitt's, perhaps their judgments may be difficult to understand; perhaps it is not easy to grant, as Johnson and Hazlitt both did, that a comedy lacking moral seriousness can be not only popularly successful but also aesthetically pleasing; and perhaps, finally, audiences no longer find pleasure in the "melting tenderness" of love songs merely tacked onto a plot with little relationship to the action. Yet there is no gainsaying the fact that *The Duenna* has a remarkably complicated but compact libretto, that it is highly amusing, and that it represents an important step in Sheridan's development.

The plot of *The Duenna* is both the most highly complex and the most highly unified, if not the most probable, of all the plots Sheridan created. The frame, of course, is provided by the four young lovers. Donna Louisa, by virtue of her sprightly grace, impish assurance, and clever trickery, is the most entertaining of these. She is matched with the handsome Antonio, whose artificial introduction with two contrasting love songs at the beginning of the opera may seem absurd and whose love and bravery are assigned, not fully developed, comic characteristics. Contrasted slightly with these two are the sober Clara and the jealous Ferdinand, yet neither is Clara so sober nor Ferdinand so jealous as to lose our interest. Sheridan may have used as lovers characters very similar to those of *The Rivals*, but he was not about to make again the aesthetic mistakes he made there. Clara's final trick on Ferdinand comically punishes his jealousy; and Ferdinand has a naïve romanticism (a characteristic easier to portray in comedy than sympathetically treated insecurity), an absolute code of Spanish brotherhood, and an essential good nature which at last makes him side with his sister against his father, even though this decision means abjuring his normal role as a Spanish brother concerned with his own and his sister's "honor." The constantly shifting relationships in which these four lovers are placed are complicated by Louisa's disguise as Clara, by Isaac's meddling, by Ferdinand's mistakes, and by the delightful trick of the two simultaneously arriving letters which resolves all three marriages. These are basically honorable young people, romantic in their love yet having typical Georgian common sense to see their financial futures safe before marrying: Louisa says to Antonio, "If we would make love our household god, we had best secure him a comfortable roof" (3.3.44–46). They are portrayed as clever enough to get their own ways in spite of strict fathers but are never made particularly witty or given complex personalities with serious internal flaws to be removed. Indeed, only Ferdinand among them has anything like a comic flaw—his jealousy. Interest in the four lovers is important. But the real pleasure in the plot, taken as a whole, comes from the complications provided by three other characters: Don Jerome, Margaret the Duenna, and Isaac the Jew; their physical and psychological idiosyncrasies conflict to create the situations most skillfully designed to evoke laughter. As in *The Rivals*, it is character that is most enjoyable in *The Duenna*, but here the character is tied much more closely to the action.

Of these three idiosyncratic characters, Margaret the Duenna is the least comic. She is an ugly old woman whom Don Jerome has hired to protect his daughter's chastity: "I thought that dragon's front of thine wou'd cry aloof to the sons of gallantry—steel traps and spring guns seem'd writ in every wrinkle of it" (1.3.131–33). Margaret is not funny for her own foibles—she never believes, for instance, when she is pretending to be the young and beautiful Louisa, that she really is young and beautiful—but for her clever manipulation of others to expose their idiosyncrasies. Knowing Don Jerome's dictatorial constitution, she is able to engineer the perfect escape for Louisa. Guessing Isaac's avarice, she can turn his cupidity into the motive for a secret marriage. Her venomous tongue displays itself in the last scene when she finally has her chance to revenge herself on Isaac for his insults: he abuses her, swearing he will not endure being locked up for life with a woman old enough to be his mother and as ugly as the Devil, and she replies:

> Dares such a thing as you pretend to talk of beauty—a walking rouleau—a body that seems to owe all its consequence to the dropsy—a pair of eyes like two dead beetles in a wad of brown dough. A beard like an artichoke, with dry shrivell'd jaws that wou'd disgrace the mummy of a monkey.
>
> [3.7.89–93]

Though she makes several witty comparisons here, Margaret is not comic for her speech; rarely does she have lines similar to the last, although she does make great use of "condescension" as a farcical synonym for ugliness in her first meeting with Isaac (2.2).

The most fun of the whole opera is that which is funniest
about Margaret—the ongoing sight gag she represents. This
technique, common to farce and the basis of a great deal of
enjoyment in characters like Bob Acres, sets up a whole series
of misunderstood exchanges between Don Jerome and Isaac
concerning her beauty. The audience has a visual memory of
the old ugly Duenna, shared by Isaac, as Don Jerome describes the beauties of his daughter, whom Isaac takes Margaret to be. This sort of purely situational comedy of exchanged identity is one of the major techniques used in the
scenario.

The tradition out of which Don Jerome springs is clear;[18] he
has little to differentiate him from hundreds of other strict
fathers, including Sir Anthony Absolute and Justice Credulous. Like most old fathers, he is crusty, testy, and financially
motivated. His cynical realism opposes the idealism and love
of his children, and of course they eventually turn the tables
on him, pitting flexibility against rigidity and asserting the
power of clever youth to take over and create the new social
order. He is never really a serious threat to the happiness of
the young people. When we first meet him, we already know
of the planned elopement and the disguises that will be used
to trick him; when we see him thereafter, he appears foolish
for having been tricked and not knowing it. And if he is not
clever enough to represent an insurmountable obstacle, so he
is not villainous enough, either. Like Sheridan's other old
fathers, and like those of late eighteenth-century amiable
comedy, even when overreached he proves good-natured. In
the end, he has been tricked by his daughter. But her new
husband honorably offers to return her fortune. Don Jerome
answers Antonio's offer with an amiableness more characteristic of the sort of ultimately benevolent comedy he appears
in than of the testy self-interested personality he has displayed
earlier:

> Why, gad take me, but you are a very extraordinary fellow, but
> have you the impudence to suppose no one can do a generous
> action but yourself? Here Louisa, tell this proud fool of yours,
> that he's the only man I know that wou'd renounce your
> fortune; and by my soul, he's the only man in Spain that's

worthy of it—there, bless you both, I'm an obstinate old fellow when I am in the wrong; but you shall now find me as steady in the right.

[3.7.114–20]

But before this unconvincing conversion, Don Jerome, in his cynicism and absolutism, and his ignorance of the true situation, speaks the funniest lines of the piece. He instructs Louisa to prepare herself to marry Isaac and banish all other lovers, especially those who serenade her, and sounds remarkably like Sir Anthony Absolute inveighing against circulating libraries or young men's choices in marriage: "I come to tell you, madam, that I'll suffer no more of these midnight incantations, these amorous orgies that steal the senses in the hearing, as they say Egyptian Embalmers serve mummies, extracting the brain thro' the ears" (1.3.36–40). He does not care if she hates Isaac, for she is Isaac's choice and "choice on one side is sufficient—two lovers shou'd never meet in marriage—be you sour as you please, he is sweet temper'd, and for your good fruit, there's nothing like ingrafting on a crab" (1.3.65–68). When Ferdinand protests that he can think of no one he wants less for a brother-in-law than Isaac, and no one he wants more than Don Antonio, testy Jerome replies: "If you happen to have e'er a sister, who is not at the same time a daughter of mine, I'm sure I shall have no objection to the relationship" (1.3.89–91). Then he explains his view of marriage. Ferdinand asks, did he not love his wife, their mother, when he married her?

Why I must confess I had a great affection for your mother's ducats, but that was all, boy—I married her for her fortune, and she took me in obedience to her father, and a very happy couple we were—we never expected any love from one another, and so we were never disappointed—If we grumbled a little now and then, it was soon over, for we were never fond enough to quarrel, and when the good woman died, why, why—I had as lieve she had lived, and I wish every widower in Seville cou'd say the same . . . .

[1.3.99–107]

However predictive these lines might be of the sort of cynical wit that graces Sheridan's masterpiece, *The School for Scandal*, these few examples are unfortunately the only ones that may be drawn from this character and the best ones from the whole comic opera. By almost all standards, this is only marginally witty; as cynical wit, it is clearly a failure, for the softening of the last sentence would never stand in a truly biting, sardonic comedy. But *The Duenna* is not a comedy of wit, and Don Jerome is not basically a witty character.

The one character around whom this comic opera may be said to revolve is Isaac, the conceited, covetous Jew who seeks to marry Louisa. The audience sees him compounding his egotism and avarice while they know all the while that eventually he will discover his mistakes and receive the come-uppance he so richly deserves. He is a comic villain, but never clever or strong enough to represent a real threat; his faults blind him too completely to allow him to damage the sympathetic characters. Still, his position in the play permits him at any moment, through accident if not through cleverness, either to prevent his own comic punishment (which would disappoint the audience's expectations for him) or to expose the lovers to Don Jerome's wrath (which would seriously discomfit them, but might not prevent their marrying). But any concern that may be felt for the lovers is outweighed by amusement at Isaac's absurdity, which is set up well in advance of his first appearance. Aside from not being Louisa's choice, he is distasteful for his past behavior. Ferdinand and Louisa, in a fast-moving, contrapuntal dialogue with Don Jerome, describe Isaac's faults. First, he is a Portuguese. No, answers Don Jerome, he has forsworn his country. Then, says Louisa, he is a Jew. No again, answers Don Jerome, he has been a Christian for six weeks.

> FERDINAND. Ay, he left his old religion for an estate, and has not had time to get a new one.
> LOUISA. But stands like a dead wall between church and synagogue, or like the blank leaves between the Old and New Testament.

Isaac's insincere conversion, motivated by avarice, is typical of his general duplicitous behavior, says Ferdinand.

FERDINAND. But the most remarkable part of his character, is his passion for deceit, and tricks of cunning.

LOUISA. Tho' at the same time, the fool predominates so much over the knave, that I am told he is generally the dupe of his own art.

FERDINAND. True, like an unskilful gunner, he usually misses his aim, and is hurt by the recoil of his own piece.

[1.3.51–61]

This preparation for Isaac's first appearance makes believable the avarice and absurd conceit there displayed. Accompanied by his friend and servant Carlos (who sings the most beautiful songs in the play, all of them quite unconnected with the action[19]) and gazing into a mirror at the Jewish beard he cannot bear to cut, Isaac is an easy target for the imposture Louisa plays upon him. Crowing to himself, "Ah! this little brain is never at a loss—cunning Isaac! cunning rogue!" (1.5.124–25), he arranges to deliver the putative "Donna Clara" into Antonio's hands, thus guaranteeing from the outset his eventual downfall. Throughout the comedy, Isaac's continual asides and continuing conceit and cupidity predict with joyous certainty his self-deception.

All these characters are somewhat interesting and Isaac especially amusing, but none of them are particularly striking, original, or clever, and none are drawn with sufficient psychological or comic depth to stay in our minds beyond the setting in which they appear. Perhaps not surprisingly in a comic opera, they are primarily types, flat place-holders who provide vehicles for the display of mostly stock comic situations. And the most frequently employed technique of the comic opera is comedy of situation. As it was used in *The Rivals* and *St. Patrick's Day*, this technique of concealing vital information from one or more of the characters is frequently used in *The Duenna*, though never with the same multilayered effect obtained in *The Rivals*. Consider a scene nearly analogous to Jack's deception of Mrs. Malaprop (*The Rivals*, 3.2): Donna Louisa's first tricking of Isaac (1.5). Like Mrs. Malaprop, Isaac errs not just because the truth is concealed from

him, but because he is effectively blinded by his own comic
faults. He makes three mistakes in the scene. First, he does
not recognize Donna Louisa as Donna Louisa but accepts
unquestioningly her self-identification as Donna Clara: this
mistake anyone could make, though the fact that Donna
Louisa's suitor should make it is ludicrous. Second, Isaac
fancies she is in love with him: this mistake only a comically
absurd character could make, since Louisa gives him no
provocation for such an opinion. Third, at her own request,
he arranges to deliver Louisa into the hands of Antonio.
Believing as he does that she is Donna Clara, this third
mistake is natural for Isaac. Most honorable men in the same
situation would do the same thing, but here the action is
comic because Isaac's motive is base: he thinks to rid himself
of Antonio, a rival for Louisa's hand, and in his own plan
finds himself abnormally clever. His third mistake, of course,
is exactly the action which will prevent his marrying Louisa,
while he ironically thinks it to be the one which will assure his
marrying her. Like Mrs. Malaprop, Isaac prides himself on his
own cunning, while as with Mrs. Malaprop, it is his least
effective trait. Like Jack, Louisa manages to use the person
who is her most obvious obstacle against gaining what is her
most cherished desire in order to gain that desire. The clever
young people appear resourceful in their posturing; the butts
appear ridiculous in their overconfidence and conceit. The
mode of achieving the comic effect is concealing the truth of
the situation from the butts, but not from the clever young
people or from the audience.

Particularly in those scenes surrounding Isaac's actions, such
techniques are frequently used. Isaac is both the character
most in need of comic punishment and the one who is directly
misled by the central comic falsehood of the scenario—that
Louisa is Clara and Margaret is Louisa. As a result, every
scene into which Isaac enters is some variation on this joke of
disguise. When he introduces Antonio to Louisa, the joke
begins in anxiety that Antonio, knowing he does not love
Clara and thinking that she is the person to whom Isaac
proposes introducing him, will give away the truth; but by the
end, the anxiety has disappeared and Antonio and Louisa

take advantage of their superior knowledge to allow Isaac to
show off his ignorance. Or again, when Isaac argues with Don
Jerome concerning Louisa's beauty, we know he refers to the
ugly Margaret while Don Jerome refers to the truly beautiful
Louisa. And again, in the last scene, when Isaac confidently
presents himself and Margaret as the happily married young
daughter and son-in-law to Don Jerome, we know the exposure of his stupidity is imminent, while Isaac thinks only of
his cleverness in marrying "Louisa" without having made a
settlement. In this sense, *The Duenna* is a one-joke comedy.
But then, so are many great comedies. Sheridan's brilliant
stroke was to exploit this one joke to its fullest possible extent.
And his favorite technique here—allowing Isaac multiple
asides in which he praises himself and his cleverness, explains
his intended actions, weighs his possible alternatives, and
never recognizes the cleverness, action, or alternatives as precisely the things which guarantee his downfall—intensifies the
comic dramatic irony.[20]

I have said almost nothing of some of the other comic
effects of *The Duenna*. A few of Antonio's songs, for instance,
are highly amusing for their witty cleverness, while some of
Isaac's songs are wonderfully whimsical for his ironic ignorance of himself. The great (and in Sheridan's time, mildly
controversial) scene, completely unrelated to the otherwise
close-knit plot, in which Father Paul and the other friars sing
over a bottle of wine, calling it their sun rising over their
table, or that in which Isaac and Jerome (anticipating Ogden
Nash) declare that "A bumper of good liquor/ Will end a
contest quicker,/ Than justice, judge or vicar" (2.3.127–29),
are most amusing.

In a comic opera, a certain frivolity obtains that is not
necessarily present in a regular comedy. Thus, the comic
analogue of fear here is not even serious anxiety; we are
prepared to see the worst occur because, if it did, we know it
would be reversed. And it is very unlikely to occur, because
Isaac and Don Jerome are portrayed from the start as
singularly inept: upon their first entrances they are already set
up to be tricked, and we know both the method and the
probable result long before the actual process of trickery

begins. Characters as bumbling as these appear in straight dramatic comedy, as does the sense of a benevolent providence that provides such happy opportunities for favorable misinterpretations as the perfect wording and arrival of the two letters to Don Jerome. But the sense of comic safety provided by comic opera is not just one of a benevolent providence operating; it can be more. For instance, in *The Beggar's Opera*, it expresses itself as a temporary suspension of dramatic rules, artificial and ironic heavy-handedness which effectively squelches any real anxiety we might have. In *The Duenna*, the same suspension of rules appears by a total artificiality in the portrayal of action, characters, and meetings. Thus Lopez, Ferdinand's servant, mocks his own dramatic function as the first expositor of the comedy; or Don Carlos appears on stage merely to sing, and after one or two scenes, every auditor knows it. Isaac himself bustles in and out of the last scenes on cue; we know he will never arrive when it would be possible for him to discover Louisa's masquerade as Clara. This sense of comic safety provided by the artificiality of the form, combined with the total ineffectiveness of the villains, gives *The Duenna* its frivolous flavor.

The frivolity of *The Duenna* is matched by the characteristic amiability of the dénouement. But for Sheridan first the frivolity, then to a lesser extent the amiability would disappear, and its disappearance would coincide not only with Sheridan's own growth, but with his removal from Covent Garden to his installation as co-patentee and manager of Drury Lane, from the home of "low" comedy and comic opera to the house of "high" and "wit" comedy. Henceforth, Sheridan would show more concern with carefully structured plot (as he is doing in *The Duenna* in comparison to *The Rivals* and *St. Patrick's Day*), more concern with wit, more concern with satire. However entertaining his later works may be, none of them are merely frivolous.

CHAPTER IV:

A Trip to Scarborough

> AMANDA. Plays, I must confess, have some small
> charms, and would have more, would they re-
> strain that loose encouragement to vice, which
> shocks, if not the virtue of some women, at least
> the modesty of all.
> LOVELESS. But, 'till that reformation can be wholly
> made, 'twould surely be a pity to exclude the
> productions of some of our best writers for want
> of a little wholesome pruning; which might be ef-
> fected by any one who possessed modesty
> enough to believe that we should preserve all we
> can of our deceased authors, at least 'till they are
> outdone by the living ones.
> *A Trip to Scarborough*, 2.1.17–26

> DANGLE. Now, egad, I think the worst alteration is
> in the nicety of the audience.—No double en-
> tendre, no smart innuendo admitted; even Van-
> brugh and Congreve obliged to undergo a bun-
> gling reformation!
> *The Critic*, 1.1.132–34

> PUFF. The pruning knife—zounds the axe!
> *The Critic*, 2.2.524

THE PORTION of the Drury Lane patent which Sheridan
in association with his father-in-law Thomas Linley and
their friend Dr. James Ford purchased from David Garrick in
1776 was in some ways overvalued. Drury Lane was the
larger, more popular, and financially more successful of the
two winter patent houses, but the retirement of its part-owner
and manager was also the retirement of its most lucrative
asset. David Garrick's acting, particularly in a period when
many went to see his final performances, was a tremendous
factor in the theater's popularity and monetary stability. In
1774–75, for instance, Garrick appeared twenty-two times; on

those occasions, the house receipts averaged over £246, while
on the 123 other nights not featuring an actor's benefit the
take was only £183. In 1775–76, despite the amazing seventy-
five-night run of *The Duenna* at Covent Garden, the forty-
seven performances by Garrick for which we have reliable
figures garnered an average of more than £266, while on the
twelve occasions when his appearance was either announced
as or was the last in a role, the average was more than £275.
These figures contrast sharply with those of 1776–77, Sheridan's first season as a manager. In 151 nights (excluding the
thirty-four nights given over to benefits), Drury Lane averaged only £191; in the 133 non-benefit nights at Covent
Garden, the average was £212.[1]

The sale of part of the patent to Sheridan and his associates
led observers to assume that Sheridan's pen and practical
abilities would compensate for the loss of Garrick. Sheridan
was to be not only the best playwright of the age, but the best
manager of the post-Garrick era. The newspapers were buz-
zing with speculation as to what Sheridan would do and expressing implicitly a great expectation of and faith in his
abilities. By December 1776, if not earlier, Sheridan had
succeeded Garrick in the eyes of the practicing playwrights as
the managerial monarch to be courted: Mrs. Elizabeth Griffith, for instance, published her translation of *The Barber of
Seville* in December 1776, addressing it to Sheridan as author
of *The Duenna* and the writer most capable of utilizing Beau-
marchais's materials for the English stage.

But while Sheridan was willing to exercise his native abilities
as an administrator and artistic advisor, he was either unwilling or unable to provide Drury Lane audiences with a new
play immediately. The kindest explanation is that he was too
busy. *The Duenna* had opened in November of the previous
year; a new son, Thomas, had entered the world at nearly the
same time. The negotiations for the patent had taken a great
deal of the 1775–76 winter. Simply to make himself familiar
with Drury Lane's practical operations must have absorbed
most of his energy for the seven months before the theater's
opening 21 September 1776. Certainly his threat to dissociate
himself from the active management of Drury Lane was
instrumental in bringing about a settlement with Willoughby

Lacy, the co-owner of the patent, when squabbles arose early in the first season;[2] that dispute must have further interrupted any literary activity. And the daily effort to present acceptable stage pieces, despite the continuity of the company, must have been very time-consuming.

Though it was evidently disappointing to the audiences, Sheridan's first season as a manager was generally productive. Seven new short pieces appeared and one new tragedy,[3] but the principal changes in the Drury Lane repertory were all products of Sheridan's creative hand. He redirected *The Old Batchelor* and *Love for Love*, advertising them "with alterations," although his changes were minor;[4] he cut down Garrick's *A Christmas Tale* to an afterpiece and presented it thirty-two times; he offered a refurbished version of the popular pantomime *Harlequin's Invasion* twenty-seven times; he redirected *The Rivals* with a Drury Lane cast. More important, he did a thorough revision of *The Relapse*; and most important, at the very end of the season and in spite of all this essentially work-a-day theatrical busyness, he presented to the world *The School for Scandal*. The influence this tyro manager had on Drury Lane can be seen in the fact that eighty-four of the 187 nights on which plays were presented in the 1776–77 season featured something directly or indirectly from his pen, mainpiece or afterpiece. And as the principal acting manager, Sheridan had his hand in every new prelude, mainpiece, or afterpiece, as well as every redirected or refurbished piece, since it was his responsibility to act in the capacity of what we would now call an "artistic director." If we add those evenings in which his service as a director may be seen, fully 179 nights featured something filtered through his creative talents.[5] When we remember that Sheridan had pacified Willoughby Lacy by granting his demand to appear on five different occasions as the hero of tragedy (an experiment in which the performances of the egregious actor brought less than £137 on the average), that the stock comedies and tragedies which depended so much for their popularity on Garrick's performances had to be greatly curtailed, and that the season was hampered by disagreements among actors and managers and by the natural problems of adapting to new managerial personnel, the average £189 which Drury Lane brought in

each night before the appearance of *The School for Scandal*
seems surprisingly high. Indeed, of the mainpiece comedies in
which Sheridan clearly had a major hand, only the revival of
the "smutty" *The Old Batchelor* averaging £178 must be
counted a failure; *Love for Love*'s average of £193, *The Rivals*'s
average of nearly £217, *A Trip to Scarborough*'s of more than
£195, and especially *The School for Scandal*'s of nearly £234 are
more nearly indicative of the ability of Sheridan to prevent a
disastrous financial decline of Drury Lane after Garrick's exit.
It was not a highly profitable season; but it was not a complete
loss.

There were clearly mistakes and false starts. Sheridan
should have had a major production ready early; the introduction of *The School for Scandal* on 8 May 1777 was far later
in the season than customary or profitable. The revivals of
Congreve's two comedies were done without extensive revisions and with little evidence of Sheridan's artistic control,
except as director;[6] the attempt to employ the spectacle of
afterpiece, to rely on musical or scenic additions to stock
pieces, and to run momentarily diverting pieces too long
suggests that Sheridan's Drury Lane might possibly have gone
bankrupt in its first season by underestimating the intelligence
of its audience. Something genuinely new was needed. Sheridan's first major effort, the revision of *The Relapse* as *A Trip to
Scarborough*, appeared on 24 February 1777.

The final line of *A Trip to Scarborough* belongs to Berinthia:
"You may be assured, that while the intention is evidently to
please, British auditors will ever be indulgent to the errors of
the performance" (5.3.328–30). Since the line is in the manuscript copy sent to the Lord Chamberlain for approval before
performance, it can hardly have been conscious irony on
Sheridan's part, though it might have been a jinx, for his
revision was not successful in its early presentations largely
because of the "errors of the performance." The casting as
Sheridan planned it was strong. Dodd, who had recreated
Acres for the Drury Lane revival of *The Rivals*, was to do Lord
Foppington; Moody, the veteran of two feisty characters in
Sheridan's two Congreve offerings and the recreator of Sir

Lucius O'Trigger, would perform Sir Tunbelly Clumsey; Frances Abington, Sheridan's choice for Laetitia Fondlewife, Miss Prue, and Lydia Languish, would portray Hoyden. The only inexperienced person in the cast was the beautiful Mary "Perdita" Robinson as Amanda; actors like Reddish, Smith, Brereton, Parsons, and Mrs. Yates could be counted on for competent performances.

In fact, the play failed to coalesce on stage in its first two performances principally because the actors failed to do their jobs.[7] Some were fine, Mrs. Abington especially; and Mrs. Robinson, though apparently the victim of stage fright in the early scenes, improved; but Dodd was not sparkling as Lord Foppington, Moody did not know his lines as Sir Tunbelly, and after the fourth performance, John Palmer was called upon to take over Reddish's role as Tom Fashion.[8] Despite the early difficulties, Sheridan's adaptation survived to play ten times that season, grossing more than £1,950, and managed to enter the repertory. For the rest of the century it replaced its original; the last performance of Vanbrugh's play (already cut greatly) had been in the 1769–70 season.

The Relapse; or, Virtue in Danger (1696) is Sir John Vanbrugh's sequel to Colley Cibber's *Love's Last Shift; or, The Fool in Fashion* (1696). Cibber's play is generally conceded, if not to mark the beginning of the moral revolt against the licentiousness of high Restoration comedy, at least to signal the coming triumph of eighteenth-century "sentimental" comedy. After four acts similar in tone and action if not in brilliance and wit to other Restoration comedies, Cibber converts his rake-wit hero in the fifth act from a life of adultery and dissipation to a new sense of virtue and a quiet country retreat. The manner of the conversion conflicts so acutely with the matter of the play as to destroy any unity of tone the piece might have had; Loveless's conversion is not probable or necessary to his character or to the action of the play.

Vanbrugh evidently thought it absurd. In his sequel, which uses the names of Cibber's characters but little more, he comically discusses conversions to virtue and reaches far different conclusions. He exposes Loveless's conversion as short-lived; one serious temptation and the former rake returns to his old philandering habits. Vanbrugh's Amanda—who in Cibber's play had waited ten patient years, virtue intact, for her Loveless to return, who seduced him in disguise, and who then gave all her fortune and life back to this adulterous husband, effecting thereby the absurd conversion—finds herself cheated by her spouse and attracted to a handsome man, ironically named Worthy. She does not know that the woman who is carrying on an affair with her husband is her cousin and her best friend, the gay and witty Berinthia; but her husband's perfidy, combined with Worthy's carefully timed arrival (he and Berinthia have arranged for Amanda to discover Loveless's infidelity in order to make her a susceptible target for Worthy's charms), create serious gaps in her armor of virtue. By physically escaping Worthy, however, she avoids rape. Then, with a rapture of lyrical argument, she converts Worthy by offering him her heart, though not her body. Overcome by her poetic persuasion, Worthy declares himself entranced, and agrees not to force her. In soliloquy, he opines that "there's divinity about her" that cools his "wild flame of love," but significantly owns that "How long this influence may last, heaven knows" (5.4.168, 170, 176).[9] The matter is allowed to stand there, but in the final scene of the play, in which all four fashionable lovers—Amanda, Worthy, Loveless, and Berinthia—appear but hardly speak, an elaborate wedding masque is presented. Cupid and Hymen argue, Hymen telling Cupid that marriage leads but to variety, while both agree that "constancy's an empty sound" (5.5.116). The nature of the Loveless-Amanda-Worthy-Berinthia relationship becomes clear, though Amanda's eventual fall is held in abeyance. As in *The Provok'd Wife*, where we know Lady Brute will face further assaults from the handsome and witty Constant, so here we are led to believe that Amanda may be pressured into giving body as well as heart to her gallant. The sequel to *The Relapse*, as Arthur Friedman once suggested to me, might be *The New Relapse; or, Virtue Done-In*.

While this main plot is often very amusing and gives the play its title, the subplot carries most of the interest of the piece and is actually the major action of the play dramatically.

The newly-created Lord Foppington (Cibber's Sir Novelty Fashion) is ridiculed for his abuse of nature; his younger brother Tom Fashion, a rake with a small amount of conscience, cleverly outwits his cruel and selfish sibling.[10]

The counterpoint of the brothers provides the entertainment here. Tom has dissipated his small portion of the inheritance, the bulk of which went to Foppington by the laws of primogeniture. Clearly the younger brother is at fault; Vanbrugh's interest, however, resides not in Tom's high living, which he never explicitly criticizes, but in the discrepancy between Tom's situation and Foppington's. In Tom's power lies one course which inevitably would bring him relief: accepting Foppington's standards of behavior. Lory, Tom's faithful servant, tells him how to approach Milord: "Say nothing to him. Apply yourself to his favorites, speak to his periwig, his cravat, his feather, his snuffbox, and when you are well with them, desire him to lend you a thousand pounds. I'll engage you prosper" (1.2.82–85). Tom cannot flatter, however, and Foppington cheerfully invites his brother to eat with his servants: "The lards I commonly eat with are people of nice conversation, and you know, Tam, your education has been a little at large. But if you'll stay here, you'll find a family dinner. Hey, fellow! What is there for dinner? There's beef, I suppose my brother will eat beef" (1.3.159–64).

Then means both to revenge himself on Foppington and to relieve his strained financial conditions are presented to Tom by Coupler, a decayed lascivious homosexual who has learned that Foppington does not intend to pay him for having arranged his marriage to an heiress of £1,500 a year.[11] Since Vanbrugh wished to stress Foppington's avarice and heartlessness, Tom, suffering moral scruples, goes to ask aid of his brother yet again before accepting Coupler's offer. Foppington responds by suggesting Tom was happy to hear of his duel with Loveless, by abusing their dead father who "starved" Foppington, by equating women with "pad-nags" who are bought and sold simply for pleasure (Tom wants a woman's heart), and finally by claiming to be out of pocket, for "these are damned times to give money in .... I have been forced to retrench in that one article of sweet pawder till I have braught

it dawn to five guineas a manth" (3.1.89–94). Tom's conscience is assuaged and he resolves to trick his older brother.

With Coupler's letter of introduction, Tom passes himself
off as Lord Foppington at Sir Tunbelly Clumsey's and by
means of a bribe secretly marries the amoral selfish little
country chit, Hoyden, Foppington's intended. But the real
Foppington arrives unexpectedly, and though Milord is temporarily discomfited by not being immediately recognized,
Tom is eventually forced to flee without his marriage being
acknowledged. Miss Hoyden, her Nurse, and the Chaplain
who performed the ceremony decide to conceal the fact and
Hoyden is married again, this time to the real Foppington.
But in the last act, Coupler and Tom bribe the Chaplain and
Nurse to tell the truth. With them swearing to Tom's previous
marriage to Hoyden, Foppington is confounded before he can
consummate; Sir Tunbelly, disappointed at being treated in a
surly manner by a lord and at finding his real son-in-law to be
a mere squire, stalks out unreconciled while Foppington
decides to put on a "philosophical air[,] . . . the most becoming
thing in the world to the face of a person of quality"
(5.5.252–53). And though we have no reason to think Tom
and Hoyden's marriage will be happy, at least now Tom will
have what he most wants and deserves: money.

In this subplot, Vanbrugh succeeds in two ways. First, he
presents in Foppington perhaps the best foppish rake in all
English comedy. Milord's confusion of appearance, affectation, emotion, and reality makes for a delightful comic subject,
and the excesses of libertine behavior are well parodied in his
character; he is a singer who knows the words but cannot
catch the melody. Second, Vanbrugh has presented for "the
first occasion in Restoration comedy . . . the predicament of
the younger brother" confronting the legal, though not moral
right of the elder to the estate; "unquestionably, Vanbrugh,
though delighting in the presentation of his superb affectation, meant nevertheless to show the insurmountable difficulty
which just such a character offered to the needs of a younger
brother, however legitimate they might be."[12] The problem is
never stressed: Vanbrugh is certainly not writing a satire
against primogeniture. But the use of the problem as the

main motivation for the subplot suggests some interest in it. Vanbrugh's success dramatically in this subplot may be seen by its popularity with eighteenth-century viewers in afterpieces and revisions.

The only potential aesthetic flaw in *The Relapse* is its lack of dramatic unity, and this will probably disturb no one on stage. Beyond a similarity of tone in the two plots—both present a world typical of high Restoration comedy where fashion in moderation and wit used properly are virtues and where adultery with discretion is no vice—there is little to connect the Foppington-Fashion subplot to the Amanda-Loveless plot. For instance, the Amanda-Loveless characters do not participate in the Foppington-Fashion difficulties. They are present at Foppington's wedding levee, but for reasons that are most obscure. Among them they have only one line, a mere piece of badinage spoken by Loveless. Certainly they are not there to aid the resolution of the plot, for they have nothing to say or do. Again, Foppington comes into their lives early in the piece, but his visit is neither motivated nor connected with the action of either plot. The scene serves only to display his character: Loveless and Berinthia allow him to talk simply because they are amused by him; Amanda pities him but is corrected by her husband and the woman she takes to be her best friend. "Pity those whom nature abuses, but never those who abuse nature" (2.1.156–57), says Loveless. Milord's very amusing conversation is followed by his rudeness to Amanda, which she answers by slapping him. This precipitates the brief duel with Loveless. The visit serves in no way to advance either story. It does help to characterize Foppington, the great fop; it does show both Loveless and Berinthia capable of the subtlety of appearing friendly to a person they admit they despise and will not pity for his weaknesses; and it does portray Amanda as so naturally sympathetic as to be concerned that a man would be thus exploited, so polite as to permit this coxcomb to display himself, and so virtuous as to resent the lascivious verbal gestures of a fool while surprised to find herself unoffended by those of Worthy. But we would know this much about all three of these characters without this scene with Foppington.

Of course, plots may be connected for reasons other than action. For instance, they may deal with similar subjects in different ways so as to shed the fullest light on the problems. Or they may be similar in their diction on the poetic level of metaphor or wit as expressed through dialogue. But there is no such connection here. The occasion of the Foppington-Fashion plot is very different from that of the Loveless-Amanda plot; its dramatic question is, how is a younger brother to find financial security when the elder brother refuses to help him? The dialogue of the Foppington-Fashion plot is of three sorts: self-display through unconscious self-caricature; witty commentary on that display; and witty dialogue used for other reasons. The Loveless-Amanda plot contains dialogue of the second sort, but little of the first. The primary metaphors of the Foppington-Fashion plot depend upon discrepancy between appearance (outer man) and reality (inner man) and between the artificial (in dress, education, social behavior) and the natural (country living, amorality). Those of the Amanda-Loveless plot depend upon the language of romance and love poetry: the primary metaphor is of the love-wound motif, the secondary of the body-soul motif. Only in the broadest sense (that both use language conveying meaning both on the denotative and poetically— and wittily—connotative levels) are the languages of the two plots linked.

But the lack of connection between two plots in a play need not be construed as a fault. Of Vanbrugh's other full-length comedies, most have plots concluded satisfactorily by a single resolution and only *Aesop* shows a similar separation of lines of action. Yet while *The Provok'd Wife* (Vanbrugh's only other wholly original play) is as successful a comedy as *The Relapse*, the other comedies with unified plots—*The False Friend*, *The Confederacy*, and *The Mistake*—are clearly derivative and boring. The presence of two distinct lines of action unified by probable or necessary links and resolved by a single resolution, or of a single, highly unified line of action, is thus no guarantee of artistic achievement: the rather meager ties among the various lines of action in *As You Like It*, for instance, are hardly reasons to damn the comedy. Yet surely a unified plot can achieve effects unavailable to a work like *The Relapse*: the special power of a play like *The Way of the World* is achieved largely through mutual, morally determined causation where all action tends toward one end and where everything contributes to the metaphor underlying the play-as-poetry. And the special power obtained through both the causal connection of and metaphoric comparison among the four lines of action in *A Midsummer-Night's Dream*, for instance, is unavailable to a work whose plot lines are so separable. Of course, only the unusual auditor seeing a production of *The Relapse* would ask himself what the Foppington-Fashion characters have to do with the conflicts of the Amanda-Loveless characters, but in the design of the play that potential for dissatisfaction is present.

The changes Sheridan made in *The Relapse* when he adapted it as *A Trip to Scarborough* indicate his awareness of its beauties and of its weaknesses. He simplified the Foppington-Fashion plot and redesigned the Amanda-Loveless plot. He invented ties between the two groups of people that make the Amanda-Loveless entrance into the Foppington-Fashion affair probable and necessary, and the entrance of the Foppington-Fashion group into the Amanda-Loveless affair probable, though not necessary. In removing the licentiousness of dialogue and motivation, he destroyed much of the wit, and his redesign of the moral world indicates his own and his time's tastes. In effect, he attempted to make a witty "genteel" comedy of manners with a "low" subplot.

The Foppington-Fashion plot of *A Trip to Scarborough* is lifted almost intact from *The Relapse*. Tom arrives penniless in Scarborough (the new setting substituted for London) with Lory, his faithful servant. He asks his foppish brother for financial aid, but appeals on his own terms, not in the flattering tones that probably would get him some help. He is rejected; learns how he can get both revenge and an improvement in his fortunes; suffers a change of conscience; approaches his brother for a second time and is again rejected. Going to Sir Tunbelly's house, he passes himself off as Lord Foppington; then he bribes the Nurse for an early marriage with Hoyden and is married. Foppington arrives, is called an imposter, and suffers the same comic punishment as in the original (chains, the ruin of his fine clothes, the failure of the "low" people to recognize his nobility by his appearance). At this point, Sheridan changes the Foppington-Fashion plot. In *The Relapse*, Vanbrugh invented Sir John Friendly, a neighbor of Sir Tunbelly's who knew Foppington, to identify the foolish lord. Sheridan omits Sir John and brings in the Amanda-Loveless group. Foppington is sure they will identify him, but they are in the story with Tom, and in a pleasant and probable way they greet Tom as Lord Foppington and so uphold his claim: the real Lord Foppington suffers further comic punishment. When a new group of wedding guests arrives to threaten Tom with exposure, he admits his imposture. Foppington is released and turns to vent his rage on Sir Tunbelly.

> Now, Sir Tunbelly, that I am untruss'd, give me leave to thank thee for the very extraordinary reception I have met with in thy damn'd, execrable mansion, and at the same time to assure thee, that of all the bumpkins and blockheads I have had the misfortune to meet with, thou art the most obstinate and egregious, strike me ugly! . . . Thou wilt find to thy unspeakable mortification, that I am the real Lord Foppington, who was to have disgraced myself by an alliance with a clod; and that thou hast match'd thy girl to a beggarly younger brother of mine, whose title deeds might be contain'd in thy tobacco-box.
>
> [5.2.259–70]

Sir Tunbelly's reaction to this abuse is not unusual in Georgian comedy.

> SIR TUNBELLY. Puppy, puppy!—I might prevent their being beggars if I chose it;—for I cou'd give 'em as good a rent-roll as your Lordship.
> TOWNLY. Well said, Sir Tunbelly.
> LORD FOPPINGTON. Aye, old fellow, but you will not do it; for that would be acting like a Christian, and thou art a thorough barbarian, stap my vitals.
>
> [5.2.271–75]

At the urging of the Amanda-Loveless characters, Sir Tunbelly meets Milord's challenge by offering his blessing to the young couple; Foppington makes to himself the same argument concerning appearance he uses in *The Relapse* to motivate his congratulating Tom, but stalks out unreconciled with Sir Tunbelly.

Sir Tunbelly's change of heart is typical of the amiable comedy of Sheridan's time. In *The Relapse*, Sir Tunbelly was justly furious with the perfidy of his daughter and his household servants (the Nurse and the Chaplain); he had been made a party to the destruction of his hopes to gain respectability by buying a titled husband for the daughter he had kept locked up, away from society's temptations. Of course, Sheridan does not give the character enough lines to characterize him fully. He removes a scene between Tom and Sir Tunbelly which, in *The Relapse*, characterizes Sir Tunbelly's impatience with counter suggestions, his drunkenness, and his gluttony—bestial qualities which for Vanbrugh stand for the coarse animal nature of the country just as Foppington represents in both plays the coarse excess of artificiality of some parts of town society. And so Sheridan's Sir Tunbelly becomes a stock character. His acceptance of Tom and Hoyden is typical of the amiable man; abused by Foppington, he is goaded into exposing what is his basic good nature, and he joins the rest of the characters in becoming aware of Foppington's selfish qualities. We are evidently supposed to believe that now he can accept with equanimity being the "main bungler at a long story." Tunbelly's line "Ecod, I don't know how I came to be in so good a humour" (5.2.317–18), reflects Sheridan's failure to motivate his change of mood adequately: *we* don't know either. But motivated or no, it is the ending of a typical eighteenth-century amiable comedy, and just as Bob Acres, Sir Lucius, Mrs. Malaprop, Justice Credulous, and Don Jerome can find themselves satisfied after being tricked and exposed, so can Sir Tunbelly. Except for Lord Foppington's exit—surprisingly like that of Isaac Mendoza—the punitive tone of the ending of *The Relapse* disappears.

Sheridan makes several other changes in the Foppington-Fashion plot necessary to accommodate the squeamish tastes of his age and typical of the comedies popular in his time. He removes, for instance, the homosexual Coupler and replaces him with the matronly Mrs. Coupler; dramatically she functions identically with her brighter original, but she lacks the spark that every character of a truly great comedy must have, that all the characters of *The Rivals* or *The Duenna* possess. Sheridan also generally cleans up the language and the more blasphemous references. Thus, Foppington refers to his watching the ladies rather than the entertainment at the opera; in *The Relapse* he ogled the women at church. Or, when discussing how his heart cut a caper in his mouth, Foppington refers to his happiness at the death of an uncle (whose heir he became), not a father. Serringe—whose name is too evidently associated with the instrument for internal cleansing and not with what we now call the hypodermic—becomes Probe. The Chaplain disappears, along with his selfishly motivated blasphemy; the Nurse's advice concerning bigamy is dropped; and Hoyden's amoral attitude toward marrying a second Lord Foppington vanishes with her frankly amoral physical desires.

Another change typical of Sheridan's own style in his original plays is the general emphasis on expectation rather than surprise as the main basis for comedy. I have discussed his reliance on this technique in *The Rivals* and in *The Duenna* at length; clearly as a creator of comic situations Sheridan generally preferred to raise the expectations of the audience for comic conflict rather than surprise them with a totally unexpected reversal. Thus, in *The Relapse*, Foppington's arrival just after Tom had married Hoyden was unexpected; he was not supposed to come down to Tunbelly's for a fortnight, but came early instead on a whim. In *A Trip to Scarborough* he is readying himself to go to his future father-in-law's even when Tom comes to request aid for the second time. Tom does not know that Foppington plans to go so soon, but the audience does, and that knowledge heightens anxiety; Tom's marriage is awaited with the comic analogue of fear. When Tom is finally married, anxiety is allayed, and at the expected arrival of Foppington the emphasis is on the lord's discomfiture. As Sheridan does in *The Rivals* when he announces the identity of Ensign Beverley in the first scene and outlines Sir Anthony's plans for his son in the second, or in *The Duenna* when he makes clear Margaret's imposture and allows Isaac to disclose all his foolish plans, so here he stresses anticipation of situation and discomfiture of the characters over comic surprise of the auditors.

Another important change is also structural. The two plots are tied more closely together than in *The Relapse*, mainly through the character of Colonel Townly. Worthy, a holdover at least in name from Cibber's play, is metamorphosed into the amiable Townly, a friend of Tom who in the first scene of the play visits him and lets us in on the probable action of the next several acts. Townly tells Tom of Foppington's infatuation with Amanda and of the impending marriage to Hoyden; thus Tom conceives of his plan to marry the country heiress before he meets with his brother while we are also given the chance to anticipate Foppington's wooing of Amanda (an action that is only barely motivated in *The Relapse*). Townly establishes Tom's friendship with Loveless and vows to enlist Amanda and her husband in Tom's cause should Foppington refuse to aid him.

This meeting early in the play simultaneously makes the lines of connection between the two plots more probable and removes other difficulties Vanbrugh encountered. Consider for instance how it improves the probability of a single exit. In the second act of *The Relapse*, following Foppington's delightful self-exposition, foolishly misdirected love-making, and abortive duel with Loveless, Worthy enters, says two or three unimportant lines, and begs Loveless's company to "go to the place I spoke to you of t'other day" (2.1.408–9). Clearly Vanbrugh wanted to empty his stage so that his two heroines could discuss the questions of love, virtue, and marriage that form the central causes for conflict of the Amanda-Loveless plot. In adapting the play, Sheridan also needed to empty his stage for similar discussion. His Townly enters, says approximately the same unimportant lines, but offers a better motivation for his exit with Loveless: "Tom Fashion, is come down here, and we have it in contemplation to save [Foppington] the trouble of his intended wedding; but we want your assistance. Tom would have called, but he is preparing for his enterprize, so I promised to bring you to him—so, sir, if these ladies can spare you—" (2.1.273–77). Loveless and Townly can now comforta-

bly leave the stage to the ladies; at the same time, they have
established again a connection with the Foppington-Fashion
plot. This changed motivation is a small point, but the edifice
of a well-made play is constructed from small building blocks.
Sheridan's concern for such detail helps to explain the excellencies of his great comedies.

Sheridan adds several other such clues to connect the plots.
For instance, Foppington tells his servant in the third act,
before Tom enters to plead a second time for aid and after he
has duelled with Loveless: "and heark thee, tell Mr. Loveless I
request he and his company will honour me with their
presence [at Sir Tunbelly's], or I shall think we are not
friends" (3.1.13–14). We are allowed again to anticipate
Amanda and Loveless's company at the wedding dinner in the
fifth act. Townly comes to spend two hours before the
company leaves for Sir Tunbelly's, not as in Vanbrugh the
several hours that Loveless plans to be away at an unexplained
midnight supper. When the party arrives at Sir Tunbelly's, we
know they have heard Tom's plans and will support him over
Foppington: we can anticipate the noble fop's being crossed
by the very group he is so sure will support him.

The integration of the two plots alleviated one potentially
unsatisfactory element in Vanbrugh's design and made Sheridan's adaptation, if not a more artistic work, certainly a more
unified creation. The simplification of the Foppington-Fashion
plot removed the difficulties of bigamy and amorality represented in Hoyden's decision to conceal her prior marriage to
Fashion and also caused the omission of what some delicate-
minded auditors would have found unacceptable criticism of
ecclesiastics in the character of the Chaplain. Making Sir Tunbelly into an amiable character instead of the beastly country
squire Vanbrugh paints was another result of Sheridan's
simplification of the Foppington-Fashion dénouement. We
lose Vanbrugh's revelatory view of human nature from these
changes, unfortunately: Sir Tunbelly as an amiable humorist
is never as entertaining as Sir Tunbelly the gluttonous old
father; the deletion of Coupler's delightful antics is keenly
felt; and the omission of that wonderfully cynical scene in
which Tom and Coupler bribe the Nurse and Chaplain to tell

the truth removes much of Vanbrugh's coldly realistic ap-
praisal of human nature. But Sheridan's was a different time
from Vanbrugh's, and the good rather than the evil in human
beings was to be emphasized in comic art as well as life; the
essential good nature and benevolence of all men followed
from an age which largely accepted the doctrine of sentimentalism.

So Sir Tunbelly has become an amiable humorist; but Tom
has undergone a more subtle change. He was obviously meant
to be a primarily sympathetic character in Vanbrugh's play;
his attitude toward Hoyden, whom he views as an irrational
creature deserving the trick which he plays upon her, is
normative for the comedy. His behavior with Coupler is less
acceptable, but realistic. If he makes a mistake in *The Relapse*,
it is to admit Lord Foppington into Sir Tunbelly's house, for
the beastly baronet is ready to scatter the "imposter" baron
and his retinue to the wind; but Tom is "resolved to brazen
the business out and have the pleasure of turning the imposter upon his lordship" (4.4.54–56). The inopportune arrival of
Sir John Friendly spoils Tom's pleasure and he is forced to
flee, mildly punished for desiring perhaps more discomfiture
of his brother than warranted and for failing in his cleverness
to anticipate this turn of events. His final pleasure will not
come until the end. Sheridan's Tom also wants to "turn the
imposture upon" Lord Foppington. But here the plot shows
the older brother, not Tom, overreaching himself. Tom's mild
comic fault in Vanbrugh becomes a comic virtue in Sheridan.
With Tom's real affection for Sheridan's softer, more attractive Hoyden, his closer ties with the people of real fashion,
and the excision of such dubious qualities of conscience as
Vanbrugh's Tom's willingness to perjure himself in order to
enter the army (he is a Jacobite) and to exploit Hoyden solely
for monetary reasons, Sheridan's young Fashion becomes an
amiable, completely sympathetic, and mildly clever late eighteenth-century comic hero, basically good-natured. Who but
such a character could express his faith in Townly's essential
honor by declaring that the Colonel's friendship with Loveless
"will prevent your pursuing [Amanda] too far" (1.1.117)?

While Sheridan's adaptation of the Foppington-Fashion line

of action is typical both of his skills as a dramatist and his
acceptance of his period's morality, the most extensive
changes to *The Relapse* were in the adaptation of the Amanda-
Loveless plot. When read with a humorless eye, this line of
action in *The Relapse* seems very similar to those in such
sentimental plays as Frances Sheridan's *The Discovery* (DL, 3
Feb. 1763) or such nearly sentimental comedies as Arthur
Murphy's *The Way to Keep Him* (DL, 10 Jan. 1761). How will
Amanda keep Loveless? How will she preserve her own virtue
against the *agent provocateur* tactics of Berinthia? Comic anxiety enters here, and the overly serious reader or auditor
might be inclined to feel fearful during the duel scene,
particularly if Amanda plays her "What has my folly done?"
and "Now on my knees, my dear, let me ask your pardon for
my indiscretion" lines with seriousness, and if Lord Foppington is made to appear a powerful swordsman, an interpretation not entirely unlikely. We are certainly not brought to
tears by anything in this line of action, but the insensitive
reader or the obtuse auditor at a production of *The Relapse*
which fails to stress the irony of Vanbrugh's mocking love
metaphors and purposefully stale romantic language might be
led to accept in all seriousness much of the dialogue between
Amanda and Loveless in the beginning and that between
Amanda and Worthy near the ending. The latter, especially,
may be read didactically; and the kind of Georgian critic who
disapproved of Congreve and Farquhar (like Francis Gentleman, author of *The Dramatic Censor* [1770]) might just approve
of Amanda's "noble lesson in virtue" to Worthy—especially if
the actor portraying him fails to emphasize his "How long this
influence may last" line properly. Played this way the main
plot has many of the "genteel" appeals of Hugh Kelly's *False
Delicacy*. Happily, Sheridan did not emphasize these features;
unfortunately, he did little to give his changes a life of their
own.

The first major change was merely mechanical. Recognizing
that *The Relapse* was no longer to be enjoyed as commentary
on its moribund predecessor, Sheridan separated it completely
from any connection with *Love's Last Shift*. Loveless and

Amanda have had no marital difficulties of any sort. Though they speak of having somewhere a "retreat," we are given none of the exposition preceding the trip to town that began Vanbrugh's play. We first see them in the second act, already lodged in Scarborough, and discussing the merits of the local theater. Our clue to their identity is provided in the first act by Townly in his conversation with Tom Fashion: they are "old friends" of Townly and Tom.

Second, as Sheridan removed the Amanda-Loveless plot from its connection with Cibber's play, so did he change extensively the motivation that occasions the sexual games. The heart of the difficulties, typical of Georgian comedy, lies in a misunderstanding between Berinthia and Townly. He is her honorable lover and has been courting her for some time. They had arranged to meet in Scarborough, but through a mixup she failed the appointment; he was piqued at first, but now protests that his interest in Amanda makes him no longer care for her. Principally to divert himself, he "offers up chaste incense" to Amanda's beauty and intelligence. By coincidence, Berinthia is the attractive woman Loveless tells Amanda he saw at the theater. Amanda is worried at his attraction to the unknown woman, but dismisses it when Berinthia, who is her cousin, enters. After Loveless and Townly leave, Amanda discloses to Berinthia that Townly has been flirting rather heavily with her. Her language further confuses Berinthia, who also had wondered at Townly's missing his appointment, but she keeps her love for him secret even from her cousin. Amanda tells her that she "did not start at his [Townly's] addresses, as when they came from one [Foppington] whom I contemned" (2.1.370–71), and Berinthia unwarrantedly fancies that Amanda is enjoying Townly's advances. Amanda protests how much she loves her husband, and how faithful she knows him to be; Berinthia is piqued, convinced that Amanda means to have Townly and keep her husband in line, too. In soliloquy, Berinthia discloses her motives:

> Base Townly!—at once false to me, and treacherous to his friend! and my innocent, demure, cousin, too! —I have it in my power to be revenged on her, however. Her husband, if I have

any skill in countenance, would be as happy in my smiles, as
Townly can hope to be in her's. —I'll make the experiment,
come what will on't.

                                                [2.1.401–5]

The whole plot depends not upon a discussion of morality
and sex shown through the exposure of character, but upon
putting the right people in possession of the right information. All the love games will stop together: when Berinthia
learns that Townly is angry because she missed their appointment, but really loves her, she will turn to him; when Loveless
learns that Berinthia would prefer to be true to Townly and
has flirted with him only to anger his wife and to pique
Townly, he will stop his half-hearted pursuit; and when
Amanda learns that Townly is Berinthia's honorable lover, she
will push him in the right direction. In other words, the
comedy is not one of moral decision to be made concerning
sinning or not sinning, but of situation whose resolution lies
only in allowing each participant to know what the true
circumstances are. This resolution is cheerfully provided by
Sheridan at the beginning of the fifth act, and the innocuous
flirtation that has gone on for the previous three acts resolves
in an easy return to the proper partners.

   To demonstrate the dull confusions and mean misunderstandings which lead to the moonlit garden scene (5.1) where
these lovers' embarrassments are resolved hardly seems necessary. Let me say only that in Sheridan's play we have a guilty,
adolescent Loveless who seems incapable of either the per-
suasive or the physical aspects of seduction, an unwilling
Berinthia who will resist anything like sexual contact, a pale
Townly who flirts out of pique, and a completely virtuous
Amanda who is meant to merit the "divinity about her"
(5.1.87) which converts Townly. To complicate and resolve the
misapprehensions and perplexities, Sheridan must rely on two
scenes of concealment and eavesdropping—rather cheap
coups de théâtre in comparison with those of his other comedies. Neither is amusing, and each ends with reflections too
nearly and too sincerely epigrammatic to please anyone but
those who enjoyed Faulkland's self-induced mortification or
who revelled in the delicate, "genteel" distresses of Hugh

Kelly's Lord Winworth, Lady Lambton, Miss Marchmont, and Charles Sidney. The second of these situations is the fifth act recognition scene which presents Amanda chastizing Townly for pursuing her, Townly chastizing himself for neglecting Berinthia, and Loveless and Berinthia overhearing both. These imagined adulterers "steal forth two very contemptible creatures" (5.1.97–98) and vow to confess their errors to their respective partners. Loveless closes the scene, revealing that "When truth's extorted from us, then we own the robe of virtue is a graceful habit" (5.1.125–26; originally Worthy's speech).

This resolution is certainly internally consistent with the tone of the rest of the piece. But it is unsatisfying because of the moral and intellectual poverty of its design. No human heart is exposed in the Amanda-Loveless plot of *A Trip to Scarborough*; no truth about human nature is revealed through artistic exploration of the soul. In the elegant dance-like structure of the verbal sparring of Loveless and Berinthia in *The Relapse*, the selfishness that is the center of their existence is comically shown. In Sheridan's adaptation there is embarassment, not comic exposure; mild flirtation, not fully achieved fornication. It is unsatisfying because the stakes are so small; the characters become mildly discomfited, not by their own natures, but by misunderstanding, by situations.

Clearly, the Sheridan who two months later oversaw production of the brilliant screen scene of *The School for Scandal* was capable of utilizing these materials for a comically satisfying and almost licentious effect. But in the Amanda-Loveless plot of *A Trip to Scarborough*, Sheridan was either unwilling or unable to lavish the care necessary to create a masterly or even a tolerably farcical recognition scene, largely because he could not adapt either the intellectual or the moral qualities of Vanbrugh's world to the tastes and suppositions of the Georgian stage and audience.

If *A Trip to Scarborough* fails because of the poverty of its intellectual and moral design, it also fails from its destruction of the wit of *The Relapse*. Vanbrugh's play is indeed funny chiefly for what Sheridan's age called its licentiousness. Coupler is brilliant; the Nurse and the Chaplain are delightful; the seduction of Berinthia by Loveless is the crowning jewel in Vanbrugh's piece. Who can fail to enjoy Berinthia's soft little protest: "Help, help, I'm ravished, ruined, undone! O Lord, I shall never be able to bear it" (4.3.78–79)? The contrast between what she says and what she does is perfect. But Sheridan's "genteel" comedy of manners, particularly in the Amanda-Loveless plot, could not bear such expressions. In removing these licentious but entertaining beauties, Sheridan destroyed much of Vanbrugh's dialogue. So far as I can find, only one witty speech of any interest in *A Trip to Scarborough* may be attributed to Sheridan. It is of the mildest sort. In *The Relapse*, Loveless draws out Lord Foppington on his activities in the House of Lords.

> LOVELESS. But your lordship is become a pillar of the state; you must attend the weighty affairs of the nation.
> LORD FOPPINGTON. Sir, as to weighty affairs, I leave them to weighty heads. I never intend mine shall be a burden to my body.
>
> [2.1.256–59]

Sheridan improves this.

> LOVELESS. But is'nt your Lordship sometimes obliged to attend the weighty affairs of the nation?
> LORD FOPPINGTON. Sir, as to weighty affairs, I leave them to weighty heads; I never intend mine shall be a burthen to my body.
> BERINTHIA. Nay, my Lord, but you are a pillar of the state.
> LORD FOPPINGTON. An ornamental pillar, Madam; for sooner than undergo any part of the burthen, rat me, but the whole building should fall to the ground.
>
> [2.1.163–70]

In general, however, the wit suffered, and instead of new wit we find "sentiments." Worthy's "robe of virtue" speech becomes an epigram in Loveless's mouth; Berinthia can justify her jealousy on the grounds that "the woman who can forgive the being robb'd of a favour'd lover, must be either an ideot or a wanton" (2.1.405–7); and Amanda can declare that "while I am myself free from guilt, I will never believe that love can beget injury, or confidence create ingratitude" (5.1.79–80). Happily such "sentiments" are few, and in some ways the dialogue is improved, if no longer licentiously witty. Sheridan wisely excised most of Vanbrugh's often wretched blank verse and shortened a great many long, stilted, and dramatically unfocussed speeches. But he lost more. For instance, his scene of Loveless wooing Berinthia is pale beside the beautifully worked love-wound metaphor of Vanbrugh—a metaphor which runs throughout the play and which, while it is not ironic to the characters, certainly is ironic to the auditors. The delightful songs that carry so much of the connotative poetic meaning of the dialogue of *The Relapse* are gone: they are, presumably, too licentious for Sheridan's time.

What Sheridan created in adapting *The Relapse* as *A Trip to Scarborough*, then, was a simplified playing piece, typical of much comedy popular in his time. The more unified action it achieves and the softening of tone make it a complete if rather "genteel" performance. He saw the failure of *The Relapse* to coalesce as a single action, or at least, as two actions mutually dependent on one another in some important way; he saw the difficulty of maintaining ties with a play by Cibber that was by now, for the most part, moribund. But he failed to realize that the beauty of Vanbrugh's play lay in its very licentiousness, for that licentiousness was the heart of the comic criticism, its exposure of the selfishness that is in most souls (or at least is seen to be in a time not highly influenced by the doctrine of sentimentalism); and in tidying up the plot, he substituted, for brilliant comic discussion of adultery and virtuous conversions, innocuous situation comedy with little artistic power, mild comic embarrassment for comic revelation of human nature. One of the oldest critiques of *A Trip to Scarborough* is in many ways still the best short assessment.

> In reading the original play, we are struck with surprise that Sheridan should ever have hoped to be able to defecate such dialogue, and, at the same time, leave any of the wit, whose whole spirit is in the lees, behind. The very life of such characters as Berinthia is their licentiousness, and it is with them, as with objects, that are luminous from putrescense,—to remove their taint is to extinguish their light. If Sheridan, indeed, had substituted some of his own wit for that which he took away, the inanition that followed the operation would have been

much less sensibly felt. But to be so liberal of a treasure so precious, and for the enrichment of the work of another, could hardly have been expected from him. Besides, it may be doubted whether the subject had not already yielded its utmost to Vanbrugh, and whether, even in the hands of Sheridan, it could have brought to bear a second crop of wit.[13]

Moore's view is moralistic, but essentially correct. And yet the revison did satisfy its time, though as anything more than a practical playing piece, we can rank it only slightly higher than St. Patrick's Day or The Camp.

But even while Sheridan was redesigning this comedy for presentation to his late eighteenth-century audiences, he was creating the comedy that would do all this could not do and would become the best playing comedy of manners in the English language. Two and a half months later it would appear.

CHAPTER V

The School for Scandal

SNEER. *Writes himself!*—I know he does—
The Critic, 1.1.210

T HE HIGH expectations which London audiences had of the young playwright who had so entertained them with *The Rivals* and *The Duenna* but whose management of Drury Lane had yet to produce the sparkling successes they desired were answered 8 May 1777 with the introduction of *The School for Scandal*. Because of the extremely late date in the season of the opening,[1] actors' benefits were nearly concluded, and in a week the Haymarket would open for the summer while people of fashion retired to their country retreats and many performers began tours of the provinces. The previous winter season had ended with unusually large crowds elbowing their way in to see the great Garrick in his last performances; once again, unwontedly late in the season, came the crush of excited theater-goers. So tumultuous were the laughter and applause which greeted the fall of the screen that Frederick Reynolds (then a journalist and later a dramatist) ran for his life as he passed Drury Lane, fearing that the building was collapsing.[2] The managers had reason to congratulate themselves, too. Twenty performances of *The School for Scandal* were given before Drury Lane closed for the summer on 7 June 1777; on every night but five, receipts ran well over £200, even with heavy "papering" of the house in the early performances.[3] The average for all performances the first season was well over £233, and the forty-five performances of the comedy in the 1777–78 season averaged a staggering £255 per night. Financially, the success of Sheridan's great comedy was equalled in recent seasons only by Garrick's final appearances. Artistically, it had not been matched since the days of Con-

greve, a fact which an approving public noted by granting to
its author that misleading sobriquet of the "modern Congreve."

Like those of *The Rivals*, the circumstances of composition,
selection of performers, and initial reception of *The School for
Scandal* have been often reviewed. And the play as a play has
received a great deal of comment: the practical aspects of Sheridan's artistry are evident in the comedy's being "a supremely
theatrical play, acting better than it reads,"[4] or "a drama of
extraordinary theatrical skills; an acting play, and what is not
quite the same thing, a play for actors."[5] Clearly, in this play
"Sheridan wrote for the actor as Handel wrote for the singer,
setting him a combination of strokes which, however difficult
some of them may be to execute finely,"[6] provide magnificent
opportunities for individual and ensemble playing. The casting was brilliant: John Palmer, in real life "as famous for his
hypocrisy as for his acting"[7] as Joseph Surface, Thomas King
as Sir Peter, and Frances Abington as Lady Teazle were
particularly notable for their performances.[8] Unlike *The Rivals*, *The Duenna*, and *The Critic*, this comedy had reached
perfection before its opening.

Simply because *The School for Scandal* is such a finished
theatrical masterpiece, it has always posed difficult questions
of interpretation. Like any great work of art, it offers to every
generation a mirror in which to reflect human nature as that
era perceives it. Like any great acting drama, it provides a
vehicle for production that turns into an elegant coach and six
on one stage, and a swift-charging hackney coach on another.
One actor can portray Charles Surface lost in a reverie of old
days and old kindnesses, kneeling before the settee over which
Sir Oliver's picture hangs; another can portray a pathetically
hurt old man in Sir Peter, as he views with desolate grief his
unfaithful Lady Teazle when the screen falls; yet the same
actors can, if they choose, project a manly sentiment with a
quick, brusque refusal to sell old Noll's image, and chagrin
followed by high dudgeon at finding Lady Teazle to be the
"little French Millener." Whether Sheridan meant the sentimental or the "laughing" interpretation is not clear.[9] But we
have reason to believe that he was not entirely happy with

Thomas King's "old fretful dotard" interpretation of Sir Peter. Years later Sheridan read the part to Charles Mathews, who in 1804 was called to take over the role; "so totally unlike was Mr. Sheridan's reading of the character from every other conception of it, that it was next to impossible for the actor to adopt any one of his suggestions." Sheridan was disappointed with Mathews's interpretation in performance, "as, it was said in the green-room, he had been with every previous representative of it, including King."[10] Sheridan's original direction of the auction scene must also have been sentimental, for Powell's acting of Charles Surface when he took over William Smith's part before the end of the century was heartily criticized by the papers: "His animation in the Auction Scene was, if anything, too indiscriminate, some of the passages requiring a considerable degree of sentimental effect."[11]

But these two examples may tell us more about actors than about Sheridan's original intentions for his play on stage. Actors will usually interpret their parts to gain the best reaction from their audiences; their judgments will be based not just on an understanding of their roles in relationship to their conception of the play as a whole, but on their knowledge of the expectations and desires of those who watch. As readers interested in drama as an expression of a particular artistic consciousness in a particular time influenced by particular preconceptions and practices in literary and dramatic creation, we must interpret any comedy in such a way as to avoid conflict with what we know of the historical, social, ethical, or theatrical circumstances.

A reader who brings to *The School for Scandal* a close knowledge of high Restoration comedy but little knowledge of late eighteenth-century comedy may believe that when a 1785 critic said, "By *The School for Scandal* the style of Congreve was again brought into fashion; and sentiment made way for wit,"[12] he implied that Sheridan was attempting to return to the style of high Restoration comedy. Such an interpretation will, or must, stress the intellectual wit antics of the Scandal School, the foolishness of Sir Peter, a stereotypical old bachelor marrying a young and lusty wife, the physical implications of Lady Teazle's relationship with Joseph, the hearty but undisguised (i.e., "natural") rakishness of Charles contrasted with the Tartuffe-like (i.e., "affected") hypocrisy of Joseph. Those lines which indicate Lady Teazle's frequent presence at Joseph's house will be emphasized, and those which indicate her reluctance to go there will be ignored; her confession in the screen scene will be interpreted as arising not from a genuine change of conscience after what she had heard behind the screen, but from a prudential assessment of her own situation, caught in a lie from which she cannot extricate herself gracefully. She is making a good political decision, willing to lose a little face out of pique at Joseph and Maria and out of rational calculation of all she has to gain by a reconciliation—a settlement now from Sir Peter and his fortune upon his death. The prognosis for their marriage is not cheerful: Sir Peter must learn a sober sadness and realistically admit that he will face such cuckolding or near-cuckolding all his life. These are the interpretations any reader who wishes to view the comedy as the last gasp of "high Restoration comedy" will be forced to make.

But if, on the other hand, *The School for Scandal* and all of Sheridan's works are seen primarily as products of a practical playwright working within the theatrical tradition of the late eighteenth century, and if we are as familiar with that theatrical tradition as with high Restoration comedy, another set of interpretations is available. The sentimental implications inherent in the representation will be stressed, with great emotional concern for the exposure of hypocrisy and the reward of merit. Joseph's Machiavellian plans with Lady Sneerwell for the destruction of Charles will be seen to contrast with Charles's own deserving character. A rake Charles may be, but he seduces no virtuous woman, never has, and never proposes to; constantly, even in the drinking scene, his sensitivity and good nature force him to protect the feelings of others. Similarly, Sir Peter and Lady Teazle's difficulties will seem to be based not so much upon genuine incompatibilities as upon mild faults arising from the rigidity of the former and the inexperience of the latter. As soon as Sir Peter is led to see that he has misjudged the hypocrite Joseph and has been too much the father and not enough the husband to his young wife, and as soon as Lady Teazle is forced to realize the hypocrisy that underlies the world of fashion and scandal and the genuine goodness and generosity that motivate her loving husband, the conflicts are at an amiable end.

In other words, depending upon one's particular literary prejudices and knowledge of theatrical tradition, *The School for Scandal* is seen as a brilliantly witty play exposing hypocrisy and foolishness in the cynical and often punitive manner of high Restoration comedy, or as a comedy representative of its time (albeit far better than any other), employing attitudes typical of the doctrine of sentimentalism, and while never melodramatic, appealing more to the emotions than to the intellect. Neither view by itself will completely explain the enjoyment afforded by Sheridan's comedy, but the evidence to be gained from an examination of the materials Sheridan chose to exploit, his particular handling of them, and the ethical and aesthetic values those choices and uses imply, demonstrates that his play is the quintessence of high Georgian comedy.

If there is to be found in *The School for Scandal* a principle of coherence which would explain an audience's pleasure as succinctly as the epithet "comedy of character" does for *The Rivals*, at first glance it would appear to be "punitive comedy of exposure." Like *Volpone* and *Tartuffe*, *The School for Scandal* has as its central concern the exposure of a comic villain whose hypocrisy, avarice, and lechery mixed with cleverness and roguery are curiously attractive as well as repellent. Mosca and Volpone are likeable, and their exposure is somewhat disappointing; Tartuffe's behavior may seem justified in a world inhabited by gulls as foolish as Orgon; and one almost wishes that the lesson about the dangers of misplaced trust and rigidity which Sir Peter must learn, and the reward of genuine benevolence and essential good nature due to Charles, need not coincide with the exposure of Joseph and his expulsion from the society. In a strange and peculiar way, he may arouse respect and at times even sympathy.

Joseph earns respect because he is the most intelligent

character in the play. Like the heroes of classical punitive comedy of exposure, his force of mind elevates him far above the pedestrian intellects of the other characters. Never, even in his most embarrassing exposures, is the "man of Sentiment" at a loss. The witty mind that sarcastically ridicules Sir Benjamin Backbite's efforts as a poet, that leads Lady Teazle through a diabolically clever chain of reasoning by way of a seduction, and that is finally capable of co-opting the values of his amiable relations and declaring that he will follow Lady Sneerwell "lest her Revengeful Spirit should prompt her to injure my Brother" (5.3.205–6) is rendered more effectively, more dramatically, and more intelligently than any other in the comedy.

Why Joseph may gain the sympathy of an audience, though, is less clear. In part it is because he is the victim of circumstances: only chance defeats him. Attracted to Maria's fortune, he is drawn into an affair with Lady Teazle by the chance that she can help him; he is caught in the act of seduction by chance; by chance his uncle Oliver arrives at precisely the moment his clever schemes have been exposed; and by chance Joseph fails to recognize Noll's imposture as Stanley. Because his mind can be respected, even if his values are rejected, it is a disappointment that his attractive cleverness has to be defeated at last, and that the manner of its defeat involves circumstances over which he has no control. Joseph is like a superb juggler whose skill at handling five or six objects we admire greatly; then suddenly someone throws him a seventh, the beautiful moving pattern is upset, and crashing destruction becomes inevitable. A mere piddling Blifil—wisely kept off the scene by Fielding in *Tom Jones* so that we do not dwell upon him for the largest part of the action—cannot gain such respect and sympathy; a masterful Iago, always before us with yet another magnificently evil clue and granted the nobility to choose eternal silence over compromise, draws us toward him with demonic force so that even if we know his exposure and destruction inevitable, even if we desire that destruction for the sake of characters and values we applaud, yet somehow we regret it.

But in *The School for Scandal*, the portrayal and exposure of Joseph, though the central structural concern, is not the primary reason for one's enjoyment of the play, as similar portrayals and exposures are in *Volpone* and *Tartuffe*. In *Volpone*, it is the unmasking of Volpone, Mosca, and their rapacious gulls that is important; the marriage and enrichment of the attractive young couple, Celia and Bonario, is only a probable consequence of the exposure. In *Tartuffe*, an audience may take slightly more pleasure in the prospect of Valerio's marriage to Mariana and the restoration of Orgon's material goods to Elmira and Damis; but again, the chief interest is in the ultimate circumvention of Tartuffe, particularly now that Orgon has finally been made to see his friend's hypocrisy, rather than in the readjustments of social and material circumstances which are the probable consequences of Tartuffe's exposure.

In *The School for Scandal*, however, much more of the pleasure in the dénouement arises from the prospect of Sir Peter and Lady Teazle's reconciliation and the reward of Charles (materially by Sir Oliver, socially by his marriage to Maria) than from the circumvention and exposure of the comic villain and his cohorts. Indeed, the exposure of Joseph is not a necessary precondition to either of these resolutions, though similar exposures of villains are necessary for the marriages of *Volpone* and *Tartuffe* to take place. The Teazles are well on the way to making a happy marriage before Joseph is revealed to be a villain to the rest of the cast, for Sir Peter has made adjustments in his rigid treatment of Lady Teazle, and Lady Teazle, by the pique she expresses at learning Lady Sneerwell has been spreading gossip about her and Charles (4.3.33–37), shows that she is coming to recognize the sterility and malice of the fashionable world she has been naively imitating. Similarly, by refusing to sell old Noll's picture, Charles has already guaranteed himself the continued benevolence of his uncle; Sir Oliver need not learn that Joseph is a hypocrite in order to reward Charles. Although the final exposure of Joseph adds greatly to our pleasure both in the punitive comic way and in its effect on the further stabilization of the other resolutions, it is to this extent separable from our concerns for the fates of Charles, Sir Peter, and Lady Teazle.

Upon examination, it becomes clear that in *The School for Scandal*, Sheridan blended with punitive comedy of exposure two other kinds of comedy—comedy of self-adjustment and comedy of merit rewarded—and created thereby an amiable comedy whose tone is representative of the late eighteenth century. The particular blend can be seen from the early conceptions which Sheridan had of the play and from the quality of wit and satire included in the dialogue and design. Luckily, two earlier sketches Sheridan made and amalgamated into *The School for Scandal* survive.[13] The convenient titles are "The Slanderers" and "The Teazles"; the interest each holds for us is largely in what Sheridan saved and what he rejected. All evidence shows in Sheridan an apprentice playwright whose tastes and impulses were largely of his time and a practical self-adapter whose increasing knowledge of theatrical effectiveness dictated what he would save.

"The Slanderers" is, as one of Sheridan's biographers points out, "what would now be called a sentimental melodrama."[14] Potentially thrilling scenes are provoked by a situation smacking of the melodramatic. The young lovers' dialogue is full of the unselfconscious sentiment that characterizes the excesses of the secondary lovers of *The Rivals*. Scenes demonstrative of their virtuous sufferings and often evocative of tears mark this as an early and inferior work, a product of Sheridan's naturally sentimental spirit and a reflection of his romantic adventures.

The action of "The Slanderers" begins much as does the present *The School for Scandal*. Lady Sneerwell inquires of Spatter (later to become Miss Verjuice, then Snake) if the paragraphs were inserted, and a scene of witty badinage follows. She explains her motivation for spreading slander: "I was hurt, in the early part of my life, by the envenomed tongue of scandal, and ever since, I own, have no joy but in sullying the fame of others." Beyond this psychological explanation lurks a more sinister desire: Lady Sneerwell wants Clerimont, lover of her ward Maria. She hopes to gain him

"by poisoning both with jealousy of the other, till the credulous fool, in a pique, shall be entangled in my snare." Maria
is briefly presented and not firmly drawn. Her character is
shown less by the dialogue than by the situation and generic
expectations. As ward of Lady Sneerwell, she is under the
unscrupulous lady's control. Lady Sneerwell is using Maria
nominally to help her in her own intrigue with Sir Benjamin
Backbite, whom the lady claims to love. Sir Benjamin, of
course, loves Maria and is party to Lady Sneerwell's schemes.
Maria fears she will alienate Clerimont by listening to Sir
Benjamin's pretended addresses to Lady Sneerwell. In a scene
typical of sentimental comedy, Lady Sneerwell presses Maria
to continue "helping" her: "Go, forget the affection I have
shown you: forget that I have been as a mother to you, whom
I found as an orphan. Go, break through all ties of gratitude,
and expose me to the world's derision . . . ." Maria replies in
kind: "Nay, madam, have I not done everything you wished?
For you, I have departed from truth, and contaminated my
mind with falsehood—what could I do more to serve you?"
The language of both is typical of sentimental drama. The
situation is like that of Kelly's *False Delicacy* with two essentially
honest characters there made villainous here; hence it has a
distastefully melodramatic cast, particularly since the balance
of the sketch shows no consciousness of the irony of such
exchanges. Sheridan was not creating the prototypical guilt-
provoking mother of twentieth-century comedy; he was following the melodramatic instincts that led his own mother to
create the Lord Medway line of *The Discovery*.

The presentation of Clerimont is "as little like what it
afterwards turned to as the block to the statue, or the grub to
the butterfly."[15] The original Clerimont is a compound of
Joseph and Charles Surface, without the hypocrisy of the
former or the youthful buoyancy of the latter. "He is one of
your moral fellows, who does unto others as he would they
should do unto him" is the sarcastic introduction Sir Benjamin
Backbite gives him. This young man is made grave by the
action. First, his sister who lives in the country has suddenly
eloped: he suspects Sir Benjamin, though we are not able to
learn if his suspicions are justified. Second, as soon as Lady

Sneerwell gets him out of the way, Sir Benjamin approaches his beloved Maria under the guise of addressing Lady Sneerwell through her. Clerimont has the misfortune of overhearing just that part of their conversation which leads him to suspect Maria's truth and constancy. "So, now—who can ever have faith in woman? D—d deceitful wanton! why did she not fairly tell me that she was weary of my addresses? that woman, like her mind, was changed, and another fool succeeded." To this soliloquizing, resembling too closely the self-tortures of Faulkland in *The Rivals* or Lord Clairville's similar doubts of Miss Courtney in Charlotte Lennox's *The Sister*, is coupled the opportune entrance of Lady Sneerwell, ready to press her advantage against the innocence of her ward.

Happily, Sheridan abandoned this train of action almost completely when he incorporated the scandal scenes into *The School for Scandal*. All that remains of this poorly drawn, poorly motivated story is the presentation of Lady Sneerwell and Joseph using intrigue and scandal in their efforts to gain Charles and Maria for themselves. Sir Benjamin sinks from an important, villainous character, whom Maria is nearly powerless to defeat and whom fate aids in misdirecting Clerimont, to a member—the most amusing one, indeed—of the Scandal School, and an impotent flirter with the morally upright Maria.

It would be excessive to accuse Sheridan of accepting the more melodramatic sentimentalism of Walpole's "*tragédie mitigée*" or the "mulish productions" attacked by Goldsmith. After all, this sketch is exactly that: a sketch, not intended for production, not polished for performance, certainly not the final intention of a great comic playwright. The use he made of it when he amalgamated it with "The Teazles" to create his masterpiece shows a mind keenly aware of its deficiencies and ready to capitalize on its excellencies. Though his first instincts are toward the melodramatic and the sentimental, toward the non-comedy of Frances Sheridan, Hugh Kelly, Charlotte Lennox, and Elizabeth Griffith, he leaves behind the trappings of weeping comedy, expunges the potentially melodramatic, and takes instead the brilliant, epigrammatic wit that characterizes the Scandal School.

But he keeps the morality that underlies the melodramatic and sentimental, the attitudes typical of the doctrine of sentimentalism so basic to his time. The sexual mores are those of the late eighteenth century: relationships should be made for love, not for mere economic alliance or sexual gratification, and their proper result is marriage. Moreover, in such lines as Maria's refusal to attend Lady Sneerwell's levee, where scandal is the chief *divertissement*, we see clear antecedents of the moral position taken by Sheridan in satirizing what to him was one of his society's chief vices: "I can never think that harmless which hurts the peace of youth, draws tears from beauty, and gives many a pang to the innocent."

The changes he makes in "The Teazles" also emphasize this acceptance of the morality of his day. Solomon Teazle (at first a city knight who has "left off trade," later in what are evidently second or third thoughts, "Sir Peter") has married for the third time, now to a girl thirty years his junior. His steward, Jarvis, details her extravagance: one hundred pounds to lower the seat of her coach, so that she may get her headdress in; another hundred-a-year salary to each of her footmen; fifty pounds for nosegays; five pounds a week for fruit for her monkey, and another five pounds for china for the pet; and thirty pounds for perfume. Old Teazle tells her a poor family could dine upon one of her roses and she saucily replies that a beggar could live off his gold-headed cane for a week at least. He remarks what a simple country girl she was when she married him:

SIR PETER. Then you could be content to sit with me, or walk by the side of the—Ha! ha!

LADY TEAZLE. True, I did; and, when you asked me if I could love an old fellow, who would deny me nothing, I simpered and said, "Till death."

SIR PETER. Why did you say so?

LADY TEAZLE. Shall I tell you the truth?

SIR PETER. If it is not too great a favour.

LADY TEAZLE. Why, then, the truth is, I was heartily tired of all

these agreeable recreations you have so well remembered,
and having a spirit to spend and enjoy a fortune, I was determined to marry the first fool I should meet with.—So pray
what induced you to fix on me? . . .

SIR PETER. O your youth & personal accomplishment to be
sure—

LADY TEAZLE. To say truth your Age would have been an
insuperable objection—But as I prudently consider'd that as a
maid I was then so anxious to be wife—I might even [as] a
wife wish as much to be a widow. . . .

SIR PETER. If I were to die what would you do[?]

LADY TEAZLE. Countermand my new Brocade—

SIR PETER. You might have [been a] maid still but for me—

LADY TEAZLE. Well you made me a Wife—for which I am much
obliged to you, and if you have a wish to make me more
grateful still, make me a widow.

The subjects are fairly innocuous (little sexual suggestion even
here), but the tone is harsh. There is the smell of death in
Lady Teazle's reiterated wish to be made a widow, and the
smell lingers, as this later exchange makes clear:

SIR PETER. Then, you never had a desire to please me, or add to
my happiness?

LADY TEAZLE. Seriously, I never thought about you; did you
imagine that age was catching? I think you have been over-
paid for all you could bestow on me. Here I am surrounded
by half a hundred lovers, not one of whom but would buy a
single smile by a thousand such baubles as you grudge me.

SIR PETER. But you continue to deny me—though 'tis hard a
Husband should furnish his wife with means to make a
conquest—

LADY TEAZLE. I can answer if you indulge me [? my] Vanity. . . .

SIR PETER. Then you wish me dead?

LADY TEAZLE. You know I do not, for you have made no settlement on me.

This Lady Teazle is not an unsophisticated country girl
brought to London. She has made her economic alliance with
as much cynicism as Fainall or Freeman. She knows what her
powers are—sexual—and she is willing to taunt old December
with her attractiveness and with her ability to cuckold him.
The comic world into which Sheridan could put such charac-

ters would have had to be as aloof, cold, and cynical as Manly's vision of life, for like Wycherley's Olivia, this Lady Teazle could easily become a simple thief. It was unlikely that Sheridan's Georgian audiences, unhappy with explicit sexuality and unwilling to believe that married couples should not adjust to one another's foibles, would accept such characters—and this tailor knew his customers.

So the Sir Peter and Lady Teazle of *The School for Scandal* are cut of a different cloth, clearly the amiably patterned one of the late eighteenth century. Sir Peter finds himself "the miserablest Dog ever since that ever committed wedlock" (1.2.3–4) yet cannot deny that he loves his young wife dearly. For him, being miserable is a kind of game: he will "never be weak enough to own" that he loves her (1.2.16). Arguing with her is his chief diversion: "yet with what a charming air she contradicts every thing I say—and how pleasingly she shews her contempt of my authority.... [T]here is a great Satisfaction in qua[r]relling with her ..." (2.1.100–3). The love game is his joy: his irascibility is typical of a man whose amiably comic nature softens what might otherwise be characteristics of a stock old bachelor. Besides loving his wife—an emotion no Restoration comic old bachelor would have felt—he unconsciously and pleasantly ridicules himself. Lady Teazle is at fault for their disagreements, he feels: "I am myself the sweetest temper'd Man alive and hate a teizing Temper—and so I tell her a hundred Times—a day—" (1.2.27–29). While he reproaches her for her extravagance, his reproaches are chiefly for the excess of her purchases, not for her wanting such luxuries. As long as she will be sweet to him, there is nothing he will not give her (3.1.175–76). And yet he finds real joy in argument with her, and he must debate even who starts the argument (3.1.205–20).

Like Sir Peter, *The School for Scandal* Lady Teazle is a character not of the harsher Restoration mold but of Sheridan's eighteenth century. She claims that "tho' I was educated in the country I know very well that women of Fashion in London are accountable to nobody after they are married" (2.1.4–6). Her statement exposes not the cold cynicism of the earlier Lady Teazle, but naïveté. She repeats a commonplace, but does not really live by its sentiments; it is more like a lesson in a copy book than a selfish conviction felt and acted upon. Like Margery Pinchwife, she is naturally naïve; but unlike Margery, her program to correct her naïveté arises not primarily from sexual appetite and attraction but from a desire to appear fashionable. Like Lady Teazle of "The Teazles," she was glad to escape the boring rural joys; but unlike her original, she did not cunningly calculate her escape or carefully plan her self-gratifying extravagances. Appearing fashionable is her desire; that she knows is done by having flowers in winter and a coach and six. She is an ingénue, not a practiced fortune hunter; her association with the Scandalous College (which, by the time of her entrance, we have seen) is further evidence of her lack of experience; and in her heart, she does not resemble these selfish, cynical wits. She had been kind and attentive in listening to Sir Peter's proposals, not calculating (3.1.192). When they married, while love may not yet have been there for her, still she defended her fiancé to her friends (3.1.196–200). Her comic fault is not cynicism but an uncautious inexperience. Though she argues with Sir Peter and spends his money on fashionable luxuries, there is still an essential respect, the forerunner of love.

Consider, for instance, the rendering of the wife-widow exchange as Sheridan adapted it from "The Teazles." Sir Peter of *The School for Scandal* has just finished detailing the simplicity of Lady Teazle's erstwhile country life and has contrasted it with her fashionable London living. He asks for her gratitude for all he has done.

> SIR PETER. This madam was your Situation—and what have I not done for you?—I have made you a woman of Fashion, of Fortune, of Rank—in short I have made you my Wife—
> LADY TEAZLE. Well then and there is but one thing more you can make me to add to the obligation—and that is—
> SIR PETER. My widow I suppose?
> LADY TEAZLE. Hem! hem!
> SIR PETER. Thank-you Madam—but don't flatter yourself for—tho' your ill conduct may disturb my Peace it shall never break my Heart I promise you:—however I am equally oblig'd to you for the Hint.
>
> [2.1.53–62]

The joke is still here, but the smell of death has diffused. The implication that Sir Peter's death would not distress his wife remains, but for one thing a kind of pun has entered: Lady Teazle might intend to say "there is but one thing more you can make me to add to the obligation—and that is—a settlement," but Sir Peter finishes for her—now I should make you my widow. Lady Teazle does not actually say this cruel line, as did her original; she has only the equivocal "Hem! hem!" Sheridan leaves it up to the actress to interpret the tone, and even before we can dwell on the implication of the throat-clearing, Sir Peter snaps back. He is strong enough to resist her implication, or his own inference. The very force of his reply reaffirms his life: he's a living man and will not be hurt by her lack of love for him. Do your worst, he seems to say. Moreover, his "I am equally oblig'd to you for the Hint" implies he can steel himself adequately against her wishing widowhood, while his choosing a particular manner of death —the breaking of his heart—indirectly but warmly reaffirms his love for her. The effect is not cynically comic, as in "The Teazles," but amiably comic. Finally, the motif appears but this one time; it is not, as in the sketch, dwelt upon.

In similar fashion, Sheridan's treatment of Lady Teazle's assignation with Joseph Surface has metamorphosed from a cynically sexual encounter, calculated to gratify lust and to hurt Sir Peter, to the most precipitous of unsophisticated mistakes—the near seduction of an innocent flirting with an accomplished hypocrite. Moore says of the general tone of "The Teazles": "This want of delicacy is particularly observable in the subsequent scene between Lady Teazle and Surface—the chastening down of which to its present tone is not the least of those triumphs of taste and skill, which every step in the elaboration of this fine Comedy exhibits."[16] Surface here is called "Young Plausible" and Charles Surface is "Frank Plausible." Young Plausible and Lady Teazle definitely have a relationship of long standing. She enters his study and asks, "What, musing, or thinking of me?" Her question needs no answer: he has indeed been anticipating their assignation.

LADY TEAZLE. Nay, in faith you should pity me—this old cur-
mudgeon of late is growing so jealous, that I dare scarce go
out, till I know he is secure for some time.

YOUNG PLAUSIBLE. I am afraid the insinuations we have spread
about Frank have operated too strongly on him—we meant
only to direct his suspicions to a wrong object.

This Lady Teazle evidently knows her own mind. She has
planned ahead for this meeting, and now she wants confirmation of his constancy to her, much as in the manner of the
Restoration love game. First, does he love her niece Maria?
(Evidently Sheridan planned that her comic punishment
would be the disclosure of Young Plausible's real affection for
Maria.) No, he answers.

LADY TEAZLE. But what proofs have I of your love to me, for I
have still so much of my country prejudices left, that if I were
to do a foolish thing (and I think I can't promise) it shall be
for a man who would risk every thing for me alone. How
shall I be sure you love me?

YOUNG PLAUSIBLE. I have dreamed of you every night this week
past.

LADY TEAZLE. That's a sign you have slept every night for this
week past; for my part, I would not give a pin for a lover
who could not wake for a month in absence. . . .

YOUNG PLAUSIBLE. Then let me on my knees—

LADY TEAZLE. Nay, nay, I will have no raptures either. This
much I can tell you, that if I am to be seduced to do wrong, I
am not to be taken by storm, but by deliberate capitulation,
and that only where my reason or my heart is convinced.

Lady Teazle here is taking a lover in much the same manner
that Bellinda capitulates to Dorimant's siege. Both women
have no real scruples about sinning; they only want guaran-
tees that they are desired and that their reputations will be
safe. She is ready to be convinced, even if she demands a
romanticism much like Lydia Languish's—he should not sleep
if he loves her. She is dominant in the relationship, asking the
love-game questions, conducting the love-game examination.
Her calculation of the meeting itself, with its concomitant ruin
of Frank's character, carries over into her view of illicit love.
This is hardly an unsophisticated country girl learning the
ways of sophistication.

In *The School for Scandal*, Lady Teazle is at Joseph Surface's
house for an entirely different reason. Entranced with the

false fashion of the Scandal School, she has made the acquaintance of Joseph and allows him to be her "Lover no
further than Fashion requires" (2.2.216–17). He is to her "a
mere Platonic Cicisbeo—what every London wife is entitled
to" (2.2.218–19). While using Lady Teazle to gain Maria for
himself, Joseph has suddenly found himself attracted to her,
though in her eyes his gallantry is part of the fashion of
London and little more. After another argument with Sir
Peter during which he accuses her of flirting with Charles, she
goes to Joseph's apartment. The visit is not spontaneous, but
neither is it clearly for sexual liaison: the villainy of Joseph
emphasizes her natural inexperience. Moreover, she is no
longer Joseph's ally in a plot against his brother; her actions
now come almost entirely from her momentary anger with Sir
Peter. She expresses her vexation at Sir Peter's suspicions and
her bewilderment that Lady Sneerwell would circulate reports
about her and Charles, and avows that they are "all without
any Foundation too—that's what vexes me" (4.3.36–37). We
are reminded of Joseph's participation in the spreading of
scandal; but his brilliant wit is apt to leave us in the same
amazed position as Lady Teazle. In a reversal of received
truth Oscar Wilde must have known before he created *The
Importance of Being Earnest*, Joseph inveighs not against virtue
but against innocence; his logic has led Lady Teazle to
complete the syllogism with "so that if [Sir Peter] suspects me
without cause, it follows that the best way of curing his
Jealousy is to give him reason for't."

> SURFACE. Undoubtedly—for your Husband should never be de-
> ceived—in you—and in that case it becomes you to be frail in
> compliment to his discernment.
> LADY TEAZLE. To be sure what you say is very reasonable—and
> when the consciousness of my own Innocence—
> SURFACE. Ah! my Dear—Madam there is the great mistake—'tis
> this very conscious Innocence that is of the greatest Prejudice
> to you—What is it makes you negligent of Forms and careless
> of the world's opinion?—why the consciousness of your Inno-
> cence—what makes you thoughtless in your Conduct and apt
> to run into a thousand little imprudences?—why the con-
> ciousness of your Innocence—what makes you impatient of

Sir Peter's Temper and outrageous at his suspicions?—why
the consciousness of your own Innocence—

[4.3.51–66]

Lady Teazle's response seems assured—"Tis very true" she
answers to Joseph's speech on the consciousness of her own
Innocence—but we feel she responds not to the principle of
his convoluted logic, but to the spirit of his implied attacks on
Sir Peter and social appearances. Does she follow his implications?

> SURFACE. Now my dear Lady Teazle if you would but once
> make a trifling Faux-Pas—you can't conceive how cautious
> you would grow—and how ready to humour and agree with
> your Husband.
> LADY TEAZLE. Do you think so—
> SURFACE. O I'm sure on't—and then you would find all Scandall
> would cease at once—for in short your Character at Present is
> like a Person in a Plethora absolutely dying of too much
> Health.

[4.3.68–74]

So formidable a wit is dangerous; the attacks, though all
apparently intellectual, appeal to the fashion Lady Teazle flirts
with; she is an innocent lurking near a tree of diabolical wit
far more pernicious—if more amusing—than Sir Anthony
Absolute's circulating libraries. But Lady Teazle seems to be
catching on, and the seduction begins to appear to her more
like a seduction. Her next two lines initiate a defense; her
employment of Joseph's medical metaphor shows her desirous
of a logic a bit more reasonable.

> LADY TEAZLE. So—so—then I perceive your Prescription is that I
> must sin in my own Defence—and part with my virtue to
> preserve my Reputation.—

(Note the dashes after "so—so—." Sheridan habitually uses
such dashes in an elocutionary fashion to indicate stress on
the preceding word; here the monosyllables convey a sense of
"now I see," not of "Aha!" Lady Teazle of "The Slanderers"
spoke this delightful phrase—which is scribbled several times
in the notebooks for the early sketches—with a certain sure-
ness—"So then you would have me sin in my own defence,

and part with my virtue to preserve my reputation"—that is lacking here.)

SURFACE. Exactly so upon my credit Ma'am.

LADY TEAZLE. Well certainly this is the oddest Doctrine—and the newest Receipt for avoiding Calumny.

SURFACE. An infallible one—believe me—Prudence like experience must be paid for—

LADY TEAZLE. Why if my understanding were once convinced—

SURFACE. O certainly madam your understanding *should* be convinced—yes—yes—Heav'n forbid I should perswade you to do any thing you *thought* wrong—no—no—I have too much honor to desire it—

LADY TEAZLE. Don't—you think we may as well leave Honor out of the Argument?

SURFACE. Ah—the ill effects of your country education I see still remain with you.

LADY TEAZLE. I doubt they do indeed—and I will fairly own to you that If I could be perswaded to do wrong it would be by Sir Peter's ill-usage—sooner than your honourable Logic after all—

SURFACE. Then by this Hand which He is unworthy of—

[4.3.75–94]

Now that she understands the logic, Lady Teazle demands an appeal to her reason. Superficially, Surface seems to do just that, but cleverly he takes exactly the clue he needs and attacks her again on the emotional level. She is, after all, in his library for two reasons. First, she believes having such assignations is fashionable; second, Sir Peter has accused her unfairly, and she is piqued at his treatment of her, treatment which has verged on the unreasonable. Just as they were becoming reconciled, he reminded her that their arguments proceeded from her argumentative nature. When she became angry, he falsely accused her of being scandalously linked with Charles. Joseph has attacked on both these grounds—fashion, and Sir Peter's unjust suspicions. Now he pretends to appeal to her reason. He would do nothing she *thought* wrong; he has too much honor. Lady Teazle, reminded of the dishonor her affair would bring, asks him to keep honor out of his logical arguments. Joseph is momentarily stopped, but returns to the theme that brought her there in the first place—her fear of unfashionableness. She was educated in the country, he reminds her, and must lose that residue of barbarism. She rejects logic, she replies, and would have an emotional demonstration, preferably one attacking Sir Peter. Immediately, witty Joseph offers her one, taking her hand, and about to damn her husband.

Precisely at this point they are interrupted by Sir Peter's arrival. Lady Teazle's final decison must be held in abeyance, but clearly this is not a Berinthia ready to cry softly from a Loveless's eager arms or a Margery Pinchwife naïvely driven by sexual desire and physical attraction to a stud as substitute for a flaccid old husband. Instead Lady Teazle seems as innocuous as Sheridan's revision of Berinthia or as harmless as Lydia when she discovers Beverley's identity: her anger at Sir Peter makes her susceptible to Joseph—the anger of a lover for her beloved's ill temper. She will not be won by love rhetoric, and one suspects that she recognizes Joseph's sentiments as pernicious stuff—at least she seems capable of subtly mocking his "honourable Logic"—which will not cause her to fall. Not the love-game but the travesty of the love-game is amusing here, most particularly Joseph's hypocritical, brilliant, and witty casuistry: where would an eager lover use such convoluted logic except in such a game? Where are the emotional protestations of love? They probably would not work with Lady Teazle, both because her disputes with Sir Peter are particularly amiable and because her delusion—that to be fashionable she should have lovers—seems particularly innocent.[17]

This assessment of Lady Teazle's character is confirmed by her reaction when she is so embarrassingly discovered. She has the power to sustain Joseph's arguments and her own reputation. His designs on Maria are not sufficiently injurious to her feelings to lead her to expose his true character out of piqued vanity; instead her affection for Sir Peter, her ultimate respect and love for him, forces her to reveal Joseph. "Had I left the Place without the Shame of this discovery," she tells Sir Peter in rejecting Joseph's attempt to explain away the appearances, "my future Life should have Spoke the sincerity of my Gratitude" for his generosity and love (4.3.422–23).

Significantly, she has recovered her sense. Common sense, a major characteristic postulated for many amiable eighteenth-century comic characters, tells her of Joseph's perfidy, now that her flirtation with Fashion is at an end. Sheridan abjured the cold cynicism of high Restoration comedy for the warmly human response his time had come to demand, and he himself had come to love. "The Teazles" is not the expression of the mature moral and often sentimental man. The comedy of self-adjustment is.

The pleasures afforded by the Sir Peter–Lady Teazle–Joseph Surface line of action as drawn from the two early sketches and completed in *The School for Scandal* are quite similar to those of high Georgian comedies like *The Jealous Wife* or *The West Indian*, where mildly erring characters are taught to mend their ways and more villainous characters are exposed and cast out of society. Some of the obstacles are internal and thus conducive to examination of character in depth, though neither Sir Peter nor Lady Teazle is a particularly deep study. Like his fellow Georgian dramatists Colman and Cumberland, and like Murphy and Kelly in such comedies as *The Way to Keep Him* and *The School for Wives*, Sheridan worked within the assumptions that marriage was a desirable state[18] and that improvement in character was possible to adjust to the difficulties posed by minor incompatibilities; that he made believable the changes in character (or at least the realization of culpability) is one way in which his artistry is superior to that of his contemporaries, especially those whom Goldsmith singled out for scorn. A lesser artist, as familiar as Sheridan with late eighteenth-century comedy, might have tried to convert Joseph or would have dwelt lingeringly and sentimentally on Sir Peter and Lady Teazle's reconciliation—a meeting which Sheridan wisely keeps off stage.

The early sketches tell us a good deal about Sheridan's original conception of the plot against Maria and the love-games of Sir Peter, Lady Teazle, and Joseph; however, they tell us relatively little about the comedy of merit rewarded which gives so much pleasure in *The School for Scandal*. Charles

Surface is no Clerimont, but neither is he Frank Plausible.[19] Without the melodrama of either, we are given a delightful tale of the restitution of fortune according to merit in the triumph of Charles's humanly warm values over Joseph's prudential hypocrisy.

This comedy of merit rewarded is at once the most emotionally pleasing and the least aesthetically satisfactory aspect of *The School for Scandal*. It contains the potentially improbable, the excessively sentimental, and the facilely moral. Sir Oliver's return is not improbable, but his disguises, tests, and easy acceptance of Charles appear less than highly probable; Rowley's unshakable belief in Charles is rather mawkish, while Charles's sentimental gratitude toward an uncle he has not seen in sixteen years can become maudlin; and if we accept Henry James's description of the "main idea . . . that a fine young fellow who lives freely and sociably and has a kind word for great and small is likely to turn out better, in the long run, than his older brother, who is an economist and 'a man of sentiment,' "[20] the morality is rather facile. Yet undeniably, there is great emotional satisfaction in the eventual redistribution of reward, and the audience is likely to value Charles more than Joseph in spite of the attractive repulsion they may feel for the hypocritical brother. Why?

Primarily because of contrast. Characters are judged in the early scenes of the play by the way they feel about Charles and Joseph. Generally, those of good nature side with Charles, those of selfishness with the hypocritical Joseph. Only Joseph, not Charles, appears in the early scenes; and we learn about Charles only through other characters. On his first appearance, Joseph immediately displays the hypocrisy which draws from Lady Sneerwell the exclamation, "O Lud you are going to be moral and forget that you are among Friends—" (1.1.104–5); his obvious dissimulation, policy, and selfishness constantly lead us to expect the opposite qualities in a brother who is contemned. Reckless extravagance and dissipation are the charges levelled at Charles, but he is not to be seen, and the levellers of the charges either mitigate the crimes (as does Maria) or defuse the accusations by their own failings (as do the scandalmongers and the wrongheaded Sir Peter). More-over, Charles is the victim of a plot by Lady Sneerwell and Joseph, and thereby earns the sympathy customarily given to the underdog. His strongest supporter is Rowley; his strongest detractor is Sir Peter, who shall be made to "own he has been for once mistaken" (2.3.67); when Sir Oliver arrives and immediately identifies himself with the values Rowley believes inherent in Charles's character (primarily benevolence), it is clear that Charles is safe. Rakishness in youth which does not encompass sexual profligacy, we are led to believe, is better than premature gravity, even if gravity is not hypocritical. Charles's reckless extravagance and dissipation will be for-given as long as those sentimental components—the ability to be lavish with his "*Tin* Money on the Stage" in the cause of charity, together with its attendant virtues of openness, gen-erosity, feeling, and gratitude—are intact.

The contrast with Joseph leads to obvious distinctions in characterization. Joseph is deep and dissimulating: he has com-plicated motives and plans bred of conscious policy. He is Fainall, Maskwell, and Blifil in one, the perfect comic Iago, as Walter Sichel called him.[21] His surface is just that: superficial, masking an interior of deceit and selfishness—morality plas-tered over avarice and lechery. To increase satisfaction in the eventual redistribution of reward according to merit, Sheridan had to make the discrepancies in situation and character as large as possible, while still maintaining comic expectations. The opposite of avarice is extravagance; economy is too nearly poised between, so Charles cannot be economical. The op-posite of hypocrisy is total candor; prudence, even self-efface-ment, can smack of dissimulation, so Charles cannot be pru-dent. The opposite of selfishness is benevolence; the thought-ful charity Rowley urges—paying tradesmen before relieving Stanley—is too close to policy, so Charles cannot think twice about giving rather than paying. The opposite of lechery is chastity; sexual desire, even with marriage as its only end, too nearly suggests the darker passion, so Sheridan neither can allow a scene between Charles and Maria nor can he permit Charles more than a chaste toast to express his attraction to her. Charles must be a comic but faultless Othello to Joseph's comic Iago; his openness, his expanse of soul, his natural warmth and honest generosity define his rather flat character.

The flat characterization is correct, for Charles cannot be complex. He cannot be a Mirabel to Joseph's Fainall; Mirabel —though practicing it for ends of which we approve—is too much a man of policy himself. The satisfaction of seeing Charles rewarded and Joseph punished is far more amiable and somewhat more intense (though on an emotional, not an intellectual level) than the satisfaction of seeing Fainall banished and Mirabel, with his virtues as well as his comically chastened faults, rewarded for his foresight. Since Sheridan had neither the scope to show how sexual urges, alcoholic incontinence, or gambling excesses may be redirected, nor the plan to effect a gradual change in character or shift in consciousness, he cannot like Fielding show his Tom Jones in situations which reveal genuine weaknesses or which suggest the acquisition of additional characteristics. Unlike Tom, Charles appears to learn no discretion; but also unlike Tom, Charles does nothing approaching the truly culpable. Instead he is seen drinking but remaining sober, going to gamble but not actually in the act of gambling; and these are minor failings next to the virtues of plain-dealing, cheerfulness, and generosity he simultaneously displays. Charles is what he is from beginning to end, and as a result the contrast with his politic brother is only clearer.

In this contrast, too, we can see how Sheridan went beyond creating a character whose benevolence and generosity are merely posited. Goldsmith's objections to the heroes of sentimental comedies whose faults were forgiven in consideration of the goodness of their hearts were levelled not just at characters who had real faults but at those characters with foibles whose generosity was drawn merely as a stage characteristic. Sheridan avoided this in Charles's case by enlarging his generosity to include the whole range of allied sentimental virtues. Consider the following sequence: Sir Oliver, disguised as Premium, and Moses have just entered Charles's house.

> SIR OLIVER. To Judge by the Servants—one wouldn't believe the master was ruin'd—but what—sure this was my Brother's House?

MOSES. Yes Sir Mr. Charles bought it of Mr. Joseph with the
Furniture Pictures—etc.—just as the old Gentleman left—it—
Sir Peter thought it a great Piece of Extravagance in him!

SIR OLIVER. In my mind the other's œconomy in selling it to
him was more reprehensible by half.—

[3.2.6–12]

Before we begin Charles's test, the rules are announced: has
"extravagance" or "œconomy" totally removed the warm human values of familial affection and gratitude from either
brother? Generosity is not in doubt, but virtues allied with
true benevolence are. Comic anxiety is heightened not because
we fear Charles will appear extravagant or ungenerous, but
because he might appear ungrateful. His decision to sell the
library, the plate, and the furniture was bad enough; will he
compound his error by selling his relations? He does, but he
refuses to sell "old Noll" and thus wins the day by showing
true gratitude in his effusion of sentimental feeling. Rowley's
bringing to Sir Oliver the news that Charles immediately
wants to help Stanley has no real effect upon Sir Oliver's
decision: his mind is already made up. In direct parallel, what
hardens Sir Oliver's heart against Joseph is not so much his
"French plate" in place of the "silver ore of Charity" as his
lack of gratitude toward his nabob uncle. His denial of
presents of money and his blackening of his uncle's character
enrage Sir Oliver. Joseph loses not on the ground of avarice,
but on the ground of ingratitude: there is no warmth, no
affection, no fellow feeling in the hypocrite (the real sentimental virtues which Joseph merely affects), and Sir Oliver,
whether or not we approve his behavior—and we are certainly
not invited to fault him for it—demands gratitude in return
for his money.[22]

In many ways, the contrast of Charles and Joseph on the
grounds of generosity, gratitude, and familial affection is part
of a larger contrast between natural plain-dealing and dissimulation which runs throughout all three lines of the play.
In the amiable comedy of merit rewarded, Charles is the
obvious spokesman for openness. When he first approaches
Premium, for instance, he tells him to dispense with forms:

Mr. Premium—the Plain State of the Matter is this—I am an
Extravagant young Fellow, who want[s] Money to Borrow, you I

take to be a Prudent old Fellow, who has got Money to lend—I
am Blockhead enough to give Fifty per Cent. sooner than not
have it, and you I presume are Rogue Enough to take a
hundred if you could get it,—Now Sir, you See we are acquainted at once, and may proceed to Business without farther
Ceremony.

[3.3.114–20]

When Charles comes to Joseph's house (4.3), is drawn out by
his brother, and learns of Sir Peter's concealed presence, his
immediate response is to bring Sir Peter out of hiding; when
Sir Peter reveals the presence of the "little French Millener,"
again Charles opts for openness rather than continued dissimulation.[23] In telling Noll he is glad to see him when Sir
Oliver reveals himself in the final scene, Charles is expressing
his real emotion, not hiding behind a cloak of false gratitude.
Only twice does Charles show anything like a desire to conceal
rather than reveal facts: he aids his brother in disposing of
Premium-Stanley before Sir Oliver arrives, thus sharing temporarily in the "prudence" that characterizes Joseph (Premium-Stanley's presence is, after all, an apparent threat to
Charles's receiving an inheritance); he also agrees implicitly
not to expose Joseph's relationship with Lady Teazle when his
stumbling on to the topic causes Joseph to reveal Sir Peter's
presence—and his lie to Sir Peter, saying that it was just a
joke, shows in Charles not so much dissimulation as generosity
of spirit, for he wishes to spare Sir Peter and even Joseph the
pain such a revelation would cause.

One way in which Sheridan achieves some unification
among the three lines has to do with these values, for as
Charles and Lady Teazle are linked socially by the gossip of
the backbiters, so are they linked structurally by the motif of
openness. Most of Lady Teazle's problems arise from her
attraction to fashion and the dissimulation of inner nature
which the accoutrements of fashionable London society demand; Charles has no interest in such accoutrements. In two
key scenes, openness is implicitly contrasted with prudence,
and in each, we are asked to judge Charles's and Lady
Teazle's culpability. Discussing Charles and Joseph, Sir Oliver
tells Rowley that he and his brother, the boys' father, were not

"very prudent youths," and that, "for my Part I hate to see Prudence clinging to the green Succours of Youth—'tis like Ivy round a sapling and spoils the Growth of the Tree" (2.3.24–25, 74–76). Later, Charles characterizes Premium as a "prudent old Fellow," and significantly the adjective "prudent" is not in the early drafts of the scene. Charles is never worried about prudence for he does not care what the world thinks of him; he refuses to practice Joseph's politics. Lady Teazle, on the other hand, is particularly careful to dissimulate in order to avoid imprudence while she is under the spell of the Scandalous College. Her harsher predecessor, in "The Teazles," admits to dissembling: "As I prudently consider'd that as a maid I was then so anxious to be wife—I might even [as] a wife wish as much to be a widow," she chose an older man to marry. The softened Lady Teazle is not characterized by such politic prudence until she finds pleasure in flirting with Joseph and begins to "think it would be imprudent" to visit his house (2.2.215). When she is there and is forced to hide from Sir Peter, she castigates herself for her imprudence —"if ever I am so imprudent again" (4.3.102–3)—in spite of Joseph's casuistry: "Prudence like experience must be paid for" and "what makes you thoughtless in your Conduct and apt to run into a thousand little imprudences?—why the consciousness of your Innocence" (4.3.81–82, 62–64). The least prudent course Lady Teazle could take is to admit her crimes to Sir Peter, but she is now beyond the spell of her fashionable friends. They, like Joseph, are well characterized by that prudence which is mere politic dissimulation: Sir Oliver significantly describes them as a "set of malicious prating prudent Gossips" (2.3.15–16).[24] The lesson Lady Teazle learns is not just the real love and generosity of her old husband, but the unattractiveness of the prudent hypocrisy practiced by her erstwhile friends; imprudent Charles does not need to learn such a lesson, for he is the chief practitioner of the unaffected, naturally warm, and generous social conduct the comedy upholds.

To reduce the complexities of all three lines of action to a single theme might be presumptuous, but for some the triumph of values upon which Charles is drawn and which

Lady Teazle comes naturally to accept over the prudential
hypocrisy of Joseph and his allies of the Scandal School may
provide such a principle of moral unification.

Many have considered the greatest shortcoming of *The
School for Scandal* to be Sheridan's failure to make Maria a
more attractive character. How can we believe, at the end of
the piece, that the marriage Charles plans to make is indeed a
suitable reward? The Maria who says "if to raise malicious
smiles at the infirmities and misfortunes—of those who have
never injured us be the province of wit or Humour Heav'n
grant me a double Portion of Dullness—" (2.2.179–82) seems
pale when contrasted with the lively Lady Teazle, and some
people may say that her wish has been granted in advance.
Moreover, her weeping exit after her interrogation by Sir
Peter (3.1.159) resembles all too closely an attempt to evoke
tears for the sufferings of the virtuous heroine. That Maria
does appear dull and helpless against the spirited assaults of
the Scandal School or the misguided absolutist thinking of Sir
Peter makes it difficult for audiences and readers to accept
the putative moral content of the rest of the play—that
scandal and dissimulation are despicable, that generosity,
family affection, and openness are attractive, that virtuous
love even between people of disproportionate years is possible,
or that Maria will indeed be the monitress, the gentle, virtuous guide who will lead Charles to a course of moderation.
She appears too much the melodramatic remnant of the early
"Slanderers" sketches.

Contemporary reviewers noted the absence of a scene
between Charles and Maria that would have prepared for
their unspoken agreement of marriage in the last scene.[25] The
usual explanation is Moore's, that "neither of the actors, for
whom [Sheridan] had designed these characters, was such as
he could trust with a love scene."[26] I wonder if this is true, or
if (since Moore is reporting a remark made by Sheridan) it is
a rationalization. For one thing, William ("Gentleman") Smith,
who created Charles Surface, had played under Sheridan's
direction such subtle roles as Congreve's Bellmour and Mirabel, and Loveless in *A Trip to Scarborough*. On the other hand,

we know that Sheridan wanted to use for the role of Maria
the actress Mary "Perdita" Robinson who had created Amanda
in *A Trip to Scarborough*, but she was pregnant and unable to
perform.[27] Yet Priscilla Hopkins, the actress who created
Maria, was no dramatic novice. The daughter of Drury Lane
prompter William Hopkins, she had early appeared on stage
and by 1774–75 was featured as Fanny in *The Clandestine Marriage* and Harriet in *The Jealous Wife*. Garrick thought her
work professional enough to qualify her for three relatively
important roles: Louisa Medway, the sentimental heroine of
The Discovery in the Drury Lane revival of Frances Sheridan's
play which Garrick pitted against *The Duenna* when Sheridan's
comic opera was enjoying its great initial success; Mildred, the
dutiful daughter of Charlotte Lennox's *Old City Manners* (an
unsuccessful revision of *Eastward Hoe!*, 9 Nov. 1775); and
Harriet, the sentimental lover of Hannah Cowley's mildly
successful comedy *The Runaway* (15 Feb. 1776). The young
actress who would much later become the wife of J. P. Kemble
was called upon by Sheridan to take over Silvia, the trickster
of *The Old Batchelor*, after Miss Essex (a Haymarket actress)
had failed to fulfill Sheridan's notion of that role in his
revival; later that season she also performed Foible in *The Way
of the World* and could handle Maria, the lively serving maid
of *Twelfth Night*. If Sheridan really doubted Miss Hopkins's
capacities in a love scene, why did he not call upon a more
experienced and presumably more trustworthy actress such as
Sophia Baddeley (who recreated Julia) to take the part? I
think the truth is that he never intended a love scene between
Charles and Maria, not because performers capable of handling such a scene were unavailable, but because he realized
that such a scene was aesthetically improper in the particular
kind of comedy he had designed.

Had he sought to, what kind of a love scene could Sheridan
have devised? A scene of witty banter like that of the meetings
of Dorimant and Harriet or Mirabel and Millamant would
grant a kind of dissimulation to characters other than the
comic villains or Lady Teazle, and thereby diffuse the sharp
contrasts that help maximize pleasure in the eventual redistribution of rewards according to merit. A scene of serious

love would not only slow the complicated action greatly and
be dwarfed in comparison with the witty Scandal School
scenes or the "daily jangles," but would add to Charles's
character a facet not in direct contrast with his hypocritical
brother. A scene in which Charles pleaded with Maria for
intervention with Sir Peter or Sir Oliver would make him
appear too passive; moreover, it would be out of character for
the plain-dealing Charles to sue for aid when he could appeal
for himself. A scene in which Maria chastised Charles for his
lack of moderation—as Harriet does Charles Oakly in *The
Jealous Wife*—would be far too moralistic for the atmosphere
of the rest of the piece. The only other possibility I can
imagine would involve Charles's rescuing Maria from some
unknown evil, a possibility I congratulate Sheridan on avoiding since he bowed enough toward anxiety-provoking comedy
in the Julia-Faulkland scenes of *The Rivals*.

Even if Sheridan had written such a scene, he was limited
dramatically on its placement. Since Charles's entrance must
immediately convince us of all his principal virtues—generosity, openness, affection—in spite of his minor failings of extravagance and mild dissipation, and since a love scene might
not accomplish these things, any love scene must appear after
Charles's introduction in the drinking match with Careless
and his cohorts. But any scene after this point would slow the
action at a time when Sheridan is properly concerned with
establishing the probability of a reconciliation of Sir Peter and
Lady Teazle, exposing Joseph to Sir Oliver, reconciling
Charles with his uncle, and dealing the final blow to the
Scandalous College. Thus the only economical placement of a
love scene is after the exposure of Joseph in the first scene of
the fifth act and after the self-exposure of the Scandal School
in the second scene of the fifth act: but there is hardly time
here.

Still, this does not explain why Maria stands almost silent
throughout the final ninety lines of the last scene, after she
has refused Charles on the grounds of his affection for Lady
Sneerwell and after Charles has been exonerated. Could not
Sheridan have given her more than her one line? Could not
she at least refer to her happiness in receiving Charles or in

seeing him vindicated of the many charges against him? Perhaps, but I would suspect that her saying anything could only add moralizing to an atmosphere that retains its gaiety largely because of the brilliant comic strokes of Lady Sneerwell's "May your Husband live these fifty years!" (5.3.196–97), Joseph's last "moral drop," and Snake's desire to have his good deed remain unpublished. Moreover, Maria cannot comment on Charles's former dissipations for much the same reason we cannot have a love scene in which she castigates him for his excesses: Sheridan did not mean for us to see his foibles as follies, let alone vices. They are stage qualities, not fully drawn characteristics, which temporarily lend credence to the calumny directed against him and help to define his position of openness, generosity, and fellow feeling in contrast to dissimulation, avarice, and pretended morality. The Sheridan who had ended *The Rivals* with a moral tag by the sober Julia had come to prefer the gay round that ends *The Duenna* and the direct appeal to the audience that concludes *A Trip to Scarborough.* And the Maria to whom Sheridan has granted "a double Portion of Dullness" unfortunately had to be dull in a comedy in which pleasure comes largely from the reversal of situations, regardless of its boy-finally-gets-girl conclusion.

One other source of pleasure in the play is the witty badinage of the Scandal School. Sheridan's choice of slander and scandal as the objects of his satire, and his deft handling of the subject, are largely responsible for his being called in his time "the modern Congreve" and for his being incorrectly associated today with the last of the great dramatists of the high Restoration tradition. As in all his dramatic works, so in *The School for Scandal* Sheridan is original not for his choice of materials but for his special handling of them. Slander and scandalmongering, both of the eternal sort characteristic of all mankind and of the special sort brought to devilish perfection in the paragraphs and "tête-à-têtes" of 1770s journalism,[28] had already served a number of Georgian dramatists. Charles Frankland works to blacken the character of Lady Frankland in Griffith's *The Platonic Wife* (DL, 24 Jan. 1765) so that his uncle will remain childless and he will continue to be his heir;

Mrs. Circuit in Foote's *The Lame Lover* (HM, 23 June 1770) has a set of scandalmongering friends; paragraphs in the newspapers add to the atmosphere of rumor concerning Lord Eustace's proposed marriage to Lady Anne Mountford in Griffith's *The School for Rakes* (DL, 4 Feb. 1769). The activities of Lady Haughty and her lickerish friends in *Epicoene* had taken on contemporary associations when George Colman revised Jonson's play for Drury Lane (13 Jan. 1776). The scandalmonger Dashwoud of Murphy's *Know Your Own Mind* was conceived long before Sheridan's set of slanderers took life, though he did not appear on stage until February 1777, when Murphy's play appeared opposite *A Trip to Scarborough* (Murphy had written the play nine years earlier and had laid it aside).

These instances, though, are minor, and merely indicate the late eighteenth century's continuing interest in the problems Sheridan used in his comedy. Of more import are a number of characters and situations from which Sheridan might have borrowed directly. One of the characters, Lady Riscounter, is the young second wife of the title character in Foote's *The Bankrupt* (HM, 21 July 1773); she actively seeks to plant paragraphs to destroy the reputation of her stepdaughter. The play was first acted after Sheridan had probably drawn his early "Slanderers" sketches, but not too late to influence him in choosing those early jottings rather than others for later development.[29]

Another Foote character may have had some influence. He is Domine Viper, who pierces O'Donovan's masquerade as a monk in *The Capuchin* (HM, 19 Aug. 1776) and whom O'Donovan remembers as "the doer of the Scandalous Chronicle," a scurrilous slander sheet where you (O'Donovan says to Viper) "mowed down reputations like muck; pushed yourself into the pay of Lady Deborah Dripping, produced anonymous paragraphs against her of your own composition, and got paid by her for not putting them into your paper." That Foote could offer such scenes and characters on 19 August 1776, nine months before Sheridan's play, is indicative of Londoners' familiarity with the scandalous practices both playwrights satirize.[30]

George Colman's *The Man of Business*, a comedy which failed to last beyond its first season, is notable for a variety of reasons. It was introduced at Covent Garden, 29 January 1774, just as Sheridan and his new wife returned to London from their honeymoon, when (we may assume) they were very likely to go to the theater, especially for the introduction of a new comedy. Seven of its principal actors created roles in *The Rivals* a year later (Shuter, Lewis, Lee Lewes, Woodward, Quick, Mrs. Green, and Mrs. Bulkley). Two of the characters are named Beverley and Lydia. And though the story has little or no direct similarity to any of Sheridan's works, the principal situations bear some resemblance, for there is a consummate hypocrite (Denier) who helps deprive a slightly profligate young man (Beverley) of his reputation, and the unexpected return of a nabob (Golding, called "Little Goldy") who is mistaken for another and abused in the supposed character. The code of Denier the hypocrite sounds rather like that of Joseph Surface after he dismisses "Stanley": "I love to husband my good offices: ay, ay! that's the true policy! to gain the good will of others, without touching your own property. —Make a small present to those that you are sure want nothing at all, and it turns to account, like money put out at high interest. —And ever, ever open your purse, and offer to lend to those who you know have no occasion to borrow!" (act 3). More significant in tracing the potential influence of this play is that members of the audience evidently took umbrage at a description of journalistic scandal which has little to do with the action of the piece, for Colman felt obliged in his dedication of the printed version to defend his play against accusations that it attacked the liberty of the press. The offending sentences occur in a conversation between Tropick and Fable. Fable has just told Tropick that the story circulated concerning the failure of Golding's mercantile establishment was false, that it was designed to shock Beverley, who is the principal agent of the firm, into a proper sense of his responsibilities. Tropick answers:

> It touched me to the quick to hear you were a rascal, and I could not help telling you so. —I beg your pardon again, and again, and again, my friend. You are one of the worthiest men

in the world—but, you know, there are not a more silly, empty,
insolent, impudent, ignorant, lying vermin, than your framers
of common reports and collectors of personal paragraphs—
wretches that pretend to know everything, and know nothing.
Your thoughts, words, and actions, they know them all; what
you have done, what you are doing, and what you intend to do,
they know: know what a papist tells his confessor, or the king
whispers the queen; things that never have been, will be, nor
are like to be, still they know—true or false, right or wrong,
praise or blame, they don't care a half-penny.

[Act 3]

Colman, like Foote, was content with the mere recital of such
villainies.

The example of scandalous activity which was probably the
most influential in the development of Sheridan's characters
and situations is that drawn by Colman in his adaptation of
Voltaire's *L'Ecossaise* as *The English Merchant* (DL, 21 Feb.
1767). A highly sentimental piece, Colman's play is mainly
about the relief of Amelia from her poverty through the
agency of Andrew Freeport, a noble English merchant (a part
created by Yates, who later portrayed Sir Oliver Surface).
Complicating Amelia's situation is the jealous Lady Alton
(Frances Abington), who resents the attentions of Lord Fal-
bridge toward Amelia and seeks to destroy their relationship
by means of Spatter (Thomas King, competent as fop, villain,
and amiable humorist). Spatter says: "I earned but a poor
livelihood by mere scandal and abuse; but if I could once
arrive at doing a little substantial mischief, I should make my
fortune" (act 1). The plan Lady Alton and Spatter conceive,
posting an "information" against Sir William Douglas, long-
exiled Jacobite who seeks a pardon and is Amelia's father, is
simple villainous treachery, not Lady Sneerwell and Snake's
sophisticated forgery, paragraphing, and journalistic scandal.
However, the inclusion of a single line describing Snake near
the end of Sheridan's play suggests a common characteristic
between the two: Sir Peter exclaims after Snake's exit "And
that man is a writer and critic, too!" even though Snake's
literary activities have had nothing to do with his role in the
plot and are not mentioned elsewhere. Spatter's principal
business is described by Lady Alton:

Did I not draw you out of the garret, where you daily spun out
your flimsy brain to catch the town flies in your cobweb dissertations? Did not I introduce you to lord Dapperwit, the
Apollo of the age? And did not you dedicate your silly volume
of poems on several occasions to him? Did not I put you into
the list of my visitors, and order my porter to admit you at
dinner-time? Did not I write the only scene in your execrable
farce, which the audience vouchsafed an hearing? And did not
my female friend, Mrs. Melepomene, furnish you with Greek
and Latin mottoes for your twopenny essays?

[Act 2]

Later, in soliloquy, Lady Alton admits that:

A convenient engine this Mr. Spatter: the most impudent
thorough-paced knave in the three kingdoms! . . . I was sure he
would stick at nothing. The writing of authors are public
advertisements of their qualifications; and when they profess to
live upon scandal, it is as much as to say, that they are ready for
every other dirty work, in which we chuse to employ them.

[Act 2]

A raisonneur's attitude toward Spatter's journalistic activity is
given by Sir William Douglas in answer to Spatter's conventional mouthing of the right of the press to be free of cen-
sorship.

When you deal in private scandal, have a care of the cudgel;
and when you meddle with public matters, beware of the
pillory. . . . I have the greatest respect for both [literature and
the freedom of the press]; but railing is the disgrace of letters,
and personal abuse the scandal of freedom; foul-mouthed
critics are, in general, disappointed authors; and they, who are
the loudest against ministers, only mean to be paid for their
silence.

[Act 1]

None of this suggests a very close resemblance between
Colman's play and Sheridan's much greater comedy except in
the choice of materials—but in the early drafts of *The School
for Scandal*, Lady Sneerwell's agent, like Lady Alton's, is
named "Spatter."

While he may not have been original in choosing these
particular vices and follies of his age to excoriate, Sheridan

was inventive in handling them. He was not content merely to rail against them; instead he exposed them by dramatizing them.

In dealing with the problem of prudential behavior and favoring by the plot of his comedy the openness of personal conduct associated with generosity, fellow-feeling, and genuine interpersonal affection, Sheridan also attacked the age-old follies of dissimulation and hypocrisy which contrast with the sentimental virtues and which go hand in hand with scandalmongering. But in attacking slander and scandal, he had a particular problem: it appears to be witty, intellectual fun. How can he both exploit scandal to provide good comic entertainment and at the same time expose malicious gossip as the lowest of selfish pleasures? What is the difference between "the social spirit of Raillery that used to mantle over a glass of bright Burgundy" (Charles Surface, 3.3.7–8) and the talk of "those utterers of forg'd Tales, coiners of Scandal,—and clippers of Reputation" (Sir Peter, 2.1.86–87)? How can Sheridan render the tales of the Scandalous College with "all the Pertness and flatulence of Champaine without its Spirit or Flavour" (3.3.9–10)?

In the comedy of wit, this was already an old problem. Nearly eighty years before Sheridan produced his play, Congreve had found himself dissatisfied by "that general taste which seems now to be predominant in the palates of our audience" and quit writing for the stage partly because his viewers could not "distinguish betwixt the charactor of a Witwoud and a Truewit."[31] The distinction is subtle, but for the most part (to make a rather large generality), the "wits" of high Restoration comedy talk about things and relationships among ideas, abusing people only when that abuse is clearly deserved, whereas the "witwouds," striving against the natural barriers of their own intellects and trying to ape the truewits' commentary, rely much more frequently on the murder of reputations. Thus, for instance, Olivia, Novel, and Plausible in *The Plain Dealer* are gossips; so is Tattle, the delightful but culpable witwoud of *Love for Love*. In *The Double Dealer* Cynthia (a truewit) speaks directly to the subject: "I find there are no fools so inconsiderable in themselves, but they can render other people contemptible by exposing their infirmities" (3.3, p. 155). Sheridan's problem was much the same as Congreve's, and since his "truewits"—Rowley, Sir Oliver, and Charles—are not witty in the same way Congreve's leading wits are, his problem was compounded.

To solve this problem, Sheridan designed the Scandal School scenes in a careful sequence. The first scandal scene, Lady Sneerwell's levee, offers the best wit. Maria's comments are dull beside the fast and spirited conversation of Sir Benjamin, Crabtree, Mrs. Candour, and Lady Sneerwell. Mrs. Candour appears a bit ridiculous for her "very gross affectation of good Nature and Benevolence" (1.1.159–60), and Sir Benjamin and Crabtree (fops both) are visually slightly ridiculous, but the commentary we have on them, such as Maria's parting comment—"Their Malice is intollerable" (1.1.321)—is not particularly effective. Even though the three visitors appear more ridiculous than Lady Sneerwell (she can comment that " 'tis very hard for them to leave a subject they have not quite run down" [1.1.344–45]), they are not yet objects of contempt or even disdain.

Before the slanderers appear on stage again, we hear more about them from Lady Teazle. Hers seems to be the normative view; we have reason by the end of her first "daily jangle" with Sir Peter to look upon her attitude toward her friends as more accurate than Sir Peter's, since he has shown himself to be mildly avaricious, more than slightly culpable for his failure to recognize Joseph's hypocrisy, and rather a nagging old husband. When she says, "I vow I have no malice against the People I abuse, when I say an ill natured thing 'tis out of pure Good-Humour—and I take it for granted they deal exactly in the same manner with me" (2.1.92–94), Sir Peter's objections seem peevish and ill-natured, for planting paragraphs and forging letters may be a genuine evil, but isn't a little slander-mongering essentially innocent, witty fun? It certainly seems so in comparison with pious moralizing and carping warnings.

When the slanderers next appear, however, a subtle change has occurred. We are treated to Sir Benjamin's epigram on Lady Betty Curricle's ponies, a witless, dull effort that Crabtree and Mrs. Candour obligingly applaud, and which Joseph

Surface's droll comment—"A very Phoebus mounted—indeed, Sir Benjamin" (2.2.16)—exposes as the product of a small, self-satisfied, and unexamined mind. The professors of the Scandalous College are beginning to appear to be objects of ridicule themselves. Lady Teazle enters immediately hereafter, and for a moment, the quality of wit (and abuse) picks up. Much of what she has to say relates to the efforts of women of fashion to retain their fading beauty, and much of it provides good visual as well as verbal humor: Lady Teazle obviously imitates "Miss Simper," who's proud of her teeth, and "Mrs. Prim," who's losing hers.

When Sir Peter enters and declares "A character dead at every word, I suppose" (2.2.75), Lady Sneerwell's description of him seems accurate: she tells Sir Peter that he is "too Phlegmatic [him]self for a jest and too peevish to allow wit on others" (2.2.137–39). Sir Peter's response that "true wit is more nearly allied to good Nature" (2.2.140) is drowned in two witty comparisons:

> LADY TEAZLE. True Sir Peter I believe they are so near akin that they can never be united—
> SIR BENJAMIN. Or rather Madam suppose them man and wife because one so seldom sees them together.
>
> [2.2.142–45]

And yet, Sir Peter has been effective in stopping the abuse of Mrs. Ogle—"a particular Friend of mine"—so that her character remains unscathed. Moreover, as he argues for good-natured wit, he uses just the "malicious barb" that makes his own comparison stick; the actor should glance slyly at Mrs. Candour and Lady Sneerwell as Sir Peter deprives them of their privileges: "Aye Madam—and then no Person should be permitted to kill characters, or run down Reputations but qualified old Maids and disap[p]ointed Widows" (2.2.154–56). There is a blush of truth in Sir Peter's objections, and since we do not see the Scandalous College in sesson again until the second scene of the fifth act, his objections carry more force. More than the virtuous protests of Maria or the self-exposure of Sir Benjamin, Sir Peter's turning the jest upon the slander-mongers themselves helps us, if not to differentiate between true and false wit, at least to find within the society of slanderers that which is ridiculous and perhaps objectionable.

The process is completed when Mrs. Candour, Sir Benjamin, and Crabtree all arrive at Sir Peter's following the screen scene. Much of the fashion that has turned Lady Teazle's head, fashion mostly represented by the slanderers, by now appears reprehensible. Sir Peter seems much more likeable, particularly because he has proved flexible enough to soften his position on Lady Teazle's rights as well as because he has geniunely suffered from her imprudent behavior. And the hypocrisy and selfishness that motivate Joseph and Lady Sneerwell have become fully apparent. Sir Oliver's attitudes toward the Scandal School and Charles's sideways comments on the nature of social raillery (3.3.6–10) also help to predispose the audience to dislike Lady Sneerwell's friends when they arrive at Sir Peter's, where what they say is obvious, malicious, false gossip. We saw the screen scene; we know there was no duel; we, unlike poor Mrs. Candour, are masters of all the circumstances. Sir Benjamin's garbled version of the incident, the entrance of Crabtree (who, like Fag in *The Rivals*, realizes that circumstantial accounts are more believable than a simple forged bill) with more false details, the counterpointing of Lady Sneerwell's selfish concern in the affair, all appear absurd.

The change is significant. At first, the objects of the Scandalous College's ridicule were ridiculous, and the slanderers' mode of talk did not appear as malicious as the virtuous and passive Maria would have us believe. Then the slanderers themselves became mildly ludicrous, but not wholly contemptible, largely because Lady Teazle joined with such spirit in their game. Finally, we see that the slanderers themselves are objects of ridicule, inaccurate in their knowledge, malicious in their intent, if still mildly clever in their invention. But their invention is directed at people we know and like, and Sir Oliver can give them the lie by announcing Sir Peter's healthy arrival; their only recourse is the rank abuse which, while Sir Peter in part deserves it as comic punishment, nevertheless sides us with the Teazles against the "Fiends—Vipers!—Furies!" (5.2.166) which we now know the scandalmongers to be.

Sheridan could have exposed slander no other way and still have wrought as effective a comedy. He could not, for instance, have allowed Maria to comment on the Scandal College's reports in the second scene of the fifth act: she could never hurl the imprecations of which Sir Peter is capable and which we now believe accurate. Moreover, by employing self-exposure, Sheridan has pressed his lesson more strongly. He could not have exposed Lady Sneerwell's friends in their first appearance, since to have done so would have blunted his purpose of giving us fun while giving us an object worthy of satiric attack. In effect, he has forced us to undergo the same process of growth which Lady Teazle experiences: we must see vice and think it attractive (as we presumably did before we came to the theater, in our own coteries of character defamers); only upon growing familiar with it will we realize its hurtful potentials. We are much more completely convinced than if we merely uttered the commonplaces on malice and slander we hear from Maria, for we have experienced the process which she never seems to have gone through—the attraction, the doubt, the final revulsion. Perhaps "revulsion" is too strong a word, for even in their maliciousness, we do not feel about these poor creatures as we do of the affected idiots of *Le Misanthrope*: we are inclined to pity them, not utterly revile them, and we are vastly amused by them. But like Molière, Sheridan adopted a plan which allowed him to bring us to this position without preaching, without positive didacticism. And this is perfectly in keeping with the balanced design of Sheridan's most polished play.

Because we are so amused by the slanderers, Sheridan was able to employ their full self-exposure to obtain one additional structural value. Having presented us in act 4 scene 3 with the climax of his comedy and one of the greatest farcical scenes of concealment and exposure (so reminiscent of *Tartuffe*), he needed an effective means to carry us to the final, desired dénouement with its distribution of rewards and punishments according to merit. By the conclusion of the screen scene we have reached a point of stasis in our expectations: what can follow is little more than mechanical summary, for now we know not only that our desires will be fulfilled but how they will be answered. Moreover, we are at a point of emotional emptiness caused by comic near-exhaustion. Sheridan had to bridge the gap. The Scandalous College builds this bridge with its absurd report of the events we have just seen, carries our interest across the gulf our comic relaxation has formed by seeing Sir Peter learn what he had to learn, and prepares us for the coming final exposures.

Despite the subtly effective satire and the obvious structural values, an irony about the slander and scandal scenes obtains. Except when the reference is to the epigrams and quick-thinking reverses of Joseph Surface, the "wit" of *The School for Scandal* almost always means the dialogue of the Scandalous College. Sir Peter and Lady Teazle are amusing and somewhat witty, but what is most amusing in their scenes is the interplay of character; similarly, throughout the rest of the play comedy of situation more frequently produces laughter than comedy of wit. Only in the meetings of the slanderers does the dialogue not partially or completely depend upon concealed information or upon the characterization of an agent; the slanderers' talk is brilliant, epigrammatic, witty. Like Congreve, then, Sheridan appears to have made attractive that which he was attacking.

But, as always, Sheridan was a practical, working playwright. His care in casting the slanderers shows the importance of these scenes in his conception of the play. James Dodd, brilliant as Sir Benjamin, was "the prince of pink heels, and the soul of empty eminence,"[32] tottering about on legs as slim, and coiffured in the latest foppish style with hair as long, as Lady Betty Curricle's ponies; William Parsons as Crabtree "played the wasp to Dodd's butterfly";[33] Jane Pope's Mrs. Candour was perhaps her most famous role. The only newcomer among the scandalmongers was Katherine Sherry as Lady Sneerwell. That Sheridan chose her rather than a more experienced portrayer of malicious ladies like Mrs. Elizabeth Hopkins, wife of the Drury Lane prompter, recreator of Mrs. Malaprop and effective in roles like Lady Wishfort, is interesting. But clearly Sheridan wanted the younger actress who was more capable than Mrs. Hopkins of portraying a woman of an age delicately balanced between the freshness of youth and

the sad cynicism of middle age. Lady Sneerwell is not to be
played as ridiculously lecherous in middle age, but as still
attractive enough to align youth and liveliness with malicious
slandermongering; the initial attractiveness of scandal—and
the consequent intensification of the satiric attack—comes
from her superficial sexuality and youth. Katherine Sherry
had also recently played in three roles which might have
influenced Sheridan's final conception of Lady Sneerwell:
Lady Haughty, the principal member of the college of ladies
in Colman's adaptation of *Epicoene*, the play from which
Sheridan probably took the collegiate metaphor; Lady Touch-
wood in *The Double Dealer*; and Lady Riscounter, the para-
graph-planter of Foote's *The Bankrupt*. Miss Sherry's selection,
like that of the other actors, was crucially important to his
conception.

Beyond the amiable amalgam of comedy of self-adjustment,
comedy of merit rewarded, and punitive comedy of exposure,
and beyond the carefully structured satiric attack on scandalmongering, there are many other features which help make
Sheridan's play one of the most entertaining comedies of
manners. The superb screen scene, prepared with loving care
for perfectly fulfilled expectation and surprise, its superficial
dialogue contrasting with the situation to produce absurd
comic irony, makes unimportant the carping complaints about
its one or two "careless" lines.[34] The scene is perhaps the
greatest exposure scene in English comedy, rivalling Molière's
in brilliance; even the conscious parody of melodrama in the
final scene of *The Importance of Being Earnest* must take second
place. Similarly, *The School for Scandal* is marked by the
brilliant presentation of minor characters; in *The Rivals* Sheridan demonstrated his awareness that no line and no character can be wasted on stage, and in his greater comedy, he put
that knowledge to practice. Taking a character a lesser play
would ignore—Trip—Sheridan makes Charles's servant into a
vehicle for social satire, an amusing, foppish caricature. Dealing with a usurer—Moses—Sheridan avoids a gross picture,
presenting in this Jew a not entirely unattractive view of a
social reality. Even Charles's friend, Careless, is present not

just as a convenient drinking companion but as a foil to Charles: Careless has all the excesses and extravagances of his friend but none of his true openness and generosity. The good Rowley, ostensibly merely a spokesman for prudent benevolence, becomes an amusing character himself, in spite of his structural function: his joining with Sir Oliver to twit the suffering Sir Peter in the second scene of the fifth act is perfectly amusing and perfectly in character for this sensible, sometimes grave, but definitely good-humored steward. Nothing is wasted.

And yet, despite its amazing technical and theatrical achievement, there are many who would deny *The School for Scandal* a place among the best works of dramaturgy.[35] Admittedly, the comedy does not provide us with the poetry of *A Midsummer-Night's Dream*, the savage moral power of *Volpone* or *The Alchemist*, or the cynical, intellectual wit of *The Man of Mode*. Instead it belongs generically with "laughing comedies" like *The Provok'd Wife* or *The Beaux' Stratagem*, though it is far superior to them. Like *The School for Scandal*, these theatrical pieces are rather bare intellectually or morally, and people like James or Shaw who are interested in ideas are not interested in theatrical pieces which do not treat ideas seriously.

I would be foolish to defend *The School for Scandal* against such attitudes. The play is not a "morally serious comedy." Although in the choice of scandalmongering as an external object for satire and in the decision not to attempt any reformation of Snake, Joseph, and Lady Sneerwell, Sheridan showed his awareness of the reality of evil, he certainly did not intend to leave his audience upset, unsure of their world, greatly concerned about man's social or moral obligations. When we finish reading *Tom Jones*, "we are not disposed to feel . . . that all is right with the world or that we can count on Fortune always intervening in the same gratifying way, on behalf of the good."[36] But at the end of *The School for Scandal* we are disposed to feel that, when all information is laid before such benevolent men as Sir Oliver or Rowley, all will be right for them and for those like them: Men of common sense and generosity can almost always solve their own problems. This is an amiable, a genial comic world made fortunate not by chance but by the good nature and benevolence of most people. Lady Sneerwell, Joseph, Snake, are exceptions in a world inhabited by crusty but good Sir Peters, temporarily naïve Lady Teazles, plain-dealing Charleses, and the villains are effectively neutralized by expulsion, unlike the absolutist Quakers, the selfish Lady Bellastons, and the Colonel Fitzgeralds of Fielding's moral world. There are comic glances at reality such as Snake's desire that his good deed not be exposed or Charles's refusal to mouth platitudes about an intended reformation; but these do not leave the aching doubt that the revelation of the cupidity of Volpone's judges or the continued social successes of Sir Fopling Flutter leave with us. So long as such doubt is associated with "moral seriousness," *The School for Scandal* will remain less than morally serious. It smacks too much of the doctrine of sentimentalism, the belief that most people are good and generous at base, which we today are inclined to ridicule.

But how could Sheridan create a different moral world in a drama so typical of high Georgian comedy? To emphasize further the evil of the slanderers would have been to tip the Horatian balance of delight and instruction too far in the direction of the didactic, as so many of his contemporaries did; to add excrescences of morality from which even the best comedies of his time suffered would have been equally reproachable. The balance is right. There is enough of the evil and potentially evil in this comic world without additional emphasis; more satire, like more overt didacticism, would only lessen the pleasures we take. And if we are not entirely convinced that *The School for Scandal* "professes a faith . . . in the habitual depravity of human nature," we certainly can welcome the "genial spirit of frankness and generosity about it that relieves the heart as well as clears the lungs. . . . While it strips off the mask of hypocrisy it inspires a confidence between man and man."[37] There are many ages in which such a confidence would be welcomed.

CHAPTER VI:

The Critic

PUFF. Now then for my magnificence!—my battle!—
my noise!—and my procession!—
The Critic, 3.1.313–14

IN HIS FIRST two and a half years of professional association
with the theater, Sheridan produced four major comic
pieces worthy of literary interest; in his next two and a half
years, he produced only one. From the 1777–78 season, a few
lines from a revised ending to *The Beggar's Opera* survive; they
indicate little of genius, though they are a useful gloss on the
playing emphasis of this ballad opera in the 1770s.[1] For the
1778–79 season, Sheridan wrote slightly more: an epilogue to
a tragedy at Covent Garden, some well-received dramatic
verses on the death of Garrick, a few changes to a comedy of
Fielding's produced now for the first time, perhaps part of a
scenic afterpiece, and probably the main dialogue and situations for a spectacular pastiche, *The Camp*.[2] As literature, none
of this is interesting. But as an indication of Sheridan's
willingness to exploit contemporary topics, to utilize all aspects
of theatrical talent available to him, and to avoid as far as
possible the disciplined effort and expenditure of creative
genius which might produce another masterpiece, the theatrical ephemera of these two seasons are significant.

More important, once again the need to make money
moved Sheridan's pen. The 1777–78 season at Drury Lane
was successful financially, largely because of the continuing
popularity of *The School for Scandal*, and not because of the
two new plays Sheridan offered (Cumberland's *The Battle of
Hastings*, Shirley's *The Roman Sacrifice*). More money was
grossed in 180 nights than had been brought in by the 187
nights of Sheridan's first season as manager, and the playwright felt financially secure enough by November 1777 to
look for ways to employ his profits. He urged the patentees of
the two principal houses to join together in an effort to

activate the dormant Covent Garden patent and establish a
new theater; when that attempted coalition failed, he joined
forces with Thomas Harris to purchase the King's Theatre, an
opera house.[3] Their management did not make money, however, and even though he called his long-experienced father
to take over as acting manager at Drury Lane for the 1778–79
season, Sheridan was losing ground financially.[4] *The Camp*
brought in large audiences for that season, but failed to stop
the falling off of receipts. *The Critic* was to be the piece which
would make the 1779–80 season profitable.

Plays about the theater were popular in the 1770s. Generally, they fell into two categories: the first were short entertainments of a distinctly occasional nature designed to introduce new seasons and new performers, utilizing contemporary
gossip about the stage, ridiculing general or particular dramatic practices, and often presenting actors in their own
persons; the second were medium-length burlesques, employing rehearsal framing devices, with the mildly satiric intent of
ridiculing not specific examples but dramatic categories. Four
such plays probably influenced Sheridan. Colman's *Occasional
Prelude* and *New Brooms!* and Garrick's *The Meeting of the Company* are good examples of the first sort of entertainment, and
Garrick's *A Peep behind the Curtain* is a good example of the
burlesque.

George Colman's *Occasional Prelude* first appeared at Covent
Garden 21 September 1772, "to open the theatrical campaign
and to introduce a new actress to the public."[5] After a conversation among chairmen outside Covent Garden concerning
their expected increase in business now that the theaters are
due to reopen, the scene shifts to the interior where the
Manager is portrayed preparing the bills, rallying the back-
stage people, and auditioning a new actress who succeeds
admirably as comedienne, singer, and mime. The new actress
was Jane Barsanti, the lively ingénue who three years later
created Lydia Languish. The entertainment was popular in its
first season and served Colman for a good many more years;
Miss Barsanti played her part as late as 19 September 1777 (at
the Haymarket) and Colman revised the piece to present the

talents of John Bannister, Junior, for the 1780–81 season. Even though he was preparing a collected edition of his works which would include a different printing of the *Occasional Prelude*, Colman was confident enough to publish the piece separately in 1776.

David Garrick's *The Meeting of the Company; or, Bayes' Art of Acting*, presented 17 September 1774, is more satiric in intent. Weston, Parsons, Hurst, and Miss Platt appear as themselves and discuss their activities during the summer break; Bayes (portrayed by Thomas King) appears with his treatise on acting in hand, and proceeds to detail how comic actors may be turned into tragic actors and vice versa. Eventually Bayes is run off the stage, vociferously maintaining his superior knowledge and skills. Garrick squeezed eleven performances from the piece that season, but it was never revived.

The third occasional entertainment, Colman's *New Brooms!*, was "written at the request of Mr. Sheridan"[6] to inaugurate the Sheridan-Linley-Ford-Lacy management and was first produced at Drury Lane 21 September 1776. King, Dodd, Palmer, and Parsons—each of whom would create major roles in *The Critic*—added their talents to Thomas Linley's music. Sheridan presented the piece eight times that season. The fictional frame was more complicated than those of the two earlier pieces cited, but still simple enough. Phelim (Moody, creator of Major O'Flaherty and recreator of Sir Lucius O'Trigger for Drury Lane) is an aspiring Irish performer who wants Crotchet (waspish Dodd, later to be Dangle), a theatrical amateur who has influence with the new managers, to help him to a place in the Drury Lane company. Catcall (Palmer, later to be Sneer), a cynic and critic, and Sprightly (King, later to be Puff), a playwright and theatrical hanger-on, discuss the state of the stage and mock Sir Dulcimer Dunder (Parsons, later to be Sir Fretful Plagiary), a pretentious, deaf music critic.[7] Some comically bad music and some genuinely good songs intersperse mild dramatic criticism and eulogies of Garrick. "Plays and little Roscius left the stage together," says Crotchet; all that remains are musicals and comic opera, but "Nature has nothing to do with an Opera—nor with the stage neither, now little Roscius has left it." Sprightly defends the

stage for legitimate drama—a raisonneur's attitude—opining
that music and dance are "the mere lace and fringe of the
theatre." The frame dissolves into the prologue in which King
compares dramatic writers to sportsmen and the stage to a
stage coach (reminiscent of Fielding's metaphor in *Tom Jones*,
book 18, chapter 1). Little of the piece is telling in a satiric
way; the few comments on the place of music in the drama
are only occasionally (in both its senses) amusing. But the
superficial similarity between the framing device and the kinds
of roles taken by actors here and those they took in Sheridan's
Critic three years later is quite interesting: surely this entertainment helped solidify Sheridan's final intentions.

The example of burlesque theatrical self-reflection, Garrick's *A Peep behind the Curtain; or, The New Rehearsal*, was first
presented 23 October 1767. It uses a farcical boy-gets-girl
plot: gentlemanly but impoverished Wilson woos and wins
Miss Fuz (whose heart he captured while masquerading as a
strolling actor the previous summer) to the confusion of her
poetaster mother and sluggish, gluttonous father Sir Toby;
their affair takes place behind the curtain at Drury Lane
where Glib (Thomas King) is rehearsing his absurd comic
opera, *Orpheus*. Despite the attempt at plot, the main interest
is in the burlesque of a newly popular form, burletta, with
Orpheus presented as a kind of genre-consuming artifact; the
comic wretchedness of the example obviates any explicit
ridicule of burletta in general. In the first act, the commentary
of Sir Macaroni Virtue and Lady Fuz (Mrs. Hopkins, later to
be Mrs. Dangle) further ridicules the stage, and near the end
Glib and Patent set about casting the burletta and choose King
to speak the prologue, thereby giving the character an opportunity to praise the actor who is in reality, of course, himself.[8]
As we shall see, Garrick's burlesque had important influence
on Sheridan's early unpublished efforts, and Sheridan liked
the piece enough to revive it for five performances beginning
21 December 1778, less than one year before *The Critic*.

None of these four pieces has any independent literary
merit; they are distinctly occasional, topical pieces which treat
with irreverence that which the audiences enjoy, and which
titillate mildly with real and imagined theatrical gossip. They

are the practical stuff of the professional theater, fillers of
gaps when more worthy entertainment is lacking; so it is not
surprising that professional men of the theater devised them.
Nor is it surprising that two of Sheridan's earliest efforts were
in this occasional, topical, self-reflective form, one an occasional entertainment and the other a burlesque; little remains of either. The entertainment was the "Prelude on
Opening Covent Garden next Season" (discussed briefly in
chapter 3 above); it was presented on 20 September 1775 and
was perhaps repeated once thereafter. While no copy survives,
a description given by the *London Chronicle* for 19–21 September 1775 makes clear the similarities of this piece to Colman's
successful *Occasional Prelude* for 1772:

> In the Prelude, the curtain rising, discovered the different
> performers of the theatre, comparing notes together on their
> various successes, cast of parts, droll accidents, etc. etc. which
> they experienced during their different summer excursions:—
> *Mattocks* gives an account of the Sailors levelling their great
> guns on the Liverpool theatre; when *Dunstall humorously* replied
> "they would point them much truer at a Frenchman or a
> Spaniard."—*Lee Lewis* diverts them with the manner of their
> performing Hamlet in a company that he belonged to, when
> the hero who was to play the principal character had absconded
> with an innkeeper's daughter; and that when he came forward
> to give out the play, he added, "the part of Hamlet to be left
> out, for that night;"—after a variety of these curious stories,
> Miss *Barsanti* informs them, that the Managers have totally
> mistaken her talents, as she is calculated for deep tragedy, and
> immediately gives a fair specimen of mimicry, both in voice and
> action, in which the tragical conceits of Miss Y[ounge] are ad-
> mirably hit off.
>   One of them now asks his brother if he has seen what they
> are doing at Drury-lane, telling him "they have not left a bit of
> the old covering on, and that even the Old Rose Tavern had
> put on a masquerade upon the occasion." The other, in answer,
> laments the loss of their late dapper manager, "who," he said,
> "would have forestalled all their fine similies upon this *painting*
> occasion, etc. and not left his rival a single word to say on his
> own alterations."—After this the stage being left to Mr. Hull
> and Lewes, the latter asks the former about the health of poor
> Ned Shuter; and Hull shakes his head, and tells him he fears

he is in great danger, but hopes that the candor of the town will receive their old favourite, and make allowances for so deserving an actor.[9]

The entertainment is clearly topical: a collage of stage gossip, contemporary events, and actors performing their specialties. So far as we can tell from this newspaper account, there is satire here, but muted satire. Moreover, since the prelude was not repeated more than once at the most, it must not have been particularly brilliant in any sense.

Sheridan's early burlesque is also lost. About August 1770, his acquaintance Nathaniel Brassey Halhed sent him a farcical burletta titled *Ixion*, requesting his help. The only known copy of the resulting burlesque, *Jupiter*, was seen by Thomas Moore who printed a few pages; but the manuscript of the joint effort subsequently disappeared. Both young men felt reasonably confident about the piece after its revisions, and apparently, some approaches were made to Samuel Foote concerning production, though it never was performed or printed. Sheridan's contribution was of a burlesque framing device. "Simile" (like Glib, author of *Orpheus* in Garrick's *A Peep behind the Curtain*) is the author of *Ixion*, the burletta being rehearsed; "Monop[oly]," who is the manager, together with an Irishman and a Scotsman, comment on the piece. Little remains. In one exchange, Simile explains his procedures in writing.

> SIMILE. Sir, you are very ignorant on the subject,—it is the method most in vogue.
>
> O'CUL. What! to make the music first, and then make the sense to it afterwards!
>
> SIM. Just so.
>
> MONOP. What Mr. Simile says is very true, gentlemen; and there is nothing surprising in it, if we consider now the general method of writing *plays* to *scenes*.
>
> O'CUL. Writing *plays* to *scenes*!—Oh, you are joking.
>
> MONOP. Not I, upon my word. Mr. Simile knows that I have frequently a complete set of scenes from Italy, and then I have nothing to do but to get some ingenious hand to write a play to them.
>
> SIM. I am your witness, Sir. Gentlemen, you perceive you know nothing about these matters.

o'CUL. Why, Mr. Simile, I don't pretend to know much relating to these affairs, but what I think is this, that in this method, according to your principles, you must often commit blunders.

SIM. Blunders! to be sure I must, but I always could get myself out of them again. Why, I'll tell you an instance of it.—You must know I was once a journeyman sonnet-writer to Signor Squallini. Now, his method, when seized with the *furor harmonicus* was constantly to make me sit by his side, while he was thrumming on his harpsichord, in order to make extempore verses to whatever air he should beat out to his liking. I remember, one morning, as he was in this situation, *thrum, thrum, thrum, [moving his fingers as if beating on the harpsichord,]* striking out something prodigiously great, as he thought,— "Hah!" said he,—"hah! Mr. Simile, *thrum, thrum, thrum,* by gar here is vary fine,—*thrum, thrum, thrum,* write me some words directly."—I durst not interrupt him to ask on what subject, so instantly began to describe a fine morning.

> Calm was the land, and calm the seas,
>   And calm the heaven's dome serene,
> Hush'd was the gale and hush'd the breeze,
>   And not a vapour to be seen.

I sang to his notes.—"Hah! upon my vord vary pritt,—*thrum, thrum, thrum,*—stay, stay,—*thrum, thrum,*—Hoa! upon my vord, here it must be an adagio,—*thrum, thrum,*—oh! let it be an *Ode to Melancholy.*"

MONOP. The Devil!—there you were puzzled sure.

SIM. Not in the least,—I brought in a *cloud* in the next stanza, and matters, you see, came about at once.

MONOP. An excellent transition.

o'CUL. Vastly ingenious indeed.

SIM. Was it not? hey! it required a little command,—a little presence of mind. . . .

When the rehearsal begins, Sir Richard Ixion, who is wooing Juno while Jupiter is trying to seduce Amphytrion's wife, enters on his arrival at Parnassus.

SIM. There is a fine gentleman for you,—in the very pink of the mode, with not a single article about him his own,—his words pilfered from magazines, his address from French valets, and his clothes not paid for.

MacD. But pray, Mr. Simile, how did Ixion get into heaven?

SIM. Why, Sir, what's that to any body?—perhaps by Salmoneus's Brazen Bridge, or the Giant's Mountain, or the Tower of Babel, or on Theobald's bull-dogs, or—who the devil cares how?—he is there, and that's enough.

Later, Simile misses a stage effect he had called for.

SIM. Z———ds, where's the ordnance? Have you forgot the pistol? [*To the* ORCHESTRA.]

ORCHESTRA. [*to some one behind the scenes.*] Tom, are not you prepared?

TOM. [*from behind the scenes.*] Yes, Sir, but I flash'd in the pan a little out of time, and had I staid to prime, I should have shot a bar too late.

SIM. Oh then, Jupiter, begin the song again. —We must not lose our ordnance.

Still later, Amphitryon misses his cue.

MONOP. Tom, where is Amphitryon?

SIM. Zounds, he's not arrested too, is he?

SERV. No, Sir, but there was but *one black eye* in the house, and he is waiting to get it from Jupiter.

SIM. To get a black eye from Jupiter,—oh, this will never do. Why, when they meet, they ought to match like two beefeaters.[10]

Naturally, we would like to have the full three acts of this rehearsal-framed burlesque. The timing of its creation strongly suggests a debt of invention to Garrick's *A Peep behind the Curtain*. That matters little in light of what Sheridan's play did not do: it did not repeat Garrick's irrelevant boy-gets-girl plot, but returned instead to the older form of Buckingham's *The Rehearsal*, emphasizing thereby theatrical burlesque over farce, Aristophanic over Menanderan comedy.

Theatrical self-reflection fascinated Sheridan, as one other early fragment of dialogue suggests. Moore places the piece quite early in Sheridan's career, probably while he was still in Bath, and the style, particularly the length of the individual speeches, suggests that it must be contemporaneous with Sheridan's attempted dramatization of *The Vicar of Wakefield*. In it, a Scotchman speaks to a Manager.

M[ANAGER]. Sir, I have read your comedy, and I think it has infinite merit, but, pray, don't you think it rather grave?

S[COTCHMAN]. Sir, you say true; it *is* a grave comedy. I follow the opinion of Longinus, who says comedy ought always to be sentimental. Sir, I value a sentiment of six lines in my piece no more than a nabob does a rupee. I hate those dirty, paltry equivocations, which go by the name of puns, and pieces of wit. No, Sir, it ever was my opinion that the stage should be a place of rational entertainment; instead of which, I am very sorry to say, most people go there for their diversion:[11] accordingly, I have formed my comedy so that it is no laughing, giggling piece of work. He must be a very light man that shall discompose his muscles from the beginning to the end.

M[ANAGER]. But don't you think it may be too grave?

S[COTCHMAN]. O never fear; and as for hissing, mon, they might as well hiss the common prayer-book; for there is the viciousness of vice and the virtuousness of virtue in every third line.

M[ANAGER]. I confess there is a great deal of moral in it; but, Sir, I should imagine if you tried your hand at tragedy—

S[COTCHMAN]. No, mon, there you are out, and I'll relate to you what put me first on writing a comedy. You must know I had composed a very fine tragedy about the valiant Bruce. I showed it my Laird of Mackintosh, and he was a very candid mon, and he said my genius did not lie in tragedy: I took the hint, and, as soon as I got home, began my comedy.[12]

Moore, commenting on the piece, suggests that "it is very amusing to observe how long this subject was played with by the current of Sheridan's fancy . . ." (1:24). It is amusing, and revealing: the Sheridan who aspired to financial success in the theater tried to begin his career with a self-reflective form; the Sheridan who had achieved success, but needed to solidify it, ended his career as comic dramatist by returning to the same form.

The Critic, which was first presented on 30 October 1779, is perhaps the most complete play about the theater ever written. It was both occasional entertainment and burlesque, topically oriented and aimed at posterity, a local development and an echo of an eternal form. From Aristophanes's *The*

Acharnians to Shakespeare's "Pyramus and Thisbe," to Fletcher's *Knight of the Burning Pestle*, to Buckingham's *Rehearsal*, to Fielding's *Tragedy of Tragedies* or *Pasquin*, the comic dramatic urge at self-reflection has surfaced brilliantly. But the examples from the 1770s which influenced Sheridan failed to achieve lasting fame largely because they are too local, too tied to contemporary situations and personalities; only Garrick's *A Peep behind the Curtain* approaches the proper balance between timeliness and timelessness, yet it lacks the wit, satire, and brilliance to endure. What is surprising about *The Critic*, a greater play which adopted a similar form, is that it too is very local.

Consider the raw materials of *The Critic*: an absurd, thin-skinned playwright, a silly romantic tragedy on the subject of the Spanish Armada, a theatrical entrepreneur entranced not with literary worth but dramatic stage effects, newspapers filled with gossip and concealed advertisements, critical debates about the uses and meaning of dramatic entertainment, a theatrical world populated by actors who are selfish and managers who themselves are playwrights. Stripped of contemporary associations, these subjects will be of interest as long as artistic impulses are channeled through the medium of the stage; but in Sheridan's play, each has purely local satiric applications which to a great extent determined the original success of *The Critic*, but which, it seems, would also prevent lasting fame. Both playwrights were recognized as specific individuals; the subject of Puff's tragedy held immense contemporary concern; and the critical themes were the stuff of the day.

Parsons, who portrayed Sir Fretful Plagiary, openly imitated the dress and mannerisms of Richard Cumberland, author of *The West Indian* and more recently *The Battle of Hastings*, a historical tragedy produced by Sheridan at Drury Lane 24 January 1778. On 20 March 1779 Cumberland had given a prelude to his musical piece, *Calypso*, for its Covent Garden production: that prelude was commonly known as *The Critic*. No one failed to recognize Parson's impersonation, and the *Lady's Magazine* for October 1779 went so far as to say that Sir Fretful Plagiary "exhibits one of the most harsh and severe caricatures that have been attempted since the days of Aristophanes, of which a celebrated sentimental writer is evidently the object: a great part of what is said by his representative being literally taken from his usual conversation, but with pointed and keen additions."[13] Cumberland so felt the imputation that in his *Memoirs* (1807) he avoids mentioning the character's name completely, but casts oblique aspersions on Sheridan by citing a conversation between himself and Garrick following the introduction of *The West Indian* in which Garrick supposedly counterfeited the reading of a bad review of the comedy, then revealed his joke. The implication is clear: in staging Sneer's attack on Sir Fretful, Sheridan was merely retelling a worn-out story, Cumberland would have us believe, plagiarizing it in fact from life.[14]

The other playwright of *The Critic*, Puff, was also from real life. Consider his thoughts on the subjects of drama:

> What Shakespeare says of ACTORS may be better applied to the purpose of PLAYS; *they* ought to be "the abstract and brief Chronicles of the times." Therefore when history, and particularly the history of our own country, furnishes any thing like a case in point, to the time in which an author writes, if he knows his own interest, he will take advantage of it; so, Sir, I call my tragedy The SPANISH ARMADA; and have laid the scene before TILBURY FORT.
>
> [2.1.1–7]

On 18 June 1779, Spain declared war on England; on 16 August 1779 the war came home to London in the form of reports that the French and Spanish fleets had evaded a British squadron and were in the Channel. Volunteer companies were formed, the militia mobilized, and not until mid-September did invasion fever die down. In the *Public Advertiser* and the *Lady's Magazine*, Queen Elizabeth's speech to the army at Tilbury before the arrival of the Spanish Armada was reprinted; theatrical entertainments were given on the subject; poems were printed in the newspapers; correspondents employing Roman pseudonyms offered copius advice; and Covent Garden produced a topical musical farce on the war preparations titled *Plymouth in an Uproar*.[15]

One of the theatrical entertainments on the subject is particularly interesting. During the summer of 1779 there was produced at the theater at Sadler's Wells a pantomime-pastiche, advertised as

> A new favourite Musical Piece consisting of Airs serious and comic, Recitatives, Choruses, &c., called *The Prophecy: or, Queen Elizabeth at Tilbury*. In the course of which will be introduced a variety of Machinery and Decorations, particularly an emblematical Frontispiece, at the top of which, in a small Transparency, will be represented the Destruction of the famous Spanish Armada, and the view through the said Frontispiece will be closed by a Moving Perspective, representing the present Grand Fleet. The Recitatives and Choruses by Mr. Olive, the Airs selected from the best Masters, and the Paintings by Mr. Greenwood. Rope-dancing by Signora Mariana and Mr. Ferzi.[16]

Pastiches of this sort almost always were mainly the creations of theatrical managers (Sheridan, of course, was behind *The Camp*, a similar topical exploitation piece), so we may assume that the author-director of *The Prophecy* was the manager of Sadler's Wells, who happened to be Thomas King, the great Drury Lane actor. King, veteran of Bayes in *The Rehearsal* and *The Meeting of the Company*, creator of Glib in *A Peep behind the Curtain*, created Puff, author of *The Spanish Armada*.

These local references seem by themselves enough to doom *The Critic* to mere topicality. But there is more in the way of local and domestic jokes. The manager who writes was Sheridan himself, and Mrs. Dangle is bothered by foreign singers because that same manager had recently assumed ownership of the opera house, as Sheridan had done in real life. Dangle was recognized by many as Thomas Vaughan, author of a farce produced under Sheridan's direction called *The Hotel* (DL, 20 Nov. 1776) and a theatrical amateur and "dangler" about the Green Room. Miss Pope's portrayal of Tilburina was a take-off of Mrs. Crawford's tragic acting, while the younger Bannister's acting of Don Ferolo Whiskerandos mimicked William Smith's portrayal of Richard III. Sheridan was known for writing "puffs" for Drury Lane, and the "puff direct" of which Puff gives an example was most likely a "puff preliminary" for Elizabeth Griffith's *The Times*, a comedy to be produced little more than a month after the introduction of Sheridan's afterpiece.[17]

Such topicality might assure a successful, financially rewarding run. In the previous season, Sheridan's slight pastiche, *The Camp* (15 Oct. 1778), had run for fifty-seven performances as an afterpiece and brought in an average of £228 a night for its first ten performances, an amazing achievement in a season for which non-benefit performances averaged only £183. The literary features of *The Camp* are hardly significant: a little characteristic and a little witty dialogue, a pair of national characters (Irish and French), some avaricious countrymen and their self-interested exciseman, some fine ladies, a briefly presented fop, and two minor, subordinated lines of action (one of a clever wit duped, the other the familiar boy-gets-girl sort) coexist merely to provide a theatrical visit to the military camp at Coxheath, then actually populated with soldiers and the focus of a great deal of contemporary interest. There were a few songs, some marching and dancing, and most important, splendid perspective views executed by De Loutherbourgh "which exceeds every Thing in Scenery we have ever seen."[18] It should not be surprising that when audiences would pay to see such drivel, Sheridan would give them more—and he did, in another pastiche, *The Wonders of Derbyshire*, later the same season. *The Critic*, in a similar fashion, has topical subjects, local and domestic jokes, songs which were popular enough to warrant separate publication, and De Loutherbourgh scenery which "seems to bring nature to our view, instead of painting views after nature."[19]

And yet, *The Critic* is obviously a great deal more than just a topical burlesque. "Whoever, delighting in its gaiety and wit, remembers that *The Critic* was written in one of the darkest hours of English history" when invasion seemed imminent?[20] We may no longer view Sir Fretful Plagiary as a caricature of Cumberland, or know that Puff is Thomas King, veteran actor and theater manager; but who fails to be delighted by timelessness encased in timeliness? The very brilliance of *The Critic* arises because its informing design is not topical, because its ridicule is not specific satire but general comic criticism. *The Critic* is clearly burlesque in its widest sense, rarely parody, the most topical form of burlesque.

Parody is a subspecies of satire, the direct mockery by imitation of a given, specific, external object. In one of the precursors of *The Critic, The Rehearsal*, numerous speeches, lines, and situations echo and ridicule speeches and situations from contemporary Restoration heroic plays. The viewer of that play today, or even the mid-eighteenth-century auditor, is unlikely to derive the pleasure contemporary audiences felt; even the reader of a good annotated edition will probably fail to enjoy all the literary satire Buckingham intended. *The Rehearsal* lasted on stage because its timeless frame permitted massive changes in its parodied content. Cibber and Garrick injected contemporary commentary, mimicked the behavior of contemporary actors, in essence made the play of their time in spite of its origins. They, and modern producers, must do so because true parody—specific satire of a specific object—is lost when the object it mocks is lost: *Shamela* without *Pamela* is not very amusing and even the early chapters of *Joseph Andrews* seem misleading to many who do not know Richardson's novel. Burlesque, however, is not parody—not specific satire— but general ridicule of classes of objects. Parody takes the characteristics of specific objects, redefines them to expose their absurdity, and moves toward damnation of the whole class through damnation of the objects; burlesque creates the characteristics of the whole class by granting characteristics to an absurd imaginary individual example which in and by itself has no direct resemblance to any individual member of the whole class. Parody is particular, burlesque is general; parody is almost always highly topical; burlesque may have some topical features, but as a whole, is barely topical in itself.

The burlesque of *The Critic* has lasted longer than that of *The Rehearsal* or *The Tragedy of Tragedies* because *The Critic* chose as its objects those of a larger, less definable, less topical class. Buckingham's play mocks a rather local group of objects, heroic plays; Fielding's play attacks nearly the same set of rather local phenomena. But Sheridan's play mocks a large, amorphous class: *The Spanish Armada* is absurd not just as heroic drama, historical drama, domestic tragedy, or romantic tragedy, but as poorly conducted serious drama of any time. Unprepared discoveries, clumsy exposition, wild coincidences, pretentious dialogue, excessive spectacle are faults not of any single genre but of any kind of wretched play. Obviously, both *The Rehearsal* and *The Tragedy of Tragedies* burlesque the general as well as parody the particular; but insofar as they ridicule the particular they remain local. *The Critic*, even encased in topical references, has more endurance precisely because it ridicules the general more consistently.

This is one reason why, for instance, searching for passages from other eighteenth-century plays parodied in *The Critic* is such a fruitless business: there are very few if any because Sheridan was not attacking specific plays. This is one reason why Puff, and not Sir Fretful Plagiary, is the author of *The Spanish Armada*: Sir Fretful's association with Cumberland was too strong, and to ridicule Cumberland's *Battle of Hastings* was to tie *The Critic* to a merely local event; the association of Puff as the author of the tragedy with King as the author of an entertainment on a similar topic is convenient, but not necessary to make the satire against bad drama effective.

Moreover, *The Critic* is not just an attack on bad drama, but a comic castigation of sloppy theatrical practices in general. Literature is not Sheridan's target, as it was largely for Buckingham and Fielding; instead, his aim is to ridicule the excesses of professional, practical theater, and not just theater in production but theater in all its aspects. Dangle is every theatrical hanger-on—the amateur of dubious influence, the critic of unsure tastes, the hypocrite of uncertain loyalties. Sneer is every dramatic critic—self-interested for the two plays he brings to Dangle, but cynical concerning anyone else's efforts. Sir Fretful is every thin-skinned author, and he became Cumberland not so much because Sheridan's text called for it as because Parsons chose to emphasize it: later actors have played the role successfully without reference to the sentimental playwright.[21] Puff is beyond correction, a hackneyed playwright and a spectacle-monger. The Italian visitors come unprepared, ignorant of language, naïvely trusting in their own talents—a perfect reflection of many theatrical hopefuls. The self-interested managers, the upstaging actors and actresses, the practical designers and prompters are theatrical characters of all time. The aim of *The Critic* is clear, and the barb hits and sticks to the theatrical target.

Yet, as in *The Rivals* or *The School for Scandal* where sentimentality seems approved of as well as damned, many have doubted the aesthetic integrity of *The Critic*. The tacking together of the manners scenes of the first act with the more highly artificial burlesque rehearsal of the second and third acts seems a cynical attempt to utilize materials on hand, not to create a unified work capable of achieving the aesthetic integrity Sheridan sought (and failed) to give *The Relapse* or successfully lent to his other comic masterpieces. Early reviews remarked that Sheridan would have done better to play the first act as a prelude, or to integrate it with the second and third.[22] It is, of course, a kind of prelude already. Yet its duration is such that it overshadows much of the rehearsal: it might have been integrated, but only at the possible expense of vitiating the effects of the rehearsal. Moreover, the attacks on newspaper puffery, on the selection of plays, on the influence of amateurs, and on the vanity and hypocrisy of authors and critics that constitute the satire of act one seem in many ways irrelevant to the attack on theater in production that constitutes the satire of acts two and three. Of course, Sheridan was attacking theater in all its aspects; his failure, if there was one, was to separate the various aspects of his target so completely that in acts two and three we lose sight of theater as a whole while we focus only on theater in production.

The serious use of spectacle might be considered a flaw; De Loutherbourgh's scenes and effects were lavishly praised for their verisimilitude, not their mockery of theatrical effect: *The Critic* was in part successful for many of the same reasons *The Camp* was—for its magnificence, battle, noise, and procession. Clearly, the representation of the defeat of the Spanish Armada by the English fleet, chorused with the popular and rousing song, "Britons Strike Home," evoked surprise, delight, and patriotic sentiment; and the procession that followed of "*all the English rivers and their tributaries*" was a theatrical extravaganza matching Garrick's *Jubilee*. Puff's final "Well, pretty well—but not quite perfect—so ladies and gentlemen, if you please, we'll rehearse this piece again to-morrow" (3.1.332–33) would be hard pressed to bring things into burlesque perspective. But I suspect Sheridan was laughing at his audience and their desires, that he was saying in effect "Here you have it, and you have nobody to blame but yourselves if you fail to see the self-satisfied stupidity of your tastes." In his time the line was his joke; in our time the joke is ours, for no modern production of *The Critic* fails to burlesque the final flourish with scenery and props falling and colliding. Moreover, Sheridan's ridicule of the theater in all its aspects would be complete only if the audience, the most important constituent, received its corrective lash, too. They did, and that is yet another reason why *The Critic* is the most complete satiric play about the theater yet created.

The informing principle of *The Critic*, then, is broad burlesque of theater in all its aspects. Such a work should not be judged by standards of unity induced from works not designed according to the same principle. Students of the play would be wrongheaded to attack *The Critic* because some characters are drawn inconsistently or because some characters disappear from the representation or because the "plot" lacks unity of tone, just as readers would be wrong to criticize *The Dunciad* for ridiculing nonliterary targets like education or to fault *Tristram Shandy* for its failure to bring all aspects of its narrative to a probable conclusion. Pope's work, designed to ridicule intellectual dullness in all its aspects, had neither to fulfill the demands of an allegorical satire on learning like *The Battle of the Books* by focusing specifically on literary matters nor to satisfy the principles of narrative coherence and characterization of an allegorical and personal satire like *Mac-Flecknoe*. Sterne's work, designed as a uniquely personal expression employing a fictive "I" narrator burlesquing a wide variety of literary forms including the periodic essay, the novel, and the confession while telling a "story," had neither to achieve a principle of narrative coherence similar to that of *Clarissa* or *Tom Jones* nor to create a sense of closure arising from the resolution of the instabilities in the relationships among characters similar to the sense of closure created in Richardson's or Fielding's novels. Just as we value *Tristram*

Shandy though it is not a novel, or *The Dunciad* though it is not strictly a satire on literature, so we should value *The Critic* though it is not just a burlesque of theatrical literature, as are *The Rehearsal* or *The Tragedy of Tragedies*.

For what should we praise *The Critic?* How can we explain the unique pleasures derived from its reading or representation? The answers lie largely, I think, in the succession of comic "moments," into which Sheridan packed all the comic techniques he had developed in his earlier works. In a manner characteristic of his indolent genius, he chose only the loosest of informing principles—that of burlesque of all aspects of theater—to bring them together.

As we have seen elsewhere in this study, Sheridan's greatest skills lay in the creation of comic moments. He could unify them around and through action and character as in *The Rivals, The Duenna, A Trip to Scarborough,* or *The School for Scandal,* but even in those works problems remain. The two most unified by plot—*The Duenna* and *A Trip to Scarborough*—fail to reach the heights of great comic literature; *The Rivals,* though a great work of comic art, nevertheless has aesthetic problems, largely of unity; *The School for Scandal* is great unified comic art, but fails as "morally serious comedy." The maker of moments could only barely bring his moments together. In a sense, Sheridan was always making parts— sketching scenes but not plots, writing dialogues to ideas, not to characters in conflict; and the sheer mass of short uncompleted fragments he left, if not the works into which he molded some of these moments, confirm that this was his method of creation.[23] The moments of *The Critic* show particularly his great skill as a maker of comic dialogue. Sheridan's comic dialogue, indeed the dialogue of all great creators of dramatic comedy, is amusing for one of four principal approaches used either separately or in combination: character, situation, manifest absurdity, or wit.[24]

In amusing dialogue based on character, the faults or foibles of the character are displayed in a comic way, so that we smile not at *what* the character says but at the fact that *he* says it. Verbal tics, dialect oddities, and comically repetitive or predictable assertions of belief all fall into this category. To utilize a stage Jew or Irishman, to display an irascible father, a disappointed old bachelor, or a ridiculous fop is to employ dialogue based on character.

Nearly as frequently encountered among comic kinds is dialogue based on situation. We laugh through our superior knowledge of the circumstances and enjoy the dramatic irony of the concealed facts which we, and perhaps some of the other characters, share. The reiteration of belief in an adulterer *manqué* while the partner in his sin is to our knowledge concealed on the scene, or the imposition by means of disguise of a clever person on a stupid one, are good situational techniques which may lead to the development of amusing, ironic dialogue.

Manifest verbal absurdity is the basis for a third kind of comic dialogue. Puns, intentional or otherwise, mistakes of grammar, excessive, inappropriate or badly designed comparisons are the most commonly encountered comic verbal absurdities. Here the character need not himself be amusing—though most frequently he is—for he can be so briefly displayed as not to develop any character, he can report the words of others, or he can make mistakes which are not truly an aspect of his character as we perceive it.

Historically the most valued of amusing comic dialogue is that based on wit. Wit, that intellectual excellence which we can admire apart from character (hence our admiration for the witty speech of even those characters by whom we are not amused), employs unusual or apt comparisons and irony in obvious or subtle manners. Like manifest absurdity, wit can be an aspect of characterization; and like amusing dialogue based on character, wit can be made an aspect of situation, as when a speaker who is witty ironically comments to a butt who fails to recognize the irony. (Note that manifest absurdity is not the same thing as false wit; false wit amuses largely as an aspect of character, for it is intentional, i.e., intended as wit.)[25]

Of these four kinds of comic dialogue, those based on character and situation are the most commonly employed, that based on manifest absurdity the least attempted, and that founded on wit the least frequently achieved. As a general principle we can say that the great and memorable scenes of comic dramatic literature employ at least three and often all four kinds of comic dialogue in concert. Indeed, the failed attempts of a good many third-rate dramatists of Sheridan's day as well as the successes of many comic dramatists of genius in all times suggest a corollary, quantitative principle: the more aspects or different representatives of amusing character, the more ironic levels of comic situation, the more manifest absurdity, and the more striking and original wit all used in concert, the more probable the creation of memorable, amusing comic dialogue. Two scenes I have touched on frequently in this study—Jack's imposition on Mrs. Malaprop, and the screen scene of *The School for Scandal*—demonstrate both the concert and the quantitative principles admirably, for both scenes depend upon widely different and striking characters, several levels of situational irony, manifest absurdity (to a lesser extent), and wit all used together. Both principles underlie the success of the dialogue in the moments of *The Critic*.

Take the famous roasting scene of Sir Fretful Plagiary. The scene begins with an immediate situational irony, prepared for by witty characterization, so that we await with pleasure the arrival of "the sorest man alive . . . [who] shrinks like scorch'd parchment from the fiery ordeal of true criticism" (1.1.171–72). Dangle's attempt to second Sneer's remarks on Sir Fretful are stopped by the playwright's entrance.

> DANGLE. Ah, my dear friend!—Egad, we were just speaking of your Tragedy.—Admirable, Sir Fretful, admirable!
> SNEER. You never did anything beyond it, Sir Fretful—never in your life.
> SIR FRETFUL. You make me extremely happy;—for without a compliment, my dear Sneer, there isn't a man in the world whose judgment I value as I do yours.
>
> [1.1.182–88]

Sneer's cynical double entendre is answered by Sir Fretful's so that we are led to expect a battle of wits. Mrs. Dangle's immediate complication of the scene's irony—"They are only laughing at you, Sir Fretful"—sparks the first of a series of amusing asides in which Sir Fretful reveals his character by revealing his irritation—"A damn'd double-faced fellow!"—

and we quickly see that Sir Fretful is not capable of matching Sneer's wit by insinuation, innuendo, and double entendre. As the scene continues, Dangle's lack of wit contrasts with Sneer's witty remarks. Both men are willing to discomfit Sir Fretful, and increasingly situation becomes less important than character and wit. At first Sneer's wit is chiefly in subtle ironic one-liners or occasionally, in neatly prepared jokes. Despite the fact that the subject matter of the conversation is directed outside the immediate situation, Sneer is able to turn it back on Sir Fretful, as in this exchange: Sir Fretful fears that the manager (i.e., Sheridan) might steal something from his tragedy were he allowed to read it.

> SIR FRETFUL. And then, if such a person gives you the least hint or assistance, he is devilish apt to take the merit of the whole.—
> DANGLE. If it succeeds.
> SIR FRETFUL. Aye,—but with regard to this piece, I think I can hit that gentleman, for I can safely swear he never read it.
> SNEER. I'll tell you how you may hurt him more—
> SIR FRETFUL. How?—
> SNEER. Swear he wrote it.
>
> [1.1.228–35]

Situational irony is added to wit and character as the basis for the amusing dialogue which develops as Sneer quotes the imaginary review to an increasingly discomfited Sir Fretful:

> SNEER. Why, [the critic] roundly asserts that you have not the slightest invention, or original genius whatever; tho' you are the greatest traducer of all other authors living.
> SIR FRETFUL. Ha! ha! ha!—very good!
> SNEER. That as to COMEDY, you have not one idea of your own, he believes, even in your common place-book—where stray jokes, and pilfered witticisms are kept with as much method as the ledger of the LOST-and-STOLEN-OFFICE.
> SIR FRETFUL. —Ha! ha! ha!—very pleasant!
> SNEER. Nay, that you are so unlucky as not to have the skill even to *steal* with taste.—But that you gleen from the refuse of obscure volumes, where more judicious plagiarists have been before you; so that the body of your work is a composition of dregs and sediments—like a bad tavern's worst wine.
> SIR FRETFUL. Ha! ha!

SNEER. In your more serious efforts, he says, your bombast would be less intolerable, if the thoughts were ever suited to the expression; but the homeliness of the sentiment stares thro' the fantastic encumbrance of its fine language, like a clown in one of the new uniforms!

SIR FRETFUL. Ha! ha!

SNEER. That your occasional tropes and flowers suit the general coarseness of your stile, as tambour sprigs would a ground of linsey-wolsey; while your imitations of Shakespeare resemble the mimicry of Falstaff's Page, and are about as near the standard of the original.

SIR FRETFUL. Ha!—

SNEER. —In short, that even the finest passages you steal are of no service to you; for the poverty of your own language prevents their assimilating; so that they lie on the surface like lumps of marl on a barren moor, encumbering what it is not in their power to fertilize!—

SIR FRETFUL. [*after great agitation.*]—Now another person would be vex'd at this.

[1.1.318–48]

Of course, we value this scene most for the wit; but the dialogue, amusing by virtue of situational irony and character as well as wit, explains why we find the scene more pleasureable than the subsequent witty exchange among Sneer, Dangle, and Puff on the art of puffery (1.2.146–281). Pleasant as this later scene is, witty and absurd as Puff's explanations of his art are, scathing as the continued indictment of newspapers and the theater becomes, the scene does not achieve the levels of comic enjoyment possible in the roasting of Sir Fretful. It is too much like those virtuoso recitations continually attempted by the characters of Samuel Foote. Sheridan could outdo Foote in this regard, but as the juxtaposition of these two scenes shows, he could also do more in blending character, situation, and wit.

The moments of the first act of *The Critic*—Mr. and Mrs. Dangle's daily jangle, Sir Fretful's roasting, the Italian singers, and Puff's art of puffery—are all bound together by their burlesque of the theater in all its aspects. Character largely informs the first scene between the Dangles; character, situation, and wit melds in the dialogue of the second; character to a very small extent, manifest absurdity, and situation make amusing the display of the Italian singers and their French-speaking interpreter; wit, and to a lesser extent, characterization make effective the satiric dialogue of the fourth scene. Any of these scenes could be removed from the burlesque; any could be exchanged with another and not disturb seriously the connections among them, for there is no significant development of character or action. Each is amusing basically for itself; each could have been, and I suspect was, written at a different time; and they were brought together here only by means of the loosest of informing devices.

The two rehearsal acts are moments in that the particular sections of the satirical target under attack at any given time could have been attacked earlier or later in the presentation; there is no principle of development underlying the satire. But the continuity of the unfolding play within the play provides a unity not to be found in the first act, and this, together with Sheridan's employment of amusing dialogue constantly based on a rich interaction of character, situation, absurdity, and wit gives to acts two and three of *The Critic* a sustained power not to be found in act one. Puff is oblivious to the quality of his play and speaks of its absurdities as if they were excellencies; his character is further revealed by his comically unjustifiable pique at the actors' cuts. We are amused too by the irony of the situation. Our own critical standards and the efforts of raisonneur Sneer reveal the concealed truth of the intellectual and creative aesthetic poverty of *The Spanish Armada* which Puff cannot recognize, Dangle only occasionally seems to notice, and Sneer sarcastically exposes. The manifest absurdities of the dialogue of the play within the play—metaphors piled upon one another with no regard to their aesthetic appropriateness, bathos where there should be pathos—are joined by the manifest absurdities of Puff's explanations. Sneer's ironic commentary adds a dimension of wit—wit of an obvious but nonetheless pleasurable sort.

Demonstration of this interaction in any of the various moments of acts two and three threatens to overwhelm even the heavy-handed irony of this section of *The Critic*. So rather

than explicate a scene or two, let me point to Sheridan's use
of three other comic devices of dialogue—repetition, diminution, and what I will call accidental wit. All reinforce the
complex interplay of the dialogue. In act one Sheridan had
used repetition to good effect with Dangle's tag lines, "tho'
he's my friend!" (see especially its last occurrence, 1.1.178–79).
In act two it becomes the principle upon which we find the
agreement of all those present on stage in *The Spanish Armada*
to pray to Mars amusing: "And me!" "And me!" "And me!"
"And me!" (2.2.206–12). Diminution—a kind of repetition for
the specific effect of reduction—adds to character in act one
as Sir Fretful's responses to the imagined criticism gradually
change from "Ha! ha! ha!—very good!" to a half-hearted
"Ha!—" (1.1.321–42); it serves both purposes of characterization and absurdity in this stichomythic exchange between two
characters of *The Spanish Armada*:

> "TILBURINA.
> "A retreat in Spain!
> > "GOVERNOR.
> "Outlawry here!
> > "TILBURINA.
> "Your daughter's prayer!
> > "GOVERNOR.
> "Your father's oath!
> > "TILBURINA.
> "My lover!
> > "GOVERNOR.
> "My country!
> > "TILBURINA.
> "Tilburnia!
> > "GOVERNOR.
> "England!
> > "TILBURINA.
> "A title!
> > "GOVERNOR.
> "Honor!
> > "TILBURINA.
> "A pension!
> > "GOVERNOR.
> "Conscience!

The crescendo of economic concerns completely deflates the
repetition:

> "TILBURINA.
> "A thousand pounds!
> "GOVERNOR.
> "Hah! thou hast touch'd me nearly!
>
> [2.2.377–404]

But perhaps the funniest lines are built on accidental wit—a combination of character, situation, manifest absurdity, and the approximation of wit. Consider just two examples, both of them Puff's explanations for problems in his play. Sneer criticizes the decorum of the dialogue:

> SNEER. But, Mr. Puff, I think not only the Justice, but the clown seems to talk in as high a style as the first hero among them.
> PUFF. Heaven forbid they should not in a free country!—Sir, I am not for making slavish distinctions, and giving all the fine language to the upper sort of people.
>
> [3.1.33–37]

Or perhaps the funniest lines of the play:

> *Enter* A BEEFEATER.
> "BEEFEATER.
> "Perdition catch my soul but *I* do love thee.[26]
> SNEER. Haven't I heard that line before?
> PUFF. No, I fancy not—Where pray?
> DANGLE. Yes, I think there is something like it in Othello.
> PUFF. Gad! now you put me in mind on't, I believe there is—but that's of no consequence—all that can be said is, that two people happened to hit on the same thought—And Shakespeare made use of it first, that's all.
> SNEER. Very true.
>
> [3.1.104–12]

Such effects make the moments of the rehearsal scenes particularly amusing. And even if the informing principle—to burlesque the theater in all its aspects—seems loose, we can be happy that Sheridan was able to cast upon it here and sorry that never again would he bring his "moments" together.

With *The Critic* we come to the end of Sheridan's achievement as comic dramatist. There would be another year or two of active work in the theater, but no more literary achievement. On 12 September 1780 Sheridan was elected Member of Parliament for Stafford, and though he remained associated with Drury Lane for more than thirty years, only one major theatrical effort was to come, the pompous and absurd *Pizzaro*. He kept his hand in, however, and not just in the till; he participated in correcting and revising other dramatists' work, in coaching and advising actors, and in organizing a few spectacular entertainments; he continually promised definitive editions of his own works and continually projected another play, especially when money was short. But never again would he produce a comedy. Perhaps Sheridan knew his powers were going or had gone; perhaps he felt he never would be able to focus the energy necessary to create another masterpiece.

Why have so many great English comic dramatists stopped writing for the stage at relatively young ages? Congreve had produced all his comedies by the time he was thirty; Etherege saw his last play on stage when he was barely forty, Wycherley when he was in his mid-thirties; Wilde's best play comes from his fortieth year, Synge's from his thirty-sixth, Jonson's four or five best from his late thirties and early forties, Coward's three or four from his early thirties, Vanbrugh's from his early thirties, Sheridan's and Farquhar's from their late twenties. Of course, one cannot give a single answer, unless one wants to invoke so vague a term as "comic spirit" or attribute to youth an exuberance many have displayed in maturer years. Congreve was disgusted with developments in popular taste; Farquhar and Synge died young; Wilde was forbidden a public forum for his wit; and Sheridan entered Parliament to embark on a new and brilliant career. Beyond these few reasons, we can only speculate. In Sheridan's case, particularly when a new comedy would have meant so much to his always precarious financial position, why did he fail to employ his obvious talents as a comic dramatist? Michael Kelly, a talented musician and performer, relates an anecdote that reveals much:

> One evening (probably in the late 1780's or early 1790's) that their late Majesties honoured Drury Lane Theatre with their presence, the play, by royal command, was the "School for Scandal." When Mr. Sheridan was in attendance to light their Majesties to their carriage, the King said to him, "I am much

pleased with your comedy of the 'School for Scandal;' but I am
still more so, with your play of the 'Rivals;'—that is my favourite, and I will never give it up."

Her Majesty, at the same time said, "When, Mr. Sheridan,
shall we have another play from your masterly pen?" He
replied, that "he was writing a comedy, which he expected very
shortly to finish."

I was told of this; and the next day, walking with him along
Piccadilly, I asked him if he had told the Queen, that he was
writing a play? He said he had, and that he actually was about
one.

"Not you," said I to him; "you will never write again; you are
afraid to write."

He fixed his penetrating eye on me, and said, "Of whom am
I afraid?"

I said, "You are afraid of the author of the 'School for
Scandal.' "

I believe, at the time I made the remark, he thought my
conjecture right.[27]

However contrived his anecdote sounds, Kelly was correct, of
course: Sheridan did not finish another dramatic comedy,
though he lived on for thirty-seven years after *The Critic*. And
Kelly was correct in another way, for though today we may
value all of Sheridan's dramatic works, he is still largely
remembered as the author of *The School for Scandal*. Beside
the greater comedy, *The Critic* seems a remnant of his youth, a
brilliant utilization of his experiences as a practical dramatist
perhaps, but more nearly the product of an exuberance and
an adolescent cynicism which the perfection of *The School for
Scandal* seems to deny. Still, *The Critic* is a more stageworthy
work than either of its major competitors in its time and in
ours, *The Rehearsal* and *The Tragedy of Tragedies*; for even
Sheridan's burlesque achieves, however artificially, a fusion of
wit which only Wilde and Coward have since reached. What a
pity that the greatest Georgian playwright would henceforth
produce only *Pizarro*.

CHAPTER VII

Sheridan's Achievement

> Whatever Sheridan has done or chosen to do has
> been, *par excellence*, always the *best* of its kind. He
> has written the *best* comedy (*School for Scandal*)[,]
> the *best* drama [*The Duenna*] (in my mind, far
> before that St. Giles's lampoon, the Beggar's Op-
> era), the best farce (the *Critic*—it is only too good
> for a farce), and the best Address (Monologue on
> Garrick), and, to crown it all, delivered the very
> best Oration (the famous Begum Speech) ever con-
> ceived or heard in this country.
>
> George Gordon, Lord Byron,
> *Letters and Journals*[1]

LORD Byron's praise reflects fairly what many of Sheridan's
contemporaries believed, though some admitted it rather
grudgingly. But to fix Sheridan's place among all English
comic dramatists requires the tact of an Addison and the
discernment of a Johnson. His work was unique as well as
derivative. While it encouraged many imitators, it produced
no dramatic heirs. Within five years English comedy was
confined once again to the false dichotomies early high
Georgian dramatists fought against, didacticism or sentimentalism, "low" and farcical or "genteel" and boring. The English comic spirit was maintained in farce, but melodrama and
the representation of social problems not easily amenable to
comic treatment doomed high comedy. To compare Sheridan's work with that of his contemporaries or his immediate
predecessors is to illuminate it but not to evaluate it against
the larger framework of English dramatic history.

Many arguments in this study have sought to separate
Sheridan's artistic achievement from that of the late Restoration comic dramatists, his predecessors by six or seven decades. The purpose of these arguments was to define more
immediate contexts within which to assess Sheridan's comedies, contexts like Georgian critical debates, Georgian dra-

matic art, and Georgian professional theatrical practices. Because they have been long ignored in defining Sheridan's
practical skills, such contexts take on added importance.

But except for a few specialists, almost no one interested in
Sheridan's comedies will judge them by reference to *False
Delicacy* or *Know Your Own Mind* or with detailed knowledge
of the Georgian stage and its critical assumptions. Such plays
as *Love for Love, The Provok'd Wife, The Beaux' Stratagem, The
Conscious Lovers,* and *She Stoops to Conquer* will endure as the
comedies by whose qualities of construction and artistic
achievement we will judge Sheridan's works. They will endure
as touchstones because we will continue to read or to see
them, not because they are any more similar to Sheridan's
comedies than are the lesser high Geogian comedies. Meas-
ured against the comic works of Congreve, Vanbrugh, Farquhar, Steele, and Goldsmith, Sheridan's comedies still stand
tall in the estimation of audiences, who have supported their
frequent revival, and should stand taller in the estimation of
critics.

For Sheridan was certainly the finest comic playwright after
Congreve and before Shaw. As a writer of theatrical burlesque, Sheridan achieved more than any predecessor or successor in this comic line. As a writer of comedy of manners,
his achievement is not so unique but just as enduring. Eschew-
ing the didactic, the melodramatic, the coldly cynical, and the
violently satiric, Sheridan charted a middle course dependent
upon original characterization, tight construction, and brilliant
dialogue. While he never reached the poetic unity or intellectual penetration of Congreve, he wrote in a wider variety of
styles, creating a distinctive "humane comedy"[2] that improved
upon the fresh boisterousness of Farquhar while avoiding the
cynicism of Vanbrugh, the lachrymosity of the later Steele,
and the improbabilities of Goldsmith.

For his subject matter Sheridan turned to his own experience largely; he chose the problems of young love and mature
affection, the battle of the sexes, and the natural rebellion of
youth against age. What he knew of these subjects and what
he learned as he matured are revealed indirectly, not as
flashes of insight into distinctly individualized, human characters but as general observations about people in society. Like

all comic writers, he was concerned with deception and trickery; but he dealt with self-deception as well, particularly in his
later comedies.

He began by structuring his plots according to the bifur-
cated forms most frequently used by his contemporaries, then
moved increasingly toward the fuller unification which
achieves most dramatic force in a single comic catastrophe.
From first to last he showed extraordinary skill in utilizing for
his original work *coups de théâtre*: no one who has seen or
read them forgets the letters of *The Rivals, St. Patrick's Day*,
and *The Duenna* or the famous scenes of concealment of these
and *The School for Scandal*. As he developed in his construction
of plot, he became less dependent upon purely physical circumstances—duels and elopements—and more capable of using the full scene for a total theatrical effect dependent upon
the movement of the actor's spirit, not upon his legs and
arms; an auction scene or a screen scene call for this display
of the soul more completely than Jack tricking his father or
Margaret imposing upon Isaac. Excepting *The Critic*, the struc-
tures of Sheridan's plots move from those which display
character for its own sake in his early works to those which
enact character for the story's sake in his later comedies.

The forms Sheridan's plots took were always distinctly
comic. Though tempted by the melodrama of Faulkland and
Julia and of his early sketches for *The School for Scandal*,
Sheridan, unlike Steele, resisted the call of *tragédie mitigée*.
Beneath all his comic excoriations of folly flows a good-
natured tolerance: he fails to be morally serious because he
chooses not to scourge vice but rather to expose foibles—a
course which will alienate none though it improves few.
Despite his insight in his last two major comic works, into
what most would call reality—a demonstration that vice is as
much a part of human nature as virtue—his evident faith in
well-intentioned men and benevolent providence to expel the
vicious from society seems unrealistic. He was a sentimentalist.[3]

For his characters Sheridan first chose stage types to which
the audience and the actors were long accustomed. Capitaliz-
ing upon familiarity from the one and skill from the other,
Sheridan molded these type characters into surprisingly orig-

inal amalgams that live in audiences' minds beyond the
frameworks in which they appear. As he became more familiar with his craft and with the actors who gave his plays
life, Sheridan ventured to complicate his characters further,
but never so far that psychological depth overwhelmed comic
effect.

His dialogue was designed primarily to give life to these
characters. It was "characteristic," his contemporaries would
have said. Only for isolated speeches in the scandal scenes or
in *The Critic* would a person reasonably familiar with Sheridan's comedies not be able to identify the speaker. The
dialogue is amusing usually because it reveals character and
complicates situation, though on occasion it is also manifestly
absurd or witty. It is brilliant not because it is especially witty
in the epigrammatic manner of a Congreve but because it is
so consistently true to character without depending merely
upon simple dialect or idiosyncratic tags. When Sheridan did
choose to use tags, he created new ones quite beyond the
grasp of an ordinary comic playwright—malapropisms, "oaths
referential," or Joseph's sentiments. Vanbrugh with his dialogue *longueurs*, Farquhar, Steele, and Goldsmith with their
more simple tags, did not reach this plateau of comic appropriateness. (The next playwright to come near was Wilde, but
he fell into the trap of wit so completely that his characters
speak sentiments they cannot possibly believe and which the
auditor could not possibly differentiate as any more appropriate to the characters than those spoken by the characters'
foils.)

Throughout his comic work, both manners and burlesque,
Sheridan's practice was to take the audience into his confidence, to share with them as much of the events yet to come
as would pique their expectations concerning the complex
situations unfolding before them. Surprise, when it came,
arose from probable consequences joyously anticipated; but
neither the expectations nor the surprises were allowed to
linger long and thereby lose their force. In this manner,
Sheridan managed to invent comedies of situation more
delicately balanced between anticipation and astonishment
than any of his eighteenth-century contemporaries were capable of creating.

In sum, Sheridan's achievement among writers of English comedy springs from his complex, fast-moving, amiably comic plots peopled by probable yet theatrical characters; from a verbal brilliance dependent not upon wit in the high Restoration comic sense but upon a full consonance of expression to character; and from a careful poise of expectation and surprise in situational comedy. "Whatever he touched," wrote Hazlitt, "he adorned with all the ease, grace, and brilliancy of his style. . . . He was assuredly a man of first-rate talents."[4]

Appendix: Two Notes on Sheridan's Compositional Practices

A. SHERIDAN, FIELDING, AND "BROCADE"

As has been noted several times, Sheridan was reluctant to waste what he considered a fine *bon mot*.[1] A phrase like Lady Teazle's famous reply to Joseph Surface's seductive casuistry, "So—so—then I perceive your Prescription is that I must sin in my own Defence—and part with my virtue to preserve my Reputation" (4.3.75–77), resulted only after repeated revisions of a kernel statement with which Sheridan experimented several times in the early sketches. The paucity of identifiable verbal echoes in Sheridan's works to contemporary or earlier pieces suggests that these brilliant sallies arose solely from his own imagination and his painstaking revision. But occasionally the playwright utilized the wit of others, transforming a bare suggestion into a *coup de maître*.

A case in point shows Sheridan lifting a pair of lines from Henry Fielding and playing with them in different contexts to achieve a momentary, striking theatrical effect. Sheridan's second produced dramatic work was the epilogue to Thomas Hull's adaptation of James Thomson's *Edward and Eleonora* (CG, 18 March 1775). In the middle section of this witty monologue is a portrait of a fashionable Englishwoman reacting to the news of her husband's approaching death:

> There are, no Doubt, tho' rare to find I know;
> Who could lose Husbands, yet survive the Blow;
> Two years a Wife—view *Lesbia*, sobbing, crying,
> Her Chair is waiting—but my Lord is dying;
> Preparing for the worst! she tells her Maid,
> To countermand her Points and new Brocade;
> "For O! if I should lose the best of *Men*

Heav'n knows when I shall see the *Club* again.
So, *Lappet*, should he die while I am out,
You'll send for me at Lady *Basto*'s Rout;
The Doctor said he might hold out 'till Three,
But I ha'n't Spirits for the *Coterie!*"

[*Dramatic Works*, p. 822]

Pope's zeugmatic line from *The Rape of the Lock* (2:107), "Or
stain her honour, or her new brocade," has been cited as a
source for Lesbia's countermanding her points and new brocade (*Dramatic Works*, p. 822, n. 1). More likely, Sheridan was
remembering and reworking a scene from Henry Fielding's
Amelia. Mrs. James is led to believe by old Colonel Bath that
her husband has just been killed in the duel with Booth. She
rushes from the interview ready to assume her widowhood,
then returns to ask Colonel Bath to send a message "to
countermand the order which she had given that very morning to make her up a new suit of brocade. 'Heaven knows,'
says she, 'now when I can wear brocade, or whether ever I
shall wear it' " (book 5, chapter 8).

That Sheridan enjoyed the brocade idea is evident from its
use in "The Teazles." An exchange between the early coarse-
featured versions of Sir Peter and Lady Teazle includes this
harsh vow:

SIR PETER. If I were to die, what would you do?
LADY TEAZLE. Countermand my new Brocade.

[*Dramatic Works*, p. 291]

Since the date of composition of the sketch is unclear, we
cannot be certain whether Sheridan first used the idea in the
sketch or in the epilogue. But, as he said in the preface to *The
Rivals* (p. 6), it was one of those "faded ideas that float in the
fancy like half-forgotten dreams": Henry Fielding "happened
to hit on the same thought—And . . . made use of it first,
that's all" (*The Critic*, 3.1.110–12). The thought suits the callow
Mrs. James and the satirized "Lesbia," but not the naïve,
good-natured Lady Teazle. For whatever reason, Sheridan
dropped the lines when he created the final version of the
Teazles' "daily jangle" in *The School for Scandal*.

B. A "Puff Preliminary" in *The Critic*

Sheridan enjoyed theatrical coterie jokes. One of the earliest in his produced works has Sir Anthony Absolute paraphrase this line first spoken a month earlier by Andrew Nightshade in Richard Cumberland's *The Choleric Man* (DL, 19 Dec. 1774): "Then, I'll not die at all; I'll live for ever on purpose to plague him . . ." (act 5; compare *The Rivals*, 3.1.8–9). I have noted others in *St. Patrick's Day*, *The Duenna*, and *A Trip to Scarborough*. But the most fertile ground for such theatrical coterie jokes was, of course, *The Critic*.

Puff gives this example of a "puff direct" in his imagined review of a performance of a friend's comedy:

> Then for the performance—Mr. DODD was astonishingly great in the character of SIR HARRY! That universal and judicious actor Mr. PALMER, perhaps never appeared to more advantage than in the COLONEL;—but it is not in the power of language to do justice to Mr. KING!—Indeed he more than merited those repeated bursts of applause which he drew from a most brilliant and judicious audience! As to the scenery—The miraculous power of Mr. DE LOUTHERBOURG's pencil are universally acknowledged!
>
> [1.2.168–75]

Obviously, this is an open-ended joke dependent upon the audience's knowledge of the actors' roles; subsequent actors portraying Puff substituted their own names and roles according to their own history and that of the performers playing Dangle and Sneer. That Sheridan had mentioned only "young Mr. Something" in the licensing copy of *The Critic* suggests that he later filled in the names and roles to take advantage of a very recent domestic joke which he could trust his actors, and his audience, to recognize.

One editor has suggested references to Sir Harry Wildair and Colonel Standard of Farquhar's *The Constant Couple*. But Dodd never appeared as Sir Harry on the London stage (it was, of course, a "breeches" part; moreover, the play was no longer very popular) and Palmer appeared only once as Colonel Standard. Palmer, Dodd, and King were in many casts together on Drury Lane's stage, but never when Palmer was a "Colonel" and Dodd a "Sir Harry" simultaneously. There might be a reference to *The Discovery*, which in Sheridan's 3 February 1779 revival included King as Sir Anthony Branville (Garrick's old role), Dodd as Sir Harry Flutter, and has a character named Colonel Medway, portrayed not by Palmer but by Brereton. Might Palmer have been asked to play Colonel Medway (which had long been Brereton's role) and have recently refused, thus garnering a sly reference from his manager? More likely, the joke was Sheridan's "puff preliminary" for Elizabeth Griffith's dull comedy *The Times* (DL, 2 Dec. 1779), probably just in rehearsal when *The Critic* was introduced. King was in that cast, and Palmer would create the role of Colonel Mountfort; a foppish character named Sir Harry Granger was featured in the original production. On 29 October, when *The Critic* appeared, Dodd, the prince of fops, could have been cast for this role; but it was eventually taken by Philip Lamash, an actor who specialized in servants and fops and whose weekly salary in 1776–77 of £1 10s. suggests that he could not afford to refuse a role the better paid Dodd (£8 in 1776–77) might have turned down. Perhaps, then, the joke was directed at Dodd. But, although *The Times* was advertised with new scenery by De Loutherbourgh like Puff's imaginary play, any list of fines paid by actors refusing roles has been lost for 1779–80; it, or some other contemporary comment, could prove conclusively that Sheridan here was joking about the theater with his actors and audience on several levels at once, something he obviously loved to do.

Notes

NOTES TO CHAPTER I

1. Except as noted, all citations to Sheridan's plays, prefaces, and dramatic poetry will be to *Sheridan: Plays*, ed. Cecil Price (Oxford: Oxford University Press, 1975), by act, scene, and line number or by page number. The texts of *Plays* are those established in *The Dramatic Works of Richard Brinsley Sheridan*, ed. Cecil Price (Oxford: Clarendon Press, 1973). I will cite ephemera and other material from *Dramatic Works* by page number.

2. Thomas Moore, *Memoirs of the Life of the Right Honourable Richard Brinsley Sheridan*, 2 vols., 5th ed. rev. (London: Longman et al., 1827; rpt. ed., 2 vols., New York: W. J. Widdleton, 1866), hereafter cited as Moore, *Memoirs*; Walter Sichel, *Sheridan: From New and Original Materials*, 2 vols. (London: Constable and Company, 1909), hereafter cited as Sichel, *Sheridan*; R. Crompton Rhodes, *Harlequin Sheridan: The Man and the Legends* (Oxford: Basil Blackwell, 1933), hereafter cited as Rhodes, *Harlequin Sheridan*. In his study, "Sheridan as Playwright, 1751–1780" (Ph.D. diss., Northern Illinois University, 1971), Leonard J. Leff has assessed seventeen of the twenty "complete" biographies of Sheridan. To his list may be added Madeleine Bingham's *Sheridan: The Track of a Comet* (London: Unwin, 1973), a popular biography which adds nothing significant to our understanding.

3. Bibliographical efforts before Price's include those of George Henry Nettleton, *The Major Dramas of Richard Brinsley Sheridan* (Boston: Ginn & Co., 1906); Sichel in *Sheridan*; Iolo A. Williams, *Seven 18th-Century Bibliographies* (London: Dulau & Co., 1924); R. Crompton Rhodes, *The Plays and Poems of Richard Brinsley Sheridan*, 3 vols. (Oxford: Basil Blackwell, 1933), hereafter cited as *Plays and Poems*.

4. Jean Dulck's dissertation, *Les comédies de R. B. Sheridan, étude littéraire* (Paris: Didier, 1962), like Jack D. Durant's volume *Richard Brinsley Sheridan*, Twayne English Authors Series (Boston: G. K. Hall & Co., 1975), could not take Cecil Price's recent studies fully into account. John Loftis's *Sheridan and the Georgian Drama* (Cambridge: Harvard University Press, 1976) appeared too late for me to incorporate its findings into the present volume. Other full-length studies are Kurt Weiss, *Richard Brinsley Sheridan als Lustspieldichter* (Leipzig: Gustav Fock, 1888), R. G. H. Niederauer's "Wit and Senti-

ment in Sheridan's Comedies of Manners" (Ph.D. diss., University of Southern California, 1966), and Carole Schauls Stahlkoph's "Rhetoric and Comic Technique in Richard Brinsley Sheridan's *The Rivals* and *The School for Scandal*" (Ph.D. diss., University of California at Davis, 1973).

5. Joseph Wood Krutch, *Comedy and Conscience After the Restoration* (1924; rpt. ed., New York: Columbia University Press, 1949), p. 252; Ashley H. Thorndike, *English Comedy* (New York: Macmillan, 1928), p. 414; Louis I. Bredvold, *A History of English Literature*, ed. Hardin Craig (New York: Oxford University Press, 1950), p. 428; A. R. Humphreys, *The Pelican Guide to English Literature*, ed. Boris Ford, 6 vols. (London: Penguin Books, Ltd., 1957), 4: 92; Allardyce Nicoll, *A History of English Drama, 1660–1900*, 6 vols. (Cambridge: Cambridge University Press, 1952–59), 3: 158. Attacking such views are Leonard J. Leff in "Sheridan and Sentimentalism," *Restoration and 18th Century Theatre Research* 12 (May 1973): 36–48, and Robert D. Hume in "Goldsmith and Sheridan and the Supposed Revolution of 'Laughing' Against 'Sentimental' Comedy," in *Studies in Change and Revolution*, ed. Paul J. Korshin (Menston, Yorkshire: The Scolar Press, 1972), pp. 237–76.

6. Harold V. Routh, "The Georgian Drama," *The Cambridge History of English Literature*, ed. A. W. Ward and A. R. Waller, 11 vols. (Cambridge: Cambridge University Press, 1914), 11: 266–73; Ernest Bernbaum, *The Drama of Sensibility* (1915; rpt. ed., Gloucester, Mass.: Peter Smith, 1958), esp. pp. 250–59; James J. Lynch, *Box, Pit and Gallery: Stage and Society in Johnson's London* (1953; rpt. ed., New York: Russell and Russell, 1971), esp. pp. 177–80, 189–91; Harry W. Pedicord, *The Theatrical Public in the Time of Garrick* (New York: Columbia University King's Crown Press, 1954); Ricardo Quintana, "Goldsmith's Achievement as Dramatist," *University of Toronto Quarterly 34* (Jan. 1965): 159–77. With some reservations, I add to this list Arthur Sherbo, *English Sentimental Drama* (East Lansing: Michigan State University Press, 1957), esp. p. 158; Sherbo's thesis forces him to understate the total effect of the doctrine of sentimentalism on Sheridan's theatrical craftsmanship.

7. A phenomenon first reported by Lynch, *Box, Pit and Gallery*, p. 23.

8. I have based these computations on the performances recorded for all London theaters for the period by *The London Stage 1660–1800, Part 4: 1747–1776*, ed. George Winchester Stone, Jr. (Carbondale, Ill.: Southern Illinois University Press, 1962) and *Part 5: 1777–1800*, ed. Charles Beecher Hogan (1968).

9. Other Shakespearean comedies which had impressive totals during the period include: *Twelfth Night* (64 performances), *All's Well that Ends Well* (24, as a "pastoral"), *Two Gentlemen of Verona* (6), and *Measure for Measure* (43). *The Taming of the Shrew* and *A Midsummer-Night's Dream* appeared in several different versions as afterpieces and were popular.

10. At the twenty different theatrical evenings offered while Sheridan lived in Bath, he could have seen the following mainpiece comedies: *The Provok'd Husband* (twice); *The Jealous Wife*; *Rule a Wife and Have a Wife*; *The West Indian* (twice); *The Country Lasses* (Charles Johnson); *False Delicacy*; *The Funeral*; *The Way to Keep Him*; *The Conscious Lovers*; *As You Like It*; *The Fashionable Lover* (Cumberland, twice); *Love in a Village* (Bickerstaff's comic opera); and *A Word to the Wise* (Kelly; damned for political reasons at its one London performance two years earlier and a sure attraction). See Frederick T. Woods, "Theatrical Performances at Bath in the Eighteenth Century," *Notes and Queries* 192 (November 1947): 489.

11. The night was 17 November 1772, when he might have seen either *The Beggar's Opera* or *As You Like It*. See *The Letters of Richard Brinsley Sheridan*, ed. C. J. L. Price, 3 vols. (Oxford: Oxford University Press, 1966), 1: 65, hereafter cited as *Letters*.

12. Stuart Tave's *The Amiable Humorist: A Study in the Comic Theory and Criticism of the 18th and Early 19th Centuries* (Chicago: University of Chicago Press, 1960), esp. chapter 5, discusses the Englishman's pride in his home-grown idiosyncratics and defines fully the term "amiable humorist."

13. "An Essay on the Theatre," in *The Collected Works of Oliver Goldsmith*, ed. Arthur Friedman, 5 vols. (Oxford: Clarendon Press, 1965), 3:210. I am indebted to Friedman's essay analyzing and applying the terms of Goldsmith's argument, "Aspects of Sentimentalism in Eighteenth-Century Literature," in *The Augustan Milieu: Essays Presented to Louis A. Landa*, ed. Henry Knight Miller, Eric Rothstein, and G. S. Rousseau (Oxford: Clarendon Press, 1970), esp. p. 252.

14. Throughout this study, unless otherwise noted, I quote from the edition of all plays as given in the microcards of *Three Centuries of English Drama*; I note quotations by act in the text. On its first mention, each play will be parenthetically identified by the place and date of its introductory performance, abbreviating Drury Lane as "DL," Covent Garden as "CG," and Haymarket as "HM," and employing the dates given in *London Stage, Parts 4 and 5*. In my citations to plays in this collection I have silently corrected gross accidentals.

15. *London Magazine* 41 (1772): 561.

16. Following Sheldon Sacks's formulations in *Fiction and the Shape of Belief: A Study of Henry Fielding—With Glances at Swift, Johnson, and Richardson* (Berkeley and Los Angeles: University of California Press, 1967), chapter 1, I will define a melodramatic action (which Sacks calls a "serious action") as that sort of plot in a novel or play in which a fortunate or unfortunate outcome does not seem clearly determined from shortly after the outset. In a comic action, a fortunate outcome seems clearly determined, whereas in a tragic action an unfortunate outcome seems so. The distinction is psychological; the sort of anxieties we feel while reading or seeing a play which is a comedy are not the same as the anxieties we feel about a play which contains a serious or melodramatic action. The three categories comedy, tragedy, and melodrama are to be considered inclusive for all kinds of plots and would encompass plots which some might identify as "ironic" or "romantic" in the categories "melodramatic" and "comic."

17. Horace Walpole, "Thoughts on Comedy," in *The Works of Horace Walpole, Earl of Orford*, 5 vols. (London: G. G. and J. Robinson, 1798), 2: 320.

18. *The Fashionable Lover* is the only comedy to which Goldsmith definitely alludes in his "Essay on the Theatre." But Oliver Ferguson questions this allusion in "Sir Fretful Plagiary and Goldsmith's 'An Essay on the Theatre,'" in *Quick Springs of Sense*, ed. Larry S. Champion (Athens: University of Georgia Press, 1974), esp. p. 117.

19. But Elder Olson in *The Theory of Comedy* (Bloomington: Indiana University Press, 1968), p. 47, would call *Much Ado About Nothing* something other than a comedy, for in a true comedy the action is "valueless," that is, on hindsight "it would seem foolish to be concerned" about the events portrayed. I agree, however, with his insistence upon some middle category, like Sheldon Sacks's (n. 16 above), to encompass works with happy endings which are not comedies in terms of the anxieties raised by the action.

20. Goldsmith, *Collected Works*, 3: 212.

21. For the best analysis of sentimentalism, see R. S. Crane, "Suggestions Toward a Genealogy of the 'Man of Feeling,'" *ELH* 1 (1934): 205–30; rpt. in *The Idea of the Humanities and Other Essays*, 2 vols. (Chicago: University of Chicago Press, 1967), 2: 188–213.

22. See Friedman, "Aspects of Sentimentalism," p. 250.

23. George Colman (the Elder), "The Gentleman," No. 6, in *Prose on Several Occasions*, 3 vols. (London: T. Cadel, 1787), 1: 209.

24. Preface to *The Good-Natur'd Man*, in *Collected Works*, 5: 13.

25. Chapter 11, "Upon Criticism," in *An Enquiry into the Present State of Polite Learning*, in *Collected Works*, 1: 320.

26. *The Monthly Review* 48 (1773): 311.

27. *False Delicacy* was the principal attraction at one of the twenty theatrical evenings in Bath when Sheridan lived there. It was probably at this time that Sheridan composed scraps such as the Scotchman's dialogue with a manager, where the remote ancestor of Sneer's famous line from *The Critic* is to be found: "The theatre in proper hands, might certainly be made the school of morality; but now, I am sorry to say it, people seem to go there principally for their entertainment!" (1.1.122–25; see also *Dramatic Works*, p. 804, and Chapter VI, p. 154). Surely this is a turn on one of the final lines of *False Delicacy*, "the stage should be a school of morality."

28. In all fairness, Kelly must be given credit for at least one fine satiric stroke. Lady Betty defends herself: "Trifles, Emmy! do you call the laws of delicacy trifles. —She that violates these—" and is answered by Mrs. Harley: "Poh! poh! she that violates:—What a work there is with you sentimental folks" (act 2). One can hear Charles Surface's "True Brother as you were going to say—" (4.3.277).

29. *The Plays of Richard Steele*, ed. Shirley Strum Kenny (Oxford: Clarendon Press, 1971), p. 299.

30. Two doctoral dissertations, both written under the direction of Professor Ricardo Quintana at the University of Wisconsin, offer similar formulations. See Robert John Detisch, "High Georgian Comedy: English Stage Comedy from 1760 to 1777" (1967) and Joseph James Keenan, Jr., "The Poetic of High Georgian Comedy: A Study of the Comic Theory and Practice of Murphy, Colman, and Cumberland" (1969).

Notes to Chapter II

1. *Letters*, 1:85.

2. Richard Little Purdy's introduction to his edition of *"The Rivals"* . . . *Edited from the Larpent MS.* (Oxford: Clarendon Press, 1935) explains much about the composition and reception of the play. It should now be supplemented by Cecil Price's introduction in *Dramatic Works*, pp. 37–66.

3. For *Miss in Her Teens* and *The Deuce Is in Him*, see Miriam Gabriel and Paul Mueschke, "Two Contemporary Sources of Sheridan's *The Rivals*," *PMLA* 43 (1928): 238; for *Polly Honeycombe* see

Plays and Poems, 1:14. Fijn P. van Draat, "Sheridan's *The Rivals* and Ben Jonson's *Every Man in his Humour*," *Neophilologus* (1932), pp. 42–56, links Sheridan's and Jonson's plays; for Farquhar and *The Old Batchelor* as sources, see Sichel, *Sheridan*, 1:484, and *Dramatic Works*, pp. 38 ff., as well as explanatory notes to *The Rivals*, passim. For the review citing similarities between Jack Absolute and Atall in Cibber's *The Double Gallant* and between Lydia and Biddy Tipkin in Steele's *The Tender Husband; or, The Accomplish'd Fools*, see the *Morning Chronicle*, 18 Jan. 1775, cited in *Plays and Poems*, 1:210 and *Dramatic Works*, p. 42; for *A Journey to Bath*, see Fraser Rae, *Sheridan's Plays Now Printed as He Wrote Them and His Mother's Unpublished Comedy "A Journey to Bath"* (London: David Hunt, 1902), esp. pp. 262–318. For *All in the Wrong*, see Sichel, *Sheridan*, and also Tuvia Block, "The Antecedents of Sheridan's Faulkland," *Philological Quarterly* 49 (1970): 266–68.

4. The meeting on the South Parade might be explained by a completely external factor: manager Harris had a splendid "prospect" scene which depicted in realistic detail that area of Bath. See Dulck, *Les comédies de R. B. Sheridan*, pp. 75 (n. 15), 82, 102–3. The press quickly noted that the meeting was unnecessary, and the scene was frequently omitted in the representation, even by 1777. See a review, in the *Morning Post*, 17 Jan. 1777, of Sheridan's production of his play when he took over as manager of Drury Lane in 1776 and presented the comedy on 16 Jan. 1777 (cited in *Dramatic Works*, p. 52).

5. Moore, *Memoirs*, 1:141.

6. *The Letters of David Garrick*, ed. David M. Little and George M. Kahrl (Cambridge: Harvard University Press, 1963), letter no. 422, August 1766, p. 532.

7. David's use of "Devon monkeyrony" is interesting for another reason: it is one of the few malapropisms, in the final revised form of the play, given to characters other than Mrs. Malaprop. See Purdy, pp. xxxii–xxxiii.

8. Like *The Rivals*, the earlier *Cross Purposes* (DL, 5 Dec. 1772) is about a pair of lovers who wish to marry but believe their parents disapprove; the parents, of course, think the marriage perfect, and eventually the misunderstandings are straightened out. The farce played regularly for several years and is as likely a source for the Jack-Lydia action as any other of the farces and plays previously mentioned.

9. In 1774–75, Lee had joined Covent Garden for the first time in a number of seasons and played roles as diverse as Bayes and Richard III, Osman (in Aaron Hill's tragedy, *Zara*), Benedick, and

old Adam in *As You Like It*. So far as I can determine, he had never performed an Irishman on the London stage. Coincidentally, he was the author of *The Man of Quality*, an adaptation of the Lord Foppington plot of Vanbrugh's *The Relapse*, the play which Sheridan adapted as *A Trip to Scarborough*.

10. Two lines from contemporary reviews are of interest. One describes the acting of Lawrence Clinch (the replacement for Lee), which "made Sir Lucius so agreeable to the audience, that the part is likely to be as fortunate to him as that of Major O'Flaherty was to Mr. Moody" (*London Evening Post*, 31 Jan.–2 Feb. 1775, cited in *Dramatic Works*, pp. 50–51). The other appears in the review of the Drury Lane production of January 1777: "Mr. Moody *O'Flahertized* Sir *Lucius O'Trigger* very laughably" (*Morning Post*, 17 Jan. 1777, cited in *Dramatic Works*, p. 52).

11. For an excellent history of the stage Irishman, see J. O. Bartley's *Teague, Shenkin and Sawney* (Cork University Press, 1954), esp. pp. 182–84. (John Moody was also the good-hearted Teague of Howard's *The Committee*.)

12. How soon Fag's part in 5.1 was cut in performance is unclear, but he does not appear in the scene as printed in Mrs. Inchbald's acting text in *The British Theatre* (1808), or thereafter in any of the acting texts. See Mark S. Auburn, "The Pleasures of *The Rivals*: A Critical Study in Light of Stage History," *Modern Philology* 73 (February 1975): 261–76.

13. But A. H. Scouten reminds me that Lessingham might have received special treatment because she was Harris's mistress.

14. One of the early acting texts makes this clear. Fag is explaining what brought them to Bath in disguise: "Why then the cause of all this is—LOVE,—Love, Thomas, who (as you may get read to you) has been a masquerader ever since the days of Jupiter" (1.1.33–35). Dolby's acting text (1814) takes the capitalized LOVE and phonetically indicates the business: "EL O VE EE."

15. See reviews cited in *Dramatic Works*, pp. 43, 53.

16. Although he was in London during the single, controversial London performance of *A Word to the Wise* in March 1770, I suspect that if Sheridan saw this play, he saw it at its Bath performance 26 May 1772.

17. Cited in *Dramatic Works*, p. 47.

18. See *Dramatic Works*, p. 803.

19. Of interest too are some other correspondences between *The Rivals* and *The Platonic Wife*. Lady Frankland is called an "eccentric comet": Bob Acres says he had travelled like a comet and Jack puns upon the common usage to call Acres an "excentric Planet"

(2.1.125). *The Platonic Wife* contains an honest older country servant like David, Nicodemus, who is rather befuddled by the foppishness of an affected French serving maid named Fontange, just as David cannot understand his master's new concern with dress; Patrick, an honest Irishman and servant to Sir William, adds to the similar theatrical types portrayed in the two comedies. An on-stage duel complicates the plot and creates visual excitement. And the prologue to Mrs. Griffith's rather didactic piece is cast as a dialogue between two Serjeants-at-law, Pompous and Placid, much in the same manner as Sheridan's first prologue to *The Rivals*. I know of no other earlier eighteenth-century prologue so designed, or of any other between *The Platonic Wife* and *The Rivals*. Sheridan probably would not have seen the play on stage since it had only six performances, all before he was fourteen; but he might have read it.

20. Like Lydia's aunt Mrs. Malaprop, Lady Louisa's aunt Lady Bridget is a ridiculous elderly matron whose speech is characterized by an affected verbal tic—in her case, ancient languages.

21. These adjectives were used to describe the performances of Miss Barsanti and Mrs. Abington in the Covent Garden and Drury Lane productions; see *Dramatic Works*, pp. 48, 52.

22. Sheridan had ample precedent for jealous lovers, and in the new Georgian comedies, for jealous lovers presented with sympathy and understanding. Beverley of *All in the Wrong* (DL, 15 Jan. 1761) is but one of many, for there are Sir John Dorilant of *The School for Lovers* (DL, 10 Feb. 1762), especially in Act 3, Wellford of Frances Sheridan's *The Dupe* (DL, 10 Dec. 1763), especially in Act 5, and Belford in *The School for Guardians* (CG, 10 Jan. 1767), all lovers whose excessive jealousy leads to excessive self-torment comically criticized by the action of the play. Dulck, *Les comédies de R. B. Sheridan*, p. 117, also points to Frances Sheridan's novel, *The Memoirs of Miss Sidney Biddulph*, as a possible source.

23. Cited in R. Crompton Rhodes, *Harlequin Sheridan*, p. 144.

24. Purdy, p. xlv.

25. Dulck, p. 104.

NOTES TO CHAPTER III

1. That Sheridan was attracting attention as a man of the theater within a very short time after the success of *The Rivals* is implied in his authorship of the epilogue to Thomas Hull's adaptation of James Thomson's *Edward and Eleonora*, 18 March 1775 at Covent Garden.

To be asked to provide an epilogue to this, a benefit performance, was a mark of artistic respect. (For more on this epilogue, see Appendix, pp. 183–84.)

2. See *Dramatic Works*, p. 151, and *Plays and Poems*, 1:139. But Sheridan could have realized money from the piece by selling the right to perform it to other actors after Clinch had had the advantage of introducing it for his benefit night. We do not know who retained the rights.

3. Foote's farce had not been performed in London when Sheridan would have been likely to see it; its most recent London performance was in November, 1770, when all the Sheridans were in Bath. But it had been published in 1756.

4. Compare *The Merchant of Venice*, 2.2.3–5: " 'Gobbo, Launcelot Gobbo, good Launcelot,' or 'good Gobbo,' or 'good Launcelot Gobbo . . . .' "

5. Imitations of the nearly inimitable Ned Shuter were not uncommon. His health was beginning to fail late in the season 1774–75, and he would perform only six times at Covent Garden in 1775–76 with five performances at the Haymarket in September 1776 being his last London appearances before his death 1 November. Richard Wilson's imitations of Shuter in the role of Don Jerome are noted in the *Morning Chronicle*, 22 Nov. 1776, cited in *Dramatic Works*, p. 207. Reviews of *St. Patrick's Day*, however, do not mention any sustained imitations of Shuter.

6. *Plays and Poems*, 1:140.

7. The claim was made in a "Programme" Sheridan drew up when he was contemplating an authorized edition of his works about 1809. See *Dramatic Works*, p. 18, and for an account of the prelude, the *London Chronicle* for 19–21 Sept. 1775, cited in *Dramatic Works*, pp. 819–20, and reprinted in Chapter VI, pp. 153–54.

8. The striking success of this frivolous piece on the Georgian stage may be gauged by the fact that the great David Garrick chose to end his career with a performance of Don Felix in *The Wonder*.

9. Both *The Wonder* and *Il Filosopho di Campagna* are among the many works mentioned by Garland F. Taylor as possible sources for *The Duenna* in his study "Richard Brinsley Sheridan's *The Duenna*" (Ph.D. diss., Yale University, 1940). "It is a work of supererogation to propose for *The Duenna* any other sources than *The Wonder* and *The Wedding Ring*" (p. 38), he writes after naming the many others— from Molière's *Le Sicilien ou L'Amour Peintre* to Dryden's *The Spanish Friar* to Garrick's adaptation of Wycherley, *The Country Girl*—which have been suggested.

10. For valuable information on this piece see Peter A. Tasch's *The Dramatic Cobbler: The Life and Times of Isaac Bickerstaff* (Lewisburg, Pa.: Bucknell University Press, 1971), esp. pp. 152–65. One of my reasons for stressing the influence of *The Padlock* is a remark of Maria Macklin who, writing to her father of *The Wedding Ring* on its introduction 1 Feb. 1773, commented that "It is like the *Padlock*" (quoted in *London Stage, Part 4*, p. 1691).

11. On 25 May 1771 and 6 Feb. 1772. See Frederick T. Woods, "Theatrical Performances at Bath in the Eighteenth Century," *Notes and Queries* 192 (15 Nov. 1947): 489.

12. Anne Catley might have been Sheridan's Donna Louisa but for her impending retirement. She was a vastly popular singer-actress at Covent Garden, but was absent in the 1775–76 season; in the 1776–77 season, she commanded the remarkable salary of £27 6s. a performance.

13. The reference is found in a letter to Quick which first appeared in the *Monthly Mirror*, 1798, as quoted in J. O. Bartley's edition of *Four Comedies by Charles Macklin* (London: Sidgwick and Jackson, 1968), p. 48, n. 1.

14. Moore, *Memoirs*, 1:156, says the opera was written during the summer recess. But Rhodes, *Harlequin Sheridan*, p. 58, and Price, *Dramatic Works*, p. 109, n. 4, cite evidence that Sheridan may have composed sketches for *The Duenna* as early as the Waltham Abbey period, August 1772–April 1773. Presumably he was gone from London following his marriage to Elizabeth on 13 April 1773, when Quick performed Beau Mordecai for the first time in the 1772–73 season on 17 April, but he could have seen him in the role before he left for Bath (i.e., 1 April 1769 and 5 April 1770) or after he returned from his honeymoon.

15. Among other Jewish characters portrayed in late eighteenth-century comedy before Sheridan are the following: "Little" Napthali, the villainous broker of Cumberland's *The Fashionable Lover* (DL, 20 Jan. 1772); Moses Mendosa and Nathan, two brokers in Foote's *The Nabob* (HM, 29 June 1772); Moses Manasses, who seeks credentials to enter fashionable society in Foote's *The Cozeners* (HM, 15 July 1774); and Reuben, another gulled Jew in Francis Waldron's one-act farce, *The Contrast* (DL, 12 May 1775). John Quick probably also created for the London stage the conceited and avaricious Isaacher, a "little Israelite" of the anonymous *The South Briton* (CG, 12 April 1774), who tries to blackmail Mowbray by "crim. con." entrapment with his Portuguese Christian wife. Contemporary interest in Jewish figures may be indicated by the advertisement of a special per-formance of *The Merchant of Venice* "in the Jewish dialect" at the Haymarket, 23 March 1775.

16. James Boswell, *The Life of Johnson*, ed. G. B. Hill, rev. L. F. Powell, 6 vols. (Oxford: Clarendon Press, 1934), 3:115–16.

17. William Hazlitt, *Lectures on the English Comic Writers* (1818; rpt. ed. Israel Gollancz, London: J. M. Dent, 1900), p. 288.

18. Portraying Don Jerome was Richard Wilson, a relative newcomer to Covent Garden who had performed a wide variety of roles in the 1775 Haymarket season and who took over many of Ned Shuter's characters. Before he created Don Jerome he had appeared in such Shuter parts as Justice Woodcock (*Love in a Village*), Peachum, Hardcastle, and Sir Anthony Absolute. His 1776 benefit mainpiece was *The Rivals*.

19. Carlos was portrayed by Meyer Leon, who under the name of Leoni sang extensively on the London stage. *The Duenna* was not performed on Friday nights in its first season because Leon was the cantor of a synagogue. Provincial companies, performing pirated versions of the comic opera, frequently had difficulty filling this virtuoso, but solely decorative, singing part, so on many occasions Carlos was cut. Leon had difficulty speaking (but not singing) English, and this fact, plus his inexperience as an actor, accounts for his paucity of spoken lines and for the carelessness with which Sheridan created his character: without any preparation, Louisa treats Carlos, the confidant of Isaac, as a friend privy to her plans in 2.4. For more information on Sheridan's intentions for Leon as Carlos, see *Letters*, 1:88–89 and *Dramatic Works*, pp. 202–3.

20. Even Sheridan's most ardent detractor, Charles Dibdin, allowed him credit for this. After demonstrating to his own satisfaction that nothing in *The Duenna* is original, Dibdin grudgingly adds: "The dialogue is by no means brilliant, but Mr. Sheridan was determined it should penetrate every where, and in particular the *aside* speeches of *Isaac*—shewing beforehand how clearly he shall himself be taken in by his different attempts to deceive others, is the most artful species of anticipation that ever was practised, and shews a judgment of theatrical effect powerful, new, and extraordinary" (*The Musical Tour of Mr. Dibdin* [Sheffield, 1788], p. 260, as quoted in *Dramatic Works*, p. 213).

Notes to Chapter IV

1. All figures in this paragraph are my computations based on the receipts given by *London Stage, Parts 4 and 5*. Benefit nights are not counted because financial records for such nights are unreliable. No financial records for Covent Garden's 1774–75 and 1775–76 seasons have come to light.

2. See *Letters*, 1:104–8, and *Dramatic Works*, pp. 302–3, 832, for more information.

3. *All the World's a Stage, A Bundle of Prologues, The Hotel, Margaret of Anjou, The Milesian, New Brooms!*, and *Selima and Azor*. The tragedy was G. E. Ayscough's *Semiramis*, based on Voltaire's play; Sheridan wrote the epilogue. Later on in the season, Sheridan also wrote a prologue to William Woodfall's alteration of Richard Savage's *Sir Thomas Overbury* (CG, 1 Feb. 1777).

4. See *Dramatic Works*, pp. 832–35. None of these alterations, or those to Garrick's *A Christmas Tale*, were extensive. They provide interesting evidence of Sheridan's continuing effort to avoid insulting the tastes of his audience with bawdry or impropriety, but not much evidence of his skills as a playwright. But see n. 5 below.

5. Sheridan's hand as a director and play-doctor could be seen in many works. Sir George Collier, in the preface to his *Selima and Azor, A Persian Tale* (printed 1784; DL, 5 Dec. 1776), records that he "was absent from England at the Time it was brought on the Stage, and he is very sensible that the uncommonly favourable Reception it met with from the Public, must be principally owing to the great Justice done the Piece by the Managers, and by the Performers; but most particularly to the Taste and Judgment of Mr. SHERIDAN, in several judicious Alterations. . ." (quoted in *Dramatic Works*, p. 775). Other alterations that season include some non-extant changes to *The Tempest* (4 Jan. 1777; see *Dramatic Works*, pp. 776–77) and a scene designed to make more acceptable the "moral" of *The Beggar's Opera* (8 Nov. 1777; see *Dramatic Works*, pp. 777–80, and n. 1, Chapter VI, p. 204).

6. But the *London Magazine*, cited in *Dramatic Works*, p. 296, praised the direction of the revisions of Congreve at Drury Lane later in the season, particularly for their casting (which, in eighteenth-century terms, means their direction), "the strength with which they were brought out, and the judicious, nay, masterly manner the parts were cast, as far as the insolence and caprice of a few capital performers would permit."

7. "Few of the performers seemed to feel themselves at ease during the representation" (*Morning Chronicle*, 25 Feb. 1777); "The performers are not yet quite perfect in their parts, and we must necessarily confess that scarcely any comedy has been so little indebted to the exertion and merit of the actors and actresses, as the *Trip to Scarborough*" (*Morning Chronicle*, 3 March 1777, as quoted in *Dramatic Works*, pp. 557, 559; see also p. 554).

8. Reddish was growing quite infirm; in early May he left the London stage for two seasons, then returned briefly. That Sheridan

cast him as Young Fashion indicates the sympathetic emphasis he intended for the part, since Samuel Reddish's specialty was in sympathetic roles. He had created the good Sir John Dormer of *A Word to the Wise*, the noble young Melville of *The Duel*, and the mildly erring Belville of *The School for Wives* in recent seasons; on the other hand, he had performed for Sheridan Valentine and Fainall—roles more devoid of sympathy, one would think—though he failed as the witty Vainlove. Palmer's specialty was made most obvious in his portrayal of Joseph Surface; Sheridan had used him in recreating Jack Absolute, and Palmer also had played Young Fashion in John Lee's abridgment of Vanbrugh's play (for which see n. 10 below).

9. Sir John Vanbrugh, *The Relapse*, ed. Curt A. Zimansky, Regents Restoration Drama Series, ed. John Loftis (Lincoln: University of Nebraska Press, 1970). All citations will be given in the text by act, scene, and line number.

10. Subsequent adapters recognized that this was the heart of Vanbrugh's play in terms of its theatricality. John Lee's three-act reduction, *The Man of Quality* (CG, 27 April 1773; later DL, 15 March 1774, where Palmer played Young Fashion), removes the Amanda-Loveless plot completely, and a three-act version of Sheridan's own adaptation, printed in *Dolby's British Theatre* (1823; vol. 4), removes all but three of the Amanda-Loveless scenes as reworked by Sheridan. "Probus" in the *Morning Chronicle*, 3 March 1777, complains that *A Trip to Scarborough* is misguided; *The Man of Quality* has already saved everything worth salvaging from *The Relapse*.

11. Coupler's reason for helping Tom is not just a desire to revenge himself on Foppington. Another motive might be past and future homosexual liaison with Tom. Tom tells Coupler he can "take possession as soon as" he pleases (1.3.206–7) in exchange for the information about Miss Hoyden, and he agrees to sup with Coupler in his lodgings for "farther instructions" (1.3.272–73); this together with Coupler's nuzzling is suspicious. Interestingly, even the late Restoration audience would probably have balked at so pointed a display of homosexuality on stage, and thus the part of Young Fashion was taken by a woman, a reversal of the usual pattern whereby an established male role later became a "breeches" part (as with, for instance, Sir Harry Wildair). By the second decade of the eighteenth century, actors were playing Fashion, but many of the homosexual references were by then excised.

12. Paul Mueschke and Jeannette Fleisher, "A Re-Evaluation of Vanbrugh," *PMLA* 49 (1934): 862–63. An essay by Lincoln B. Faller, "Between Jest and Earnest: The Comedy of Sir John Vanbrugh,"

Modern Philology 72 (1974): 17–29, illuminatingly assesses Vanbrugh's dramatic work with particular reference to *The Relapse* and *The Provok'd Wife*; he takes issue with Mueschke and Fleisher on this point.

13. Moore, *Memoirs*, 1:198–99.

NOTES TO CHAPTER V

1. Cecil Price, "The Completion of *The School for Scandal*," *Times Literary Supplement*, 28 Dec. 1967, p. 1265, cites the *Morning Chronicle*, 16 April 1777: "a pretty time of year to produce a new piece at a WINTER THEATRE!"

2. The story is told in Sichel, *Sheridan*, 2: 550, and *Plays and Poems*, 2: 15.

3. Free tickets or "orders" to persons sympathetic with a new play were common. Cf. *The Critic*, 1.1.99, where Sneer avers that "On the first night of a new piece they always fill the house with orders to support it."

4. Christian Deelman, "The Original Cast of *The School for Scandal*," *Review of English Studies*, n.s. 13 (Aug. 1962): 257.

5. Arthur C. Sprague, "In Defense of a Masterpiece: *The School for Scandal* Re-examined," in *English Studies Today: Third Series* (Edinburgh: Edinburgh University Press, 1964), p. 128.

6. George Bernard Shaw, "The Second Dating of Sheridan," in his *Dramatic Opinions and Essays*, 2 vols. (New York: Brentano's, 1913), 2: 34.

7. Deelman, "Original Cast," p. 258.

8. See *Dramatic Works*, pp. 302–3, and reviews cited pp. 312–22.

9. But Andrew Shiller in "*The School for Scandal*: The Restoration Unrestored," *PMLA* 71 (1956): 694–704, argues that Sheridan's "purpose was clear: to write a neo-Restoration high comedy of manners" (p. 694), even though he failed because of his acceptance of his time's morality.

10. A. Mathews, *Memoirs of Charles Mathews, Comedian*, 2: 6–7, as quoted in *Dramatic Works*, p. 304.

11. *Morning Herald*, 9 Jan. 1799, as quoted in *Dramatic Works*, p. 308.

12. *Universal Magazine* 77 (1785): 120, as cited in *Dramatic Works*, p. 322.

13. Alicia Lefanu said many years later that the germs of *The School for Scandal* were discussed in Bath by Richard and his sister (*Memoirs of Frances Sheridan* [London: G. & W. B. Whittaker, 1824], p. 407), thus placing the initial conception before August, 1772.

That Sheridan—who at that point had had nothing produced on stage—was named as the author of Hugh Kelly's *The School for Wives* (produced anonymously, 11 Dec. 1773) by the press might suggest that he had mentioned the title of his future work at least by late 1773. But beyond these facts, we cannot be sure of the time of composition.

The sketches have been known since Moore's biography; Moore prints a considerable portion of the rough workbooks, and my citations will be to his printing except for several short exchanges. Two of these schoolboy notebooks have survived and are owned by Mr. Robert H. Taylor, who kindly allowed me to examine them. For a description of the notebooks, see *Dramatic Works*, pp. 291–95.

14. Sichel, *Sheridan*, 1: 564.

15. Moore, *Memoirs*, 1: 146.

16. Ibid., 1: 153.

17. Shiller, "The Restoration Unrestored," errs on the side of the sentimental interpretation when he argues that "there was never the remotest possibility that [Lady Teazle] would permit herself to be seduced" (p. 699); yet he also says "she comes close to being a sentimental heroine in a domestic tragedy" (p. 702).

18. "The sanctity of this institution [of marriage] . . . is at the core of the play," writes Shiller (ibid., p. 701).

19. Here the biographical evidence is revealing, for if Charles represents anybody it is the young scapegrace Richard Brinsley Sheridan, victim of excessive drinking habits, victim of the displeasure of his father over his marriage, and the younger son in a family where the elder was given all the advantages of living constantly at home, having the father's ear and confidence, and being recommended for early preferment. The playwright who dramatized a duel and elopement, several crusty and barely sympathetic old fathers, and who poked open fun at his practices as theatrical manager in *The Critic*, was perfectly capable of dramatizing his conscious or unconscious resentment of a favored, elder brother. But, as Thomas Sheridan is said to have declared rather maliciously: "Talk about the merit of Dick's comedy, there's nothing to it. He had but to dip into his own heart and find there the characters both of Joseph and Charles" (cited in *Plays and Poems*, 2: 12).

20. Henry James, *"The School for Scandal* at Boston," in *Scenic Art: Notes on Acting and the Drama 1872–1901*, ed. Allan Wade (New York: Hill and Wang, 1957), p. 17.

21. Sichel, *Sheridan*, 1: 55.

22. Allan Rodway in "Goldsmith and Sheridan: Satirists of Sentiment," in *Renaissance and Modern Essays Presented to Vivian de Sola*

Pinto, ed. G. R. Hibbard (New York: Barnes & Noble, Inc., 1966),
argues that the test of the brothers is "a piece of structural sentimentality. . . . Scapegrace sentimentality is the price of moral satire
[of Joseph]" (p. 68). But Sheridan surely was unaware of that price
and heartily joined his audience in applauding Charles's sentimentality and damning Joseph's ingratitude.

23. Leonard J. Leff in "The Disguise Motif in Sheridan's *The
School for Scandal*," *Educational Theatre Journal* 22 (1970): 360, argues
that whenever Charles "sees disguise," he acts to remove it.

24. Sheridan also contrasts prudence against humanly warm, sentimental values in some of his other plays. In *The Camp* (2.1.22–23),
Nell tells William that "you would have been very imprudent to have
suffered" Nancy, his beloved, to marry him while he was still serving
in the army; he answers, "Aye, but prudence, you know, is not a
soldier's virtue." In *The Rivals*, one of Faulkland's self-tortures proceeds from his specious line of reasoning that Julia might be
marrying him only for his money: "O Julia! when *Love* receives such
countenance from *Prudence*, nice minds will be suspicious of its *birth*"
(3.2.89–91). In praising Mrs. Crewe as "Amoret" in "A Portrait," a
poem attached to a presentation copy of *The School for Scandal*,
Sheridan writes that Amoret is "Discreet in Gesture, in Deportment
mild,/ Not stiff with Prudence, nor uncouthly wild—" (ll. 49–50).
Prudence was evidently a value which the poet and playwright did
not hold high. Nor did the statesman: Jack D. Durant points to some
variations on "prudence" that Sheridan developed years later in his
attack on Warren Hastings in "Prudence, Providence, and the Direct
Road of Wrong: *The School for Scandal* and Sheridan's Westminster
Hall Speech," *Studies in Burke and His Time* 15 (1974): 241–51.

25. See for instance *London Magazine* 46: 228–32, cited in *Dramatic
Works*, pp. 318–22.

26. Moore, *Memoirs*, 1: 249. See also Deelman, "Original Cast,"
and *Dramatic Works*, p. 303.

27. Deelman, "Original Cast," p. 266.

28. The "Tête-à-Tête" was a particularly malicious invention of
the *Town and Country Magazine*. A sketch of a love affair, frequently
without any foundation in fact, between two prominent people
whose identities could be recognized by nicknames and subtly placed
initials, was faced by a full-page engraving in miniature of the heads
of the two accused. Mrs. Clackit, says Snake, has been behind some
of these: "Nay, I have more than once traced her causing a Tête-à-
Tête in the Town and Country Magazine—when the Parties perhaps

have never seen each other's Faces before in the course of their Lives" (1.1.17–19). Frances Abington, Lady Teazle of Sheridan's initial production, had recently been the subject of one.

29. Katherine Sherry, who created Lady Sneerwell, portrayed Lady Riscounter at the Haymarket in 1776.

30. Alicia Lefanu believed that Sheridan abandoned the name "Lady Kitty Candour" for the character who subsequently became Mrs. Candour because it too much resembled "Lady Kitty Crocodile," a caricature of the Duchess of Kingston in Foote's *A Trip to Calais*. This farce was refused license because of its scurrility, but Foote utilized everything in it except his portrait of the Duchess— who might be "Lady Deborah Dripping"—in creating *The Capuchin*. See Lefanu, *Memoirs of Frances Sheridan*, p. 409.

31. Preface to *The Way of the World*, in *William Congreve: Complete Plays*, ed. Alexander Charles Ewald (rpt.; New York: Hill and Wang, 1956), p. 292. A subsequent citation to *The Double Dealer* from this edition is noted parenthetically in the text.

32. James Boaden, *Memoirs of Kemble*, 1: 55, as quoted in Deelman, "Original Cast," p. 263.

33. Deelman, "Original Cast," p. 264. Since he lacked the resources of *The London Stage, Parts 4 and 5*, Deelman was not able to identify Katherine Sherry's qualifications to portray Lady Sneerwell.

34. Some have thought Sheridan careless to have Joseph introduce the screen at the beginning of 4.3 as a protection against the eyes of his "opposite Neighbour— . . . a maiden Lady of so curious a temper!" (4.3.14–15), and then to allow Lady Teazle to hide behind it so that she is exposed to the spinster's eyes. But note that Lady Teazle decides to hide herself there, not Joseph. The actors are well advised to play the few lines after Sir Peter's announced arrival with the greatest possible flurry; Joseph must not direct Lady Teazle to any hiding place, or perhaps, he should direct her to the closet, while she ignores his suggestions. Played this way, the line will appear anything but careless, for it is a masterly way of calling attention to the greatest prop in the history of comedy.

35. In the essays by James and Shaw cited above, each author denies *The School for Scandal* a place among masterpieces of drama on the grounds of its facile morality.

36. R. S. Crane, "The Concept of Plot and the Plot of *Tom Jones*," *Critics and Criticism*, ed. R. S. Crane (Chicago: University of Chicago Press, 1952), p. 638. "Morally serious comedy" is Crane's term.

37. William Hazlitt, *Lectures on the English Comic Writers*, p. 281.

NOTES TO CHAPTER VI

1. The emphasis was sentimental and didactic. Sheridan's additions (probably first produced 8 Nov. 1777) were designed to point the moral more closely, reprieving Macheath, but vowing he would reform: "If you suppose your Hero possess'd of *Feeling enough* to be reclaimed by such unexpected lenity—an English Audience will never find injustice in an act of mercy" (italics added). There were only about six speeches in the revision. See *Dramatic Works*, pp. 777–80.

2. The epilogue was to Hannah More's *The Fatal Falsehood* (6 May 1779). *The Verses to the Memory of Garrick. Spoken as A Monody, at The Theatre-Royal in Drury-Lane* first were staged 12 March 1779. Sheridan's small corrections to Fielding's posthumous *The Fathers* were identified by Price in Larpent MS 461 (Huntington Library): the production of 30 Nov. 1778 bore few marks of Sheridan's interest as "play doctor" or director. The afterpiece, *The Wonders of Derbyshire*, was a popular spectacle in which Sheridan's portion was minor; it appeared 8 Jan. 1779. For more on *The Camp*, see p. 161 above.

3. The matter of the dormant patent is unclear. Charles II originally granted one patent to William Davenant and another patent to Thomas Killigrew in 1660; William III granted a third license to Betterton in 1695, after the patents of Davenant and Killigrew had been consolidated in 1682, but not invalidated. For many years, Price says in *Letters*, 1: 116–21, two letters patent were associated with Covent Garden, one with Drury Lane. ("Patents and licenses have always been considered as the same," stated the Lord Chamberlain in a chancery suit in 1790, according to Hogan, *London Stage, Part 5*, p. cxxx.) Sheridan's plan was to create a new theater for the mutual interest of both the major houses, utilizing their personnel and supplies. The theater would open its doors at a later hour and be located in a more fashionable neighborhood, thus not competing directly with either Covent Garden or Drury Lane. All that came of the plan was a temporary agreement in 1778–79 for a free exchange of actors between the two houses. The opera venture was equally abortive. Harris sold his interest before the end of the first season, and Sheridan sold his in November 1781.

4. The gross receipts for the 1778–79 season were £3,000 lower than for 1777–78; those for 1779–80, £4,000 lower than for 1778–79.

5. Advertisement to the "Occasional Prelude" in *The Dramatic Works of George Colman*, 4 vols. (London: T. Beckett, 1777), 4: 247.

6. Advertisement to *New Brooms!* in *Works*, 4:321.

7. Cf. *The Critic*, 1.1.397–99: "SNEER. I thought you had been a decided critic in musick, as well as in literature? DANGLE. So I am—but I have a bad ear."

8. Cf. King as Puff with his "puff direct" in *The Critic*, 1.2.171–73: "but it is not in the power of language to do justice to Mr. KING!—Indeed he more than merited those repeated bursts of applause which he drew from a most brilliant and judicious audience!"

9. As cited in *Dramatic Works*, pp. 819–20.

10. Moore's version (*Memoirs*, 1:18–22) is the source of all subsequent reprints. Price discovered a manuscript of Halhed's burletta (BM Add. MS. 25935), but it did not contain Sheridan's revisions. See *Dramatic Works*, pp. 793–96. I have not here expanded speech prefixes, as I have done elsewhere; there is no way of knowing what "MacD" and "O'Cul" stand for.

11. Cf. Sneer, *The Critic*, 1.1.122–25: "The theatre in proper hands, might certainly be made the school of morality; but now, I am sorry to say it, people seem to go there principally for their entertainment!"

12. I reprint Moore's version of this, *Memoirs*, 1: 23.

13. As cited in *Plays and Poems*, 2: 252.

14. The anecdote is given in *Memoirs of Richard Cumberland* (London: 1806; ed. Henry Flanders, Philadelphia, 1856; reissued New York; Benjamin Blom, Inc., 1969), pp. 153–54.

15. See *Dramatic Works*, pp. 465–67, for additional information on contemporary interest in the war and its relationship with *The Critic*.

16. *The Gazetteer*, 16 August 1779, as cited in *Plays and Poems*, 2: 182. Cf. a similar advertisement from the *Morning Chronicle*, 28 September 1779, cited in *Dramatic Works*, p. 466.

17. See appendix, pp. 185–86.

18. *St. James Chronicle*, 15–17 Oct. 1778, cited in *Dramatic Works*, p. 712.

19. *London Evening Post*, 30 Oct.–2 Nov. 1779, cited in *Dramatic Works*, p. 475.

20. Rhodes in *Plays and Poems*, 2: 180.

21. Sheridan was quoted as saying that "he had drawn the character of Sir Fretful Plagiary partly from" Cumberland, but that "he did not, however, intend that Parsons should dress after Cumberland" or mimic his behavior so closely (J. C. Hobhouse, Lord Broughton, *Recollections of a Long Life* [1909], 2:138, as cited in *Dramatic Works*, p. 469).

22. And as with all his works except *The School for Scandal*, the

same reviews complained about the initial length of the piece. See those cited in *Dramatic Works*, pp. 476–84.

23. Pieces, not wholes, abound. Aside from the fragments of "The Teazles" and "The Slanderers," the fragments from the rehearsal frame for *Ixion*, and the sketches for "A Scotchman," parts of which are reprinted in this study, there are also the fragments for a dramatization of *The Vicar of Wakefield*, the sketches for an unfinished play titled *Affectation*, another titled *The Statesman*, and other pieces, cited and printed in *Dramatic Works*, pp. 801–3, 808–16, 841–43, and elsewhere.

24. None of these types of comic dialogue are necessarily comic; indeed, each of the devices I am discussing can be employed in serious or tragic situations without raising any risibility whatsoever.

25. In these comments on wit I am indebted in part to Elder Olson, *The Theory of Comedy*, esp. pp. 21–24.

26. Note the aural pleasure of the misplaced emphasis on "I" in the quotation from *Othello*.

27. *The Reminiscences of Michael Kelly*, compiled by Edward Hook (2nd ed. London: 1826; reissued New York: Benjamin Blom, Inc., 1969), pp. 343–44.

Notes to Chapter VII

1. Byron, George Gordon Noel 6th Baron, *Byron's Letters and Journals*, ed. Leslie A. Marchand, 5 vols. (London: John Murray, 1973–76), 3: 239.

2. Shirley Strum Kenny has defined the comedy of Vanbrugh, Farquhar, Cibber, and Steele in comparison to high Restoration comedy in an essay titled "Humane Comedy" (forthcoming in *Modern Philology*), which she kindly allowed me to read.

3. Since I have written these lines Jack D. Durant has kindly allowed me to see his forthcoming essay, "Sheridan, Human Nature, and Comic Catharsis," in which he creates a context for Sheridan's moral thought and argues that although Sheridan sees charity and benevolence as the prime attributes of the Christian hero, "he knows full well the misery of this world, and he proceeds resolutely to disregard it, even to fly into its face by forcing merriment from the implications of our fallen state." No mere "sentimentalist," Sheridan strives toward a realism based on the post-Latitudinarian world-view he inherited. Hazlitt's curious comment that *The School for Scandal* "professes a faith . . . in the habitual depravity of human nature" (see p. 148 above) suggests a similar Sheridan.

4. Hazlitt, "On the Comic Writers of the Last Century," in *Lectures on the English Comic Writers*, p. 288.

NOTE TO APPENDIX

1. Moore, *Memoirs*, 1: 24, 1: 155 n.; Jackson, "The Importance of Witty Dialogue in *The School for Scandal*," *Modern Language Notes* 76 (1961): 601–7; Price, *Dramatic Works*, pp. 287–312, esp. p. 310.

INDEX

Sheridan's and Shakespeare's works are indexed only under their names.

209